KATHERINE
GRAINGER
THE AUTOBIOGRAPHY

KATHERINE GRAINGER
THE AUTOBIOGRAPHY

ANDRE
DEUTSCH

Text copyright © Katherine Grainger 2013
Design copyright © André Deutsch Limited 2013

First published in hardback in 2013 by André Deutsch
an imprint of the Carlton Publishing Group
20 Mortimer Street, London W1T 3JW

Paperback edition 2014

A CIP catalogue record for this book is available from
the British Library

10 9 8 7 6 5 4 3 2 1

ISBN 978-0-233-00420-4

Printed and bound by CPI Group (UK) Ltd,
Croydon, CR0 4YY

CONTENTS

To Mum, Dad and Sarah who were there
waiting for me when I came into this world and
who have been there for me every day since.

FOREWORD

Nothing can give me greater pleasure than writing this foreword for Katherine's autobiography. Simply because having looked forward to the Olympics for so many years the one actual result I would have sacrificed every other for was for Katherine Grainger to win gold. This is not just because she is an extraordinarily talented rower, as Team GB has produced many of these. It is more down to the human qualities that she possesses, and that anyone who has ever met Katherine will be aware of. Her thoughtful and kind nature that has led her to become the heart and soul of the British Women's Rowing group. Her determination and dedication that perhaps I see reflected in my own bloody mindlessness over the years, that has taken her from the joy of her first silver medal; the satisfaction of her second and the crushing disappointment of that silver in Beijing to finally gold in her home country. I can only admire what she has achieved and her absolute resolve and utmost application to gain what she has always wanted and deserved. Katherine's story is not just one long success story, though we have to always take into account that the ability to win any Olympic medal demands truly Olympian application. Moreover it is a story that is dotted with the highs and lows that we have all experienced in our lives, and that everyone reading this book who has ever picked up an oar, racquet or club, or even played with any shaped/sized ball will relate to. It is testament to her strength and intelligence that her dream did come true in the end. The fact that she can tell this story in her own words is also a reflection of her unique intelligence and empathy that shine through to everyone who meets her.

As the dream that was London 2012 begins to fade there will be many moments that I will never forget, but shining through them will be the golden smile of Katherine Grainger's gold medal win and this I am sure – whatever Katherine goes on to do in the future – will burn very bright for many years to come.

SIR STEVE REDGRAVE

PREFACE TO THE PAPERBACK EDITION

Memory is an interesting thing. If I think back to London 2012 some of the details are so sharp, it's as if it happened in the past few days. In other ways it feels a magical moment that happened a very long time ago in a galaxy far, far away. The most wonderful thing of it all is that it regularly comes to mind when strangers I meet want to recall those heady days of summer or people I work with ask the details of what it was really like in the build up and during the Games. And every time I talk about it, it feels fresh and new and I remember slightly different aspects. I've been asked what it feels like to know that I will never be able to "beat" that moment of my career and the assumption is that it must be slightly sad or depressing, acknowledging that the best part is now behind me. But the truth is that there is nothing about that magical summer that is sad or depressing. To have had that moment in my life is something I will treasure forever, and I can go back and remember it whenever I want. It is a special privilege to have experienced what I did and shared it with so many people and it will always be a part of me, making me smile until the day I die. I will never forget and I would never want to "beat it".

But life goes on with new and wonderful challenges. The direction of my life is still unclear and I have big decisions ahead, but the options are many. The time since the Olympics has been packed with charity work, finishing my PhD, talks, honorary degrees, school visits, supporting universities and sports clubs, working for the BBC, becoming an Auntie, racing in an eight with some fantastic legends from British women's rowing covering eight Olympiads, running the marathon, climbing the Atlas mountains, and helping to ensure the Olympic legacy is strong. None of which makes for a boring existence! So life remains about setting fresh challenges, broadening horizons, laughing as often as possible, seeking inspiration, staying hungry to learn, constantly pursuing higher standards, having fun, retaining a passionate spirit and making sure there are no wasted moments... so no change there!

ACKNOWLEDGEMENTS

My main thanks go to everyone in rowing and to the wider sporting family whom I have had the privilege of knowing over the years. I have been constantly inspired by their friendship and their tireless energy.

I am grateful to Mike Pask and the team at IMG who encouraged me to take this first step into writing. The writing process was made easier by De Vere, who allowed me the use of one of their beautiful lodges on the banks of Loch Lomond which proved to be a perfect writer's retreat.

To Martin Corteel and the rest of the Carlton staff I owe huge thanks for their unfailing patience and vision for this project. I am indebted to Steve Dobell for sharing his knowledge and experience of writing and whose enthusiasm was so infectious.

I deeply appreciated all those who shared their stories, reminding me of past events. Andrew Longmore in particular was invaluable in helping me to concentrate my thoughts and in reassuring me that there was a story to be told and that I was the one to tell it.

Finally, my heartfelt thanks go to all my family and friends for their unstinting understanding and for joining me on this rollercoaster. The ride has been so much better because of them.

"It is not the critic who counts; not the man who points out how the strong man stumbles, or where the doer of deeds could have done them better. The credit belongs to the man who is actually in the arena, whose face is marred by dust and sweat and blood; who strives valiantly; who errs, who comes short again and again, because there is no effort without error and shortcoming; but who does actually strive to do the deeds; who knows great enthusiasms, the great devotions; who spends himself in a worthy cause; who at the best knows in the end the triumph of high achievement, and who at the worst, if he fails, at least fails while daring greatly, so that his place shall never be with those cold and timid souls who neither know victory nor defeat."

THEODORE ROOSEVELT

ONCE UPON A TIME

Over the years a commitment to excellence in my sport has meant an incredible level of attention to detail: the preparation and the practice have been everything. With more groundwork and planning the risk lessens every step of the way, even though the challenge might get greater.

Then I agreed to write a book. For that undertaking I didn't have any experience or development. I couldn't practise and I couldn't look back at all the lessons I might have learned from past mistakes or recent success. The only thing I had on my side was a lifelong love of words and other people's writings. And my story. I have always been an avid reader and like every child at school I had my attempts at creative writing in English class. Since then I've written academically, but those things are a far cry from writing your own story. At first there was an expectation that someone else would write this story for me, but I very quickly realized that if my story was to be told then I wanted to be the one to tell it. In my own voice. Perhaps it was a pride thing: I felt I should be able to tell my story. It was also a challenge, and I do love a challenge. Mainly, it was about loyalty. The people contained in this story are people I love, people I respect, people I care about and people I'm proud of, so the words had to be true. I've read many articles in the press that I know have contained inaccuracies. I didn't want to risk that; I wanted to write the truth.

But things aren't as simple as that. Everyone has their own version of the truth and all I can say is that this one is mine. Some may have forgotten some of these stories or remembered them differently; some might disagree with my point of view, but I take full responsibility for these words because they are all my own. With a bit of professional advice from the sidelines to help with editing I have relied on my own instinct and so I stand by my own failings.

I still have some discomfort over the concept of an autobiography. I've loved reminiscing about the people and places contained on these pages. Looking back I've realized more than ever how lucky I've been with my life so far. However there is a great difference between recounting stories for my own enjoyment and thinking that they may entertain other people.

I was overwhelmed by the incredible reaction I've received ever since the London 2012 Olympic Games, and enough people have told me that there is an inspiring story in amongst it all that maybe I felt it was a good story to tell. I also wanted to tell the story of many other people who were part of my incredible journey, whose names may not be known or whose accomplishments are not celebrated but who deserve to be part of the tale. Because it is a story of continuous challenge and of people coming together to change and improve the system. It's a story of battles lost and won, of heroes and villains, of knights and magicians. Of sacrifice, of love and loss, of heartbreak and of tragedy. There are dreams fulfilled and moments of crushing disappointments. There is laughter and tears, births and deaths, risk and daring, physical prowess and mental powers. It's a story with horses and guinea pigs. And murder.

I've always thought there is something exciting about the first page of a book, the first line that starts 'Once upon a time'. There's the feeling that everything is possible and anything could happen. For the young, or the young at heart, it's the magical beginning that can transport you to anywhere in the world, in any time. Where the ordinary rules may not exist. I love spending time in those other worlds. Like others, while I was growing up, after my mum and dad came to say goodnight and switch off the light, I would wait until I heard their footsteps fading downstairs and I would disappear under my covers with my book and a torch. One of my favourite subjects at school was Classical Studies, because we studied all the Greek and Roman myths under the watchful eye of Mrs Holmes, our Deputy Head. While terrifying us with her black cape and severe stare, she also brought to life the gods and goddesses of ancient times. Stories can be captivating in all forms; not just in books but on stage and screen too. My favourite job when growing up was the summer I spent working in a cinema, and even now I love the thrill in the theatre or the cinema as the lights dim and you enter another world.

And so here you will enter another world. It is a world all about rowing. But it is, I hope, more than that. I've been able to write it because of the great success of the summer of 2012. I'm also aware that the people contained in these pages have all helped me to achieve what I did that summer. I have truly stood "on the shoulders of giants". People throughout my life have helped, motivated, inspired and encouraged me in all sorts of ways, and to each and every one of them I owe a huge thank you. I have achieved more than I ever thought I would because of all I've been given and all that I've learned. It is because of daring to dream of great things that great things can be accomplished. Passion and purpose can help achieve far more than many people deem possible. And "daring greatly" is an option open to everyone.

CHAPTER

1

LET'S START AT THE VERY BEGINNING...

My international rowing career started with a lie. Not a bad lie. More of a fib, a white lie, possibly even just an exaggeration. It was well meaning if that makes it any better. Perhaps not, but it started the journey. "Rowing in a pair is just like being in an eight. Really, it is." I smiled as I said this, trying to ooze confidence and knowledge. Cesca frowned slightly but slowly nodded. "OK, let's give it a go," she said, while sounding firmly unconvinced. Truth be told, the two boats were miles apart in many ways, but Cesca didn't need to hear that. Francesca Zino, or Cesca as she was known, came from Cambridge University, where she had only rowed in the big eights. She had never rowed a pair in her life but the trials we were about to race in were in those small boats. She was understandably a little nervous taking to the water in such a flimsy, fragile craft, but I felt a quick exaggeration of the truth was better than a long explanation of the differences and similarities at that moment.

CHAPTER 1

We had met for the first time just a few hours before in Nottingham. The nearby Holme Pierrepont Centre was the location for the Under-23 British Rowing Team trials. Both of us had arrived without training partners, so we were put together. Cesca, like pretty much every athlete I've ever met through rowing, had a strong and distinctive character. She liked things certain ways and was hard to shift once she had made her mind up about something. She had wonderful quirks, like always taking a supermarket bag to the landing stage with her so she could easily carry all of her equipment. While the other athletes stuffed water bottles, bits of clothes, spare socks and the like down their lycras, either unaware of how they looked or more likely unconcerned about it, Cesca neatly gathered her things into some form of bag, earning her the affectionate name of "Bag Lady". She came from a wealthy background but that didn't mean she was unaware of the value of things. In fact she was meticulous about not wasting anything and would save money in every way she could. She would never leave half a pat of butter unused, and either fold it up to take it with her or find someone who was in need of butter, whether or not they realized it. For years she drove fellow athletes crazy as she refused to buy a car, relying on others to give her a lift. She always had the natural assumptive air that someone would step in to help, but then she had such a wonderful genuine manner about her that someone always did.

Meanwhile back in Nottingham we were about to take to the water for the first time in a pair. "Are you sure they're safe? They look very unstable," she asked as we gently put the boat on to the water. "Oh yes, it's very difficult to fall in from one of these," I replied, while gripping the side of the boat as she leaned over to put her blade in. Whereas an eight is big and heavy enough to sit solidly on the water, the smaller pair will flip instantly if you put too much weight on one side of the boat. As Cesca gained in confidence and leaned over to the far side to fix her equipment, my knuckles started to show white as I dropped my full weight on to the opposite rigger. "All set?" I asked, while trying to disguise the way my jaw was clenched from the force I was having to exert to keep the boat level. "Yes, I think so. And you're right, they are quite steady, aren't they?" Cesca smiled back at me.

As in a lot of things, confidence can make a vast difference in rowing. At that moment Cesca only had to feel that she could trust the boat and me – two things she had first encountered only a few hours ago. If she could have this trust, then she could apply her power and technique without any doubts in her mind. We took the few strokes away from the landing stage and the boat responded smoothly. In exchange for the more "tippy" feel, you get a wonderful instant responsiveness from a pair, far more than from the bigger boats. It is easier to feel its subtleties, and although a bad small boat can be the most frustrating and unrewarding of experiences, a good pair can be the most thrilling combination of athlete, boat and water.

We arrived at the start of the race after having enjoyed a simple and satisfying 2,000m to get there. We lined up next to the more experienced and better-known athletes and as usual had a few minutes to get organized. The silence is broken by the occasional noise of legs being slapped, throats being cleared, the murmur of last words being said between crewmates. Usually the time is filled with simple things like taking off any extra layers of kit that wouldn't be needed for the race. The person in the bows will often look behind them towards the finish and check the boat is directly in the centre of the lane. A common habit is reaching over and just checking that the nut on top of the rigger is tight. The pair in the lane next to us tried a few of those things simultaneously. As one of the girls leaned out to check her rigger the other one was taking off a t-shirt. The combination of neither athlete holding on to either the blades or boat and also the balance being pushed too far over to one side meant that in a fraction of a second the boat spun over, throwing both girls out of the boat and into the water. The brief shriek and following splash caused everyone in the race to spin around and see what was going on. There were a few gasps and laughs from the other lanes, but from my lane there was silence. I sat innocently as Cesca very slowly turned around with an aristocratic eyebrow arched. I smiled weakly. "That's *very* unusual," I said. "Honest."

Thankfully Cesca didn't let that moment affect her, but showed the same stubborn determination that made her a champion. We won the race easily, much to everyone's surprise as we had upset the predicted and expected finish order. As two unknown, untested and untried girls from outside the system, it was controversial for us to arrive and win. We were then split up and put into boats with other partners, and in every race Cesca and I would finish first and second. The biggest winning margin of the day was the first race, when we had been in the same boat together, and so when the selection decisions were made we were told we would be the Under-23 women's pair that year for Great Britain.

The meeting we had with the Team Manager, David Tanner, was enlightening. We would be racing at the "Nations Cup", the Under-23 World Championships, in Milan, Italy. We would be given two lycras, a t-shirt and a cap, and we would need to give British Rowing some money for the privilege of rowing for our country. Most of the costs would be met by GB Rowing, but there was money to be given by us too. David's words were, "I'm sure you can all find a rich uncle who would be willing to help out." I sat quietly in the meeting wondering where you found one of those.

Both Cesca and I were in our final year at University. My course finished first so I moved down to Cambridge and stayed there while she finished the year. I have snapshot memories of my time there, like when I was in the phonebox (this was before I had a mobile phone) to call Edinburgh to see if I could get my results from my final exams. I had to make the call a few times, each time nervously dialling the university number and then waiting what felt like an eternity only for the lady in the office to say, "No, results aren't back yet." Finally one day I was in the overheating box, leaning against the glass side, and after the usual delay the lady said, "OK then, let's see what you got." I had relaxed during the wait, expecting the usual "Sorry dear, maybe try again tomorrow," so when she started shuffling the information to find my specific results I went from a half-asleep relaxed athlete to a nervous, sweaty-palmed student in a second. Thankfully the news was good; all the rowing hadn't stopped me from getting my law degree, so I could call my mum and dad to share it.

There was need for some celebration, and as it happened Cesca said there was a bit of a party happening at the boathouse later that day. At the time the Cambridge Blue boats were sponsored by a gin company. We went along to the afternoon party where boxes and boxes of gin had been delivered. As it was being run by students there was far more of the free gin than there was of any of the necessary mixers that should have been bought. I remember drinking gin and tonics out of plastic pint glasses that were more gin than tonic by a long way. When we left a few hours later on the bicycles that everyone rides around Cambridge I gazed hypnotized at the wicker basket on the front of the bike as we weaved our way unsteadily around the streets. I still have no idea how we made it back to the halls of residence.

Once Cesca finished her degree we moved to Marlow, where we briefly trained with the senior girls. I can remember the last day of training there – the girls wished us luck and we loaded the boat on to the trailer ready for our first foray into international racing. It was a beautifully hot day and Cesca and I jumped into the river and swam around laughing and playing. We were excited and I don't remember there being any concerns or fears about what we were about to do. I know we wouldn't be allowed to play in the water a few days before international competition now – the possibility of picking up something nasty from the water would be seen as too much of a risk, but back then there really didn't seem to be a care in the world.

Out in Milan the temperature was a lot hotter. It was an oppressive, baking heat and as soon as we stepped out into the sunshine we were soaked with sweat and dizzy with the temperature. It also sapped energy instantly, and so we were only allowed outside for a limited amount of time. Even when it came to racing we were told to cut our warm-up short – the usual few laps around the warm-up zone was restricted to simply rowing to the start. The advantage Cesca and I had was that this was our first experience of international competition, so we didn't have anything to compare it with. Sometimes, when there's too much of an established way to do things, any change to that routine can be upsetting, distracting or more worrying than it need be. We were happily oblivious to the fact that the shortened warm-up might be a problem. That was also thanks to Hamish Burrell, who was coaching us; he was focused only on what would make us fast and didn't let us worry about anything that might detract from that. I had worked with Hamish for a couple of years and didn't yet realize that his calm, relaxed manner was a very precious and surprisingly rare trait.

The time in Milan was fun and exciting. We made it to the final and headed off to the start after Hamish pushed us off, with David Tanner watching carefully next to him. I found out years later that David had asked Hamish at that point how he thought we would do. While still watching us paddle away Hamish replied in his understated way, "They'll win." David was surprised by Hamish's confidence. It's funny to think of it now, but back then there weren't many successful

British crews, and the ones who were bringing in the medals were mainly on the men's side. Nowadays there would be trouble if the answer *wasn't* about winning, such is the mentality of success and excellence. But in 1997 it was a different world, especially in the women's team, and winning was not expected of a new, inexperienced pairing.

But the statement of winning wasn't an act of bravado from Hamish; nor was it a rebellious display of going against the classic British underdog mentality. He simply knew what he had seen over the past few days and he knew how fast we could be. One of the great things about Hamish is that he has always been able to think a little differently from the system. He has his own ideas and expectations, and he would never have thought Cesca and I wouldn't win just because it was our first international and we were inexperienced in relation to the rest of the squad. Hamish simply knew what he saw, what he believed, what his instinct told him. And it didn't matter to him if that didn't fit in with traditional thinking.

About 30 minutes later after David and Hamish's conversation we crossed the line ahead and became the first British women's crew to win gold at either a Junior, Under-23 or Senior International event. It was a wonderful moment and we were so naïve after winning that we started to head back to the landing stage where we had boated. Before we managed to get there a safety launch cut us off and waved us back. "Great Britain, please proceed to the medal podium," they called out. Cesca and I looked back at them confused. The Italians wearily pointed over to the opposite side of the lake.

My first podium in a GB vest was truly special and very memorable. Partly because of seeing the Union Jack being raised for the first time. Partly because of the pride I felt in what Cesca, Hamish and I had achieved. And partly because as the drum roll started and we readied ourselves for the National Anthem they played Queen's "We are the Champions". A brilliant piece of Italian style.

she glanced up to see us walking towards her. The look of utter disbelief and horror outdid anything the locals could summon. She looked wildly around to see if anyone else had noticed, in a desperate hope rather than anything else. When all she saw was every person staring wide-eyed at Kate, Rachel merely put her head into her hands and tried to shrink away. Undeterred, Kate marched straight to Rachel, sat next to her and threw an arm around her. "Miss us?" Kate said loudly and grinned.

Kate and Rachel were not just fantastic company; they were also fantastic athletes. Back at the trials in 1997, as the four of us rowed over to the side and waited to be told what combinations would be going out to race next, we looked at each other and agreed that it had felt like the fastest boat of the day. In seat racing the crews often have no time to practise and get used to each other, so you get a very short time to put together a good race. With this crew the boat flew fast and easily and was better than anything else we'd tried that day. We didn't know how we would fare on time and we knew that was the only real factor that would decide selection. We were told the racing was over for the day and we carried the boats in, after which there was nothing to do but hang around waiting nervously for the results. As we hoped, they chose Kate, Rachel, Cesca and me as the four who would join with the existing four to become the new British women's eight.

But it was never going to be as easy as just joining the other four. They had been racing all season, and it had to be made clear that it was worth their while to join with four others and put their energies into an eight. To prove our worth we were going to have to race the other four and would have to be within a boat length to be deemed worthy of creating the new eight. It was a tough ask as they had been winning comfortably on the international scene all summer and we had just met each other as a crew. And we were given a matter of days. The whole squad was staying at Nottingham University and training at Holme Pierrepont. Luckily the four of us had hit it off instantly and loved the challenge we'd been given. We would meet on the outdoor steps at the halls of residence and talk about our plans.

Without knowing anything about how to form teams we were unwittingly doing things right. All four of us were comfortable to give our opinions; no one outranked the others. Everyone had different strengths and we made sure we knew what those strengths were and

13

used them. Everyone could make suggestions, and after discussions the best suggestion would be the way we'd go. It was simple, all underpinned by an incredibly clear common goal, a united purpose, and with each individual feeling she added value. There was also a limited time frame, so we couldn't waste a moment or a session. We knew it was a massive challenge, but all our energies were focused on how we would do it, not whether or not we would. We didn't realize it at the time, but the simplicity was a powerful weapon. And I was relentlessly optimistic about our chances.

Every day on the last 2km of the training sessions I would run through our race plan. Although what it turned into was less race strategy and more visualization of winning. I didn't even intend it to happen the first time. We sat at the startline at the end of the lake and I described how we might be feeling and what we would be thinking about; then the gun would go and I'd talk us through the first few strokes of the race, and then I said where the other four was and how we were doing in relation to it. Rachel later said, "I thought after about a minute that there was no way you could keep that up, but you just kept going." I had to check if that was a good or bad thing, but apparently it was good. I talked through the whole 2,000m as we paddled down the course; sometimes we would be ahead, sometimes behind, sometimes level. Sometimes I'd call for better technique, sometimes more work, sometimes a change in pace. I'd describe how the other crew might be feeling and what we would be feeling.

To their absolute credit, whatever I came up with the crew would respond and be better for it. I would try to come up with something different every time so that we wouldn't have any set expectations of how the race would unfold. We had nothing to base our relative performance on, so we had to be ready to be ahead, behind, level at any point and not get either overly confident or dangerously disheartened. But one thing was always the same each time we did it. Every single time we would win. Sometimes by a long way, sometimes by the smallest of margins. And although it was at the end of a training session and just supposed to be low physical intensity and mainly a mental exercise, inevitably by the end of the row we would all be pushing a little more, breathing a little harder, with a slightly higher rate than was intended. It was a good sign.

When the day of the race came we were as ready as we could be. It was a full 2,000m race, with only two boats in the centre of the Nottingham lake. We had talked so much about the start of the race that it wasn't scary sitting there, we were looking forward to seeing what we could do. For about 1,500m the two boats were practically level, sometimes one ahead, sometimes the other; there wasn't much to separate us as we came into the last part of the race. That is often the toughest part – not mentally (that pleasure is usually reserved for the third quarter), but it's tough because you are exhausted and yet have to gather strength to sprint for the line while everything is aching and sore and tired and your mind thinks trying to go faster is a crazy idea and your technique comes under the greatest of stresses. The technique that we try to perfect in training is tested most when physically and mentally everything is tiring. And unfortunately that's when our lack of time together showed.

The other four mounted an impressive sprint finish that they had been practising in their international racing. We rallied to match them and although it was one of the strongest finishes in the sense of passion, drive and determination I have ever been part of, the mind was thinking beyond what was possible with our technique. Where the other crew showed their prowess, we showed what will happen if a crew has more passion and drive than technique and training; it got us so very far but not far enough. We dropped behind in the dying stages but crucially held on to the overlap which meant we were within the required boat length of the other crew. Although we lost and felt the disappointment of that, it was soon replaced with the thought that we had won the challenge that had been thrown at us. We were on our way to the World Championships. And, importantly, in racing in the way we had, we had won the respect of the coaches and the other four.

Unbeknownst to me, what lay ahead was one of the happiest summers of my rowing career. The memories from that time are so strong and the friendships created then continue now. We flew out to Varese, Italy, in preparation for the World Championships. Our accommodation was a monastery in the hills above the town, and we had sparse individual rooms with single beds, the sole decoration a crucifix above each bed; but the austerity didn't affect the excitement of being in Italy with the British Rowing Team, preparing for the biggest rowing event after the Olympic Games. Steve Redgrave was also on the camp, and although I had met him a month or so earlier when he awarded Cesca and me the Redgrave Trophy for the pairs event at women's Henley, here we were on the same team. Steve and Matthew had won the pairs title at the previous year's Olympic Games, and were the only British gold medallists from 1996. I had cut out a fantastic picture taken by Peter Spurrier that was in the paper shortly after their victory. It wasn't a jubilant celebration or the triumphant moment on the podium. It was a simple gesture. They were still sitting in the boat, Matthew had put his arm behind him and Steve was holding on to it with both hands, head bowed. It summed up everything in a quiet personal moment, and it took me years to fully appreciate those special few minutes alone in a crew after crossing the line in a world of noise and chaos. To train alongside the likes of Steve and Matt and James and Tim and Jurgen as they worked towards that historic win in Sydney was an enormous privilege.

But in 1997 the Sydney Games were a long way away and everything would be focused on just the few short weeks we had to prepare for Aiguebelette, the beautiful French lake that would host the World Championships. The training was tough but enjoyable. Ron Needs would be our coach and would try to steer us through to the Worlds as best he could. Ron is a legend within rowing; at the time he was in his 70s and had been in rowing as long as anyone could remember. He had supported women's rowing with his own money before funding had come in, and had done the same for lightweight rowing before that. Ron used to work in the pharmaceutical industry and was often jet-setting around the world on business. There is an infamous tale of him telling his lightweight men's crew the session he wanted them to do. It was in London on the Thames, and before he left for his meeting abroad he gave them detailed instructions about how far up the river he wanted them to row. With the coach away, the crew did most of the session but felt maybe it wasn't necessary to go quite as far as he had suggested. Ron would never know, it would all be fine. When he joined them the next day he asked how their training had been. They answered it had been good, and then Ron asked them why they had turned around earlier than he had asked them to. There was a pause as the athletes tried to work out if he was bluffing or not. How could he really know? He pointed skywards. "I had the plane divert over the river to watch where you were." As that story went into rowing legend, no one ever cut short Ron's outings; there was a sense that you never quite knew where he might be.

Ron by now was less businessman and more of a kind grandfather figure. He was still a shrewd coach, but he had softened and was very encouraging to us as his new crew. We were lucky to have him, and as he shuffled around making supportive comments we slaved under the hot sunshine. The other four girls that made up the eight were also great to row with. Lisa would be the stroke; she was the driving force and had high standards we all had to live up to. She often carried herself with the serious look of someone carrying the weight of the world on her shoulders, but she could easily be shaken from this into laughing with the rest of us. Sue was at seven and was nicknamed "Mother Hen". The thankless job she took on was to make sure everything was OK and everyone was OK. Similar to Lisa, she had a serious side, but while for Lisa it was about her own performance and that of the boat, Sue seemed to take on everyone else's performance. She wore a concerned frown much of the time but also had a wonderful sense of humour and laugh whenever she allowed herself. I referred to her room as "the clinic" because she seemed to speak to so many people there, to console, reassure, support and share. Her moods could vary with the burden she carried, but she always delivered on the water.

Alex always seemed to have a huge smile on her face and laughed easily, but valuably gave her opinion strongly whenever needed and could be relied on to raise important but difficult points whenever necessary. Libby went through her own challenges with injury that summer but generally could be found laughing somewhere and, along with Rachel, kept spirits high in the bows of the boat. And then there was Suzie. Coxes have one of the toughest positions in rowing, mainly because they fall between athlete and coach. In my mind they are one of the athletes, but their role is admittedly a tricky one. Some may do the land training with the athletes to show team spirit, but their job isn't physical and in the boat they don't do the physical work. This can lead to them being the target of exhausted and fraying tempers and getting accused of not understanding the athletes' pain. Coxes do have to work closely with the coaches, because when the coach isn't nearby and especially in races, the cox has the coach's voice, and their thinking should ideally be the same. Coxes usually have extra meetings with the coaches and can be seen as one of "them". I have known people surprised to hear that coxes get medals too, but believe me they earn it. A good cox can make the vital difference in a race. Whereas steering is an understated skill, the impact coxes can make by the words they use, the confidence they inspire and the emotions they control is enormous. Suzie would show why she was the best in Britain when it came to our final a few weeks later.

It wasn't all happy, though. When I look back through my diaries of that time, although the overwhelming reading is positive there were a few episodes along the way that stopped it from being a fairytale summer. The saddest of all of them was when we were told Kate would be leaving the group. Kate, who to me was an unstoppable force of nature, a vibrant, strong personality, had picked up a virus and hadn't been able to shake it off. Poor Kate hadn't started the camp well, and maybe we should have read the signs. When we got off the plane in Milan we took our bags to the bus and climbed aboard. After a long wait someone came on asking if anyone had seen Kate. We looked at each other and shrugged. Then we were asked if anyone had seen Kate in Italy, and when the last time we had seen her was. Her bag was going around the carousel and there was no sign of Kate. It transpired that the last sighting had been in one of the duty-free shops at Heathrow Airport. She was buying a music system and while waiting for the assistant to locate the remote control Kate missed the final boarding call and duly missed our flight. She had to catch the next flight, arrived stressed and out of sorts, and only about a week later left the camp, still stressed and now exhausted, to try to recover from pleurisy which she had been diagnosed with.

When Kate left she taught me all I needed to know about handling disappointment. She was devastated to be leaving and I found her in her room leaning out of the window, head in hands, listening to deafening music. But she never made her premature departure an issue for the rest of us. She wouldn't do anything to detract from the job we all still had to do, and she wished us well with the challenge ahead, saying we would see her again. She walked out with grace, with dignity and with defiance.

Inevitably we all moved forward. We had to. Elise Laverick had joined us and took Kate's seat. Elise had been in the Under-23 team with Cesca and me and so was a friendly, familiar face. She was stepping into big shoes, but seamlessly joined the group and became a key member of the senior team for over ten years. The eight was still going well in training, but while Kate had been having health issues we were dealt another blow when Libby was taken out of the eight with a suspected rib stress fracture. There were a few days when I went into the four, Cesca and Elise rowed in a pair and Rachel went into the single. It was a tricky time for everyone, not knowing who would be doing what and when. Sue, Lisa and Alex struggled with not knowing what would happen with their four and the impact it might have on the eight.

Finally we left Varese with Libby back, Kate gone and Elise in. It was my first World Championships and despite the rollercoaster ride to get here I wanted the next couple of weeks to go well. I was still thrilled by the kit we had been given back in Varese. I remember putting on my first tracksuit top with "Great Britain" on the back and dancing around my single room with the door shut. The others had had kit issued to them in previous years and didn't seem to be displaying the same ridiculous excitement I felt, and so I kept my embarrassing celebrations to myself.

With the kit and the arrival at the site of the World Championships other things began to sink in too. I realized that this is what the whole year was aimed towards and it would be over very quickly. All too soon we would return to the long, cold, dark, wet nights and mornings. There's a phrase much used by the coaches about "putting money in the bank". That's what the winter is for, the hours and hours every day of long water sessions, long ergos and sessions in the gym lifting weights. In Aiguebelette I appreciated those sentiments as I realized it was now too late to be longing for more time on the water or in the weights gym. I wrote in my diary, "Now it is the time to polish and perfect, not to create. Although winter may not be the glamorous side, it's definitely the backbone to it all."

Aiguebelette is a beautiful corner of France, with the lake at the bottom of a huge hill that rises up behind the water and casts a shadow over the lake at certain times of the day. The water is blue and hypnotic and the sun was out every day. We set up little tents at the side where we could relax between races or training sessions and get physio treatment if necessary. One of the physios who came with us brought his saxophone and I remember lying in the shade listening to soulful tunes next to the lapping water and thinking I had the best job in the world.

A few days before the regatta we were sitting around down at the course when Mike Spracklen, the women's head coach, walked over to us. "Did you hear the bad news?" he asked. It sounded like the first line of a joke, and yet he wasn't usually the one telling the jokes. We squinted up into the sun at where he was standing and said no we hadn't. I was worried we might have yet another injury in the crew. "Princess Diana and Dodi Al Fayed were in a car crash and…" And there was no punchline. We looked at each other in confusion and went to find out what on earth was going on. It turned out that France was in chaos as the news broke of Princess Diana being in a crash in a tunnel in Paris. The next few hours were surreal as bits and pieces of information came in and there was a general air of disbelief. Reports weren't clear as to what had happened and at first it wasn't definite that she had died. First Dodi Al Fayed was confirmed dead, and then Diana. We sat in our various rooms with the doors open and watched in shock. Suzie was in the room opposite us and I remember distraught wails crossing the hallway. It was strange being in the country where it was happening but away from the country that was experiencing the strongest reaction. Britain had been brought to a standstill and the news in France was full of pictures of the Mall being filled with thousands and thousands of flowers.

It looked at one point as if the tragedy was going to affect us directly. Many sports events had been called off in Britain out of respect. Weekend matches were cancelled and there was the suggestion we should withdraw from the World Championships. It's tough because although there is a desire to show respect, for us this was a once a year international event, not just a weekend fixture. After a nervous wait we were told we would be racing but we would wear black ribbons, and if any medals were won the Union Jack would fly at half mast. Sadly it was to be the first of three separate occasions when I would race wearing a black ribbon to mark a British tragedy.

The competition drew near and we were ready to go. It was incredible to be part of a huge team all racing under the Great Britain title. Being part of a special team is an incredible feeling and it made me even more sure I wanted us to deliver on the lake. The regatta started positively, especially with the pair and the double racing well. Dot Blackie and Cath Bishop were the British pair and two people I had looked up to for a long time. They won their heat and looked strong going forward through the regatta. But it was not to be. Cath became very ill and couldn't race in their semi-final. She didn't want to stop Dot from racing but had to move out of our hotel to be isolated in case she was contagious, enduring a miserable few days in a hotel across the road knowing the devastating impact her illness would have. It was decided Cesca would sub into the pair in her place and race with Dot.

Suzie and I went down to watch their race, knowing they just had to finish in the top three in order to go through and give Cath a chance to make it back for the final. It was heartbreaking. Dot and Cesca were in second or third position for most of the race with a reasonable margin over Denmark in the fourth position. But in the crucial last 500m they began to slip down the field. The camera showed the boat moving to one side of the lane as Dot in her desperation applied more and more power. When the camera swung back to the side view they were losing ground. There was a sharp intake of breath from both Suzie and me, and we froze until they crossed the line. In fourth place.

Suzie and I went over to help them at the landing stage and they were both in floods of tears. I had tears in my eyes as it hit home that all the year's work and training were focused on this one moment. A year is a long time for it to come to this, and for it to be so close and yet so far. It felt cruel. I could only imagine what Cath must be going through in her hotel room in front of the TV. Later, back in the room that Cesca, Rachel and I were sharing, we tried our best to cheer Cesca up. Dot walked in with half a dozen white roses for Cesca and a note that read: "Thanks, it was more than I could have asked for. Sorry I couldn't make it a double whammy for you."

While disappointment raged for some, there was celebration for others. Suzie, Rachel and I went to the grandstands to watch the women's four race. It was at this point that I learned a lifelong empathy towards friends and family watching races. I felt more nervous about the women's four race than I had ever done about my own, and I did not enjoy the heart-pounding tension as the four sat on the startline. Happily, however, they won in an impressive race, powering through the favoured Romanians in the last 250m. Their ecstatic faces on the podium said it all. Gillian and Miriam won an impressive and ground-breaking silver in the double, Guin came fourth in the single and Steve and the four also won. The four received their gold medal with their heads bowed and the Union Jack at half mast.

And then it was our turn. Lisa gave a fantastic talk about what was to come, Suzie gave us our best ever race visualization, Ron even swore in his pre-race chat. We were ready. As we boated for the race Rachel and I looked at each other, and I said, "It's a good day to die," inspired by Brad Alan Lewis's book on his 1984 Olympic experience, *Assault on Lake Casitas*, when he talks about giving everything to the race ahead. Through all the ups and downs, the highs and lows, the tears and laughter, the year ultimately gets defined by about six minutes on the water.

I sat on the start and glanced across to the boats either side of me, but didn't take much in. I just smiled a small smile, enjoying the moment and ready to do whatever it was we came here to do. After the "Attention" there was a huge gap and the silence was immense. As the green disc flipped over, a deafening clamour broke the stillness and we were off. It felt like a good start but we were sixth at 250m. This was a deciding moment for us and this is where Suzie showed her greatness. In a loud, clear, confident tone she said, "We're sixth and we're OK." It was only much, much later, long after the race, that I looked back and thought that meant we were last. The way she said it expressed only that things were going well for us and her tone matched the feeling in the boat that we were in the race and it felt good. A lesser cox might have panicked or tried to explain that sixth was actually OK, but by just the clear direction, I didn't think for even a moment that sixth might be a problem. We powered on to the next marker with confidence. I remember the race flying by, but I still had the time to listen, to recognize the markers and to relax. We soon pulled ahead of the USA and Germany and were moving into the bronze medal position. We stayed in bronze as we raced to the finish line.

Crossing the line was strange. At first I felt a slight disappointment as I'd gone out to win. But the reaction of the crew around me changed all that. They were screaming and shouting, laughing and grinning and clapping each other. We'd just won a bronze medal in an Olympic event in our third ever race together. I started to smile and hugged Cesca and Alex. We'd just managed a better result than any previous British women's eight had. There was much joking that we owed it to the Spice Girls as that was the year of international Girl Power. On the podium there were many more hugs, and when the flag was raised I just stood grinning at it until my cheeks hurt; there was no sombre stance for me. Matthew Pinsent stood at the press tent and bowed to us.

The history books show one version of the summer, but experience teaches us that there is often a different story behind the results. The year 1997 was a successful one for the British women's eight, four and double. On paper it was a non-event for Kate Mackenzie and Cath Bishop and a disappointing result for Dot Blackie. And indeed it was a heartbreaking season for all three of those athletes. The truth, however, is a little more complex. That year Dot Blackie displayed a courage and generosity of spirit that no result can express. Cath Bishop experienced a depth of grief that she had never experienced before in rowing and learned to handle the cruel disappointment of external factors cutting short her own opportunity and that of her crewmate too. And Kate Mackenzie, who when I talk about the '97 eight I always still include in the line-up without realizing, may have lost a medal but won the everlasting respect of her teammates. None of us would have had the opportunity to race that summer in the eight if she hadn't been part of the toughest four back in Nottingham. She taught us all a little of what it was to have to walk away from a dream and to do it with head held high, shoulders back and that magnificent chest thrust forward.

CHAPTER 2

THE WONDER YEARS

Within two months of graduating from University with my law degree, therefore, I was an Under-23 World Champion and the winner of a bronze medal at the senior World Championships. It wasn't at all what I had expected as I started at Edinburgh University four years earlier.

When I was leaving school I agonized over what to do. My mum and dad repeatedly tried in vain to help me with my thinking. We'd have conversations together, separately, at home, on the bus, in the car, but I couldn't pinpoint what I wanted to do. I felt I had a lot of energy and a lot of passion to be aimed somewhere, but I just couldn't identify the direction. On the wall of my bedroom I had a poster of a golden retriever leaping off the end of a jetty into the air above the water, and the caption read, "I don't know where I'm going, but I'm going." I could relate to that. I remember exclaiming in frustration, "I just don't want a boring life!" I couldn't really define what a boring life was, though, never mind explain what my idea of a non-boring life would be.

When I was much younger I wanted to be a vet. In fact I went through a stage when I believed that animals were the best things on the planet. One day I even proclaimed to my mum, "From now on I am only going to read books about animals." The enthusiastic English teacher in my mum reined in her most obvious reaction and very calmly informed me that in that case I would be missing out on a lot of great stories. Thankfully I moved past my stubborn stage and soon embraced the wider world of fiction, and my real and imaginative world were undoubtedly enhanced as a result.

Along with many young people at school at some point I filled in a questionnaire that would help me find a job that I would be suited to. I can't remember exactly how I answered, but it might have been with a childlike enthusiasm for a range of areas because the answers ranged from being a children's entertainer to a prison warden. I wasn't sure about the connection between the two (although some may disagree) and at least the questionnaires didn't appear to be limited in scope. People seemed to have suggestions like "circus performer" or "botanist in Madagascar". I'm a believer in trying as many things as possible that interest, challenge or fascinate in order to find your true passion. My interests had always been varied and I still find all kinds of things absorbing in different ways. I would far rather have someone thinking "I wonder what a deep-sea dolphin dentist does?" than be given the more obvious traditional career options.

My mum and dad were teachers and had met on the first day of their post-graduate teacher training in Edinburgh. They were both headhunted and walked into jobs as soon as they left college and soon were married. Dad's second job was in Inverness and it was there that my sister Sarah was born. According to family lore she was the perfect baby, slept all the time, straight through the night from an early age, and rarely cried. The following year, shortly before I was born, the family moved to north Glasgow, and it was there that I was almost born a single child. In the chaos of moving there were things strewn all over the house and Sarah, crawling her way around a new home, found an abandoned screwdriver and felt the best place for it was in a live socket. Somehow she survived unharmed but managed to fuse the whole house. Not to be outdone in parental attention I decided to join the world three weeks early, although I did give my mum enough time to put her Carmen rollers in before she had to leave for hospital. Thankfully my mum has never been a woman who gets flustered easily, and so having one daughter who nearly electrocuted herself and one who arrived before boxes were unpacked didn't create any problems and our family was complete.

By the time my sister and I were old enough to be aware of what our parents did, dad had moved from the classroom. He worked in national curriculum development and I learned subliminally about the value of enjoying what you do for a living. Most days my mum would come home from her school with her handbag slung over one shoulder and a big plastic shopping bag crammed with paper folders and A4 paper. She would diligently sit at our dining-room table and mark papers or do lesson plans, often entertaining us with tales from her school. She taught English and, without her needing to tell us, we knew that she loved it. I remember being in awe as she told us about her sixth-year classes, the oldest students, who were allowed to get up and make a tea or coffee in the classroom while the class discussed literature. This level of trust and responsibility was unknown to me in my own classes, and I longed for the time when I'd be treated as a grown-up while discussing Shakespeare or Tennessee Williams or Hardy.

Mum worked hard but never showed resentment or fatigue with it. She wanted to make her classes as good as she possibly could and was always working on new inventive ways to engage students about the subject she loved. Her passion was infectious and although she did spend hours on work and at work, we had the impression she was enjoying what she was doing and therefore it didn't appear onerous. My sister and I were, no doubt, seeing it all through the naïve eyes of youth, and although I'm sure mum was tired and stressed at some points in her career, from our point of view we saw someone who loved what she did and therefore didn't ever complain about working.

My dad, on the other hand, rarely worked at home. According to what we heard from my mum, dad had been a great history teacher at school and was spotted early on as having potential. He soon moved to curriculum development and, it seemed, never enjoyed the role as much as teaching. He did his job at the office, and Sarah and I weren't really sure about what he did as he rarely talked about it. In my French or German classes he became a teacher again, or sometimes a doctor, as they were easier vocabulary than "national curriculum education officer". As dad didn't seem to work when he was at home, it meant more time to sit with him as he watched Marx Brothers films and swashbuckling westerns. It was dad who gave me one of my favourite books, about Knights and Legends, and I would lose myself in the stories of the myths and retell them to dad when he came up to say goodnight.

Dad was great with DIY and made loads of toys for Sarah and me when we were young, including a massive Noah's Ark complete with all the animals imaginable. The basement room of the house was his workshop, and he had a huge circular saw set up there. Sarah and I weren't allowed to touch the saw, but we would watch nervously from the doorway with hands over our ears as dad donned his plastic safety goggles and the scream of the saw signalled work had begun on his latest creation. Dad would also make bread on a Sunday morning, and I would stand next to him at the kitchen counter when I was old enough to reach it, being allowed half of the dough to knead, after sprinkling flour on to the worktop, and then fold into the silver baking tins. I'd then watch through the oven door as the magic of baking took place and the slightly sticky concoction dad had put in was transformed into a dark golden crusty loaf. At the time it was the only bread we ate, and I eventually took it for granted, longing for the occasional slice of white bread my friends all had. But now I'd give anything for another slice of that toasted home-made bread with butter melting on it. I'm ashamed to say my cooking skills haven't progressed much over the years, although I still have hope that they might as I love the sociable aspect of food. Sarah and I did, however, inherit a little bit of dad's creative ways, and we used to spend hours with various model kits, glueing and painting all kinds of things. We also had masses of Lego and I used to love playing with my space station kit, including rocket and buggy track.

Dad has always been a fan of the outdoors and when we were growing up in Glasgow he often disappeared to climb a Munro or two. He'd pack his bag for the day and put on an array of walking gear that was well worn. The weather would be irrelevant; come rain or shine the hills were there to be conquered in all conditions. As we grew up we sometimes joined dad for a hike up the west coast mountains and then took part in the regular ritual of buffing and oiling our own walking boots. Our boots were to be looked after.

As well as learning about responsibility, mum and dad instilled a strong sense of manners into us. Although dad was the disciplinarian and mum the one to give us hugs, it was mum who would watch over us every Christmas and birthday while we sat at the dining-room table and wrote thank-you notes. Sarah and I used to groan as we were dragged away from whatever bit of fun we were having to sit and write the letters. It's only as a grown-up that I appreciate the important values we were being given.

Sarah and I were also suitably unappreciative of the holidays we went on. Every year, it seemed, we loaded up the car and drove south, stopping first at grandma and grandpa's in Upminster before boarding the diesel-smelling ferry that bellowed its way across the channel to France. As a consequence of my dad's interest in history we visited endless châteaux and the summers were filled with fromage, gîtes and stories of Kings and Queens, beheadings and intrigue. We journeyed from north Brittany to the Alps to the Camargue, where we tried archery, the luge and dinghy sailing. It was incredible, and yet Sarah and I rolled our eyes when yet again we were told we were going to France on holiday. Among the best bits for us were the few days we spent in Upminster on the way there or the way back; they always seemed to be balmy summer days with water fights in the garden.

Grandma was a small, neat woman who sat in her favourite chair watching over the house. The family story goes that when my mum was introduced to grandma after my mum and dad first began dating, mum sent grandma flying, not realizing she was behind her. As grandma grew older they had a stairlift put into the house and she'd watch, pretending to be disapproving, as Sarah and I took it in turns to take the interminably slow, but in our minds endlessly entertaining, trip up and down the stairs sitting on the seat, standing on the seat, balancing upside-down on the seat. Grandpa was an active man, and if I got my sporting genes from anywhere, it would have been from him. When he was younger he had the chance to turn professional in both football and cricket, but in the end he went into teaching, as the pay was more reliable and the job more secure. Considering the scale of football wages now, it seems funny to think that football wasn't a good career choice a couple of generations earlier.

CHAPTER 2

Every three years we would have a special trip to stay with grandma and grandpa before travelling on to Heathrow. The excitement of being woken very early to make the dawn drive to the airport was immense, as we were off for a holiday in the United States, where my aunt and uncle and two cousins, Michael and Kerron, lived. Mum's sister, my Auntie Kate, had moved out there with my Uncle Mike when she was still quite young. I loved her sense of adventure and her warm, capable manner. Everything felt possible there, and although I was the youngest in the family, Auntie Kate used to pull me on to her knee for games of Trivial Pursuit and let me be in her team as I was her namesake. Sarah and I shared a room with Kerron, and we three girls used to fall asleep with the radio playing softly in the background and the gentle whirr of the overhead ceiling fan trying to cool the humid summer evening. Sometimes we would have jam jars lighting the room with glow-worms we had caught earlier in the day. We would always be able to hear the laughter coming up from the living room along the hallway where mum and Auntie Kate would be happily reminiscing. My Uncle Mike was a larger-than-life character, both in personality and physical size. He had a big fuzzy beard and would nuzzle against us, eliciting screams of hilarity and horror as his scratchy face rubbed softly against ours.

Together we travelled all over, from their original home in Connecticut to New York, Niagara Falls, down to New Orleans, the Gulf of Mexico and Tennessee, where they later moved to. When I started rowing, Auntie Kate and Uncle Mike couldn't have been prouder, and when I won my first international race they bought me a beautiful book on rowing and dedicated it "To our gold medal niece". Sadly they both died prematurely and didn't live to see my Olympic career, but I know they'd have been there in London yelling the loudest from the stands if they'd been able to. A few months after the London Olympics Anna and I went to the Women of the Year awards and were asked to nominate a woman each who inspired us. I chose my Auntie Kate for her fearlessness and her fun and also the huge amounts of work she did for charity. Although she is gone she is constantly missed and her inspiration will always live on.

I was lucky to be surrounded by wonderfully inspirational women when I was growing up. I loved spending time with Auntie Kate and mum, and there was no doubt that they got their "can do" attitude from their mum, my beloved gran. She was a dynamic woman, always on the

30

go and never without some project or other. Even when we were sitting watching TV together, gran would be sewing or darning or knitting or writing. One summer when Sarah and I were both very young, grandad bought us a set of plastic golf clubs. They were quite bulky to carry about, so in an hour or so gran found some tartan material and stitched together perfect golf bags, complete with little pockets for the balls and tiny rows for the tees. Magic! Every summer we visited gran and grandad in Aberdeen and they would take Sarah and me to the beach for a swim in the North Sea, irrespective of weather. We'd both tiptoe into the waves, screaming as the cold water swirled around our white feet. After a while we'd come running out breathlessly and be embraced with big fluffy towels that gran and grandad would be holding open for us. We'd build endless sandcastles and then be called over to eat home-made sandwiches, crunching our way happily through the grains of sand that were inevitably blown into the bread.

Gran worked every week for 38 years in a voluntary charity shop in Aberdeen city centre. When I was visiting I loved going on the bus with her and venturing into the city to join her in the "thrift shop". I would help behind the counters, but one of my favourite bits was when we were allowed a tea break and would go through into the narrow back shop area where the kettle would be on and the tupperware box of chocolate biscuits was opened and various home bakes were brought out. I would sit with my can of juice and listen to the wonderful conversations they would have, crammed full of whispered gossip, freely given opinions, stories from the past, tales of so-and-so who had just been into the shop and "you'd never guess, but …". Gasps of surprise and raised voices of mild outrage would filter through the buzz of too many voices talking over themselves to be heard. I loved my days there, and when grandad came to collect us at the end of the day I always seemed to leave with more than I arrived with. I'd find stuffed into my bag a jumper, belt, shirt, jacket or bag that one of the ladies had laid aside because she thought it was "just right" for me.

After the Olympics, Royal Mail gave every gold medallist a gold post-box. They could have put mine in Glasgow where I was born, or Edinburgh where I learned to row or Marlow where I trained but, unasked, they put it in Aberdeen – right outside gran's "thrift shop". They had no idea of course, but they couldn't have chosen a more perfect place. She was no longer with us, but I think of it as my gran's golden reward.

Food was always on the go in gran's house and there was usually the smell of baking seeping out from the kitchen. Her shortbread and chocolate chip cookies were legendary, as well as all forms of cakes. Every Christmas her sherry-soaked trifle was a hit, and there'd be sharp intakes of breath around the table as a particularly potent mouthful hit the spot. In the evening we'd settle in front of the TV and start with one or two of the soaps that gran loved, usually *Coronation Street*, *EastEnders* or *Emmerdale*, then a bit of *The Bill* for grandad, who was an ex-policeman, and we'd inevitably finish with a good murder mystery of some sort. The library books stacked up next to gran's bed were usually crime thrillers, from Agatha Christie to Ruth Rendell, from P. D. James to Patricia Cornwell. On TV we'd watch *Miss Marple*, *Poirot*, *Columbo*, *Taggart*, *Prime Suspect*, in fact anything with a high body count and an element of intrigue. It was no wonder I ended up studying crime. At some point in the evening gran would leave her chair and disappear into the dining room next door. Sarah and I would listen for the noise of the bottom drawer being opened in the wooden sideboard which was gran's "secret" stash of chocolate bars. This was the home of Wispas and Crunchies and occasionally a Fry's peppermint cream. Gran would come back with "a little treat" for everyone.

Her generosity and hospitality were legendary, and there were stories of how when she was younger she supplied cakes to prisoners. When grandad was in the police, at one point they lived in a police house that had the jail attached to the residential part of the house. After a day of baking gran, much to grandad's horror, would take a tray of scones, biscuits or cakes down to the cells and offer them to the offenders in the lock-up. By the time Sarah and I were around, grandad had left the police, but we loved hearing stories of his days in uniform and we'd hunt out the objects he still owned from his time on the Force and play with the whistle, his little metal container for chalk and his wooden truncheon.

Grandad was the gentlest, sweetest man imaginable, always a complete gentleman. Even when he was 90, suffering from dementia, and had to move into a home, he still used to hold the doors open for the staff and looked after the old lady in the room next to his to make sure she was

OK and not too lonely or scared. When we were growing up, one of my favourite moments was when he would bring out his old-style movie projector. I loved the whirring noise of the huge machine, the smell in the air as it heated up and the dust particles that would come to life in front of the bright bulb. The whole family crammed into the room and as the numbers flashed on to the wall we'd join in the countdown: "5, 4, 3, 2, 1." Soon the wall would be full of either home movies or the bright colours of various Disney cartoons. I remember being terrified by Maleficent, the baddy in *Sleeping Beauty*, and the black crow that used to sit on her shoulder. Her arched eyebrows and long face would fill the screen, soon to be replaced by the terrifying, enormous dragon she turned into. Sarah and I would watch spellbound, holding our breath as good and evil did battle in our dining room.

It wasn't just indoors that good and evil did battle. Sarah and I would continue the stories outside when we met up with our friends to play all sorts of imaginative games. The place where I grew up was perfect from a child's viewpoint. The street we lived on was reasonably quiet, as the road that went along in front of our house doubled back on itself and came around behind the houses, ending in a cul-de-sac. The dead end bit of road at the back became the perfect place to play, with access to houses on both sides and gardens and garages. Just over a wire fence was the Mosshead Primary School playground, and beyond another fence were the fields and a park with a stream, opening up infinitely more possibilities of adventure. It was on those streets that we played football or hide and seek, learned to ride bikes and climb trees. Every afternoon and evening we would gather outside with the other kids in the neighbourhood. In a street of maybe ten houses, seven had children the same ages as Sarah and I. The summer nights especially would last for hours as the Scottish evenings never seemed to darken. Usually one of the parents would come out and shout for us, or bang loudly on the windows and beckon to us, to signal the end of the fun for another night.

It always felt incredibly safe, and none of us grew up feeling afraid or concerned to be out and about for hours on end away from parents' watchful eyes. However, there had to be some mild sense of danger to help feed a child's imagination, and in one corner of the street lay an electrical generator fenced off with warning signs, danger markings and promises of death. There was always a frenzied panic if a ball was thrown or kicked over the fence, and dares made for someone to go and get it back. No one was electrocuted to my knowledge but we feared and respected it in equal measures. That was the biggest threat we were aware of; there was no concern about stranger danger.

My best friend Kirsteen lived two doors up and she had an older sister and brother. Many nights she would shuffle over to my house having borrowed her sister Diane's shoes, big high-heeled smart patent items that were about double the length of Kirsteen's feet but didn't stop her trying to clip-clop her way around in them. Colin, one of my first boyfriends, lived next door and at the far end of the street was my other best friend Catriona and her younger brother and sister. It was an incredibly simple life and every day we would walk to school and back with bags dragging along the pavement behind us and make great plans for the weekend ahead.

Sarah and I wanted a dog. We tried all forms of childhood persuasion, from pleading to begging and sulking to unrealistic promises. When even the final desperate straw of "but it's so unfair, Kirsteen is allowed one" failed to convince our parents, Sarah and I resigned ourselves to a lifetime of watching goldfish swim around a tank. We were, therefore, ridiculously excited when we were informed we would be allowed to go to the pet shop and choose our own guinea pigs. Here were pets that we could actually touch and hold and stroke. We might not be able to take them for walks or run around in the fields with them, but at least they wouldn't flip about gasping for breath and threatening death when we changed the water. So began many years of guinea pigs, who proved to be friendly, attentive, intelligent and cuddly companions. The only downside was, as with every pet, when they eventually have to die. I remember one traumatic evening I was studying for my exams in my bedroom while my ageing and ailing guinea pig was downstairs with my mum. At one point I knew the slow footsteps on the stairs meant only one thing and I turned to see my mum in tears carrying the lifeless body of Patch, my beloved white, brown and black little friend who used to squeak at my arrival home from school every afternoon. For a while we tried hamsters and rabbits, but the attachment just wasn't the same. Sarah and I left home and, would you believe it, mum and dad have had dogs ever since.

I remember at weekends when mum would take us over to Milngavie, the nearby town, for shopping. There were untold riches there, including the pet shop, the Colpi ice cream shop legendary for the delicious vanilla nougat wafers, the shop crammed with all sorts of strange appliances that spilled out into plastic baskets on the pedestrian walkway, but my favourite was the bookshop. The door had an old fashioned bell that would ring as you walked in and there were three or four main aisles, crammed from floor to ceiling with books of all sizes and shapes and colours and ladders leaning up against impossibly high shelves. This was before the days of internet shopping when any book can be located at the click of a button, and so the piles of books seemed to hold new unknown treasures just waiting to be discovered. Mum would disappear down the grown-up section while Sarah and I would lose ourselves in a different corner. Even the smell of the new books and the feel of flicking through the crisp paper pages was exciting. It was like when we went to the local library to select our three books each to take home, but the difference here was the books could be ours forever – so the decision was even more important.

Sarah and I both had jobs growing up. I started on the "cream and egg round". Every Friday I would load up two buckets with eggs, cream, potato scones, and in winter there would be a variety of Christmas goodies like shortbread and even leather goods. Mum or dad would drop me a few streets away and for the next few hours I would walk the streets with my buckets, calling at pre-arranged houses to sell the products. It was a test of endurance. At the beginning the buckets were heavy and I'd try to keep them evenly balanced in weight and also movement because if the precious eggs were broken then they would be unsellable and I would lose valuable money. As the round went on and I sold more things the load would get lighter but the fatigue set in. The rain and cold could make it a miserable couple of hours, but the benefit was people generally felt sorry for me and usually bought more. I had to handle the cash and at the end of the night I would do the totals and decide what to order for the following week. It wasn't the easiest way to make money, but it taught me about sales, customers and just how much weight it is possible to carry in your arms for hours at a time. It also brought me my next (and easier) job, babysitting. Some of the customers who got to know me over time then asked me to babysit.

That money seemed easy to me – reading bedtime stories and then sitting in the warmth watching television while occasionally checking on the sleeping forms upstairs.

One woman who asked me to babysit, Candy, was a solicitor and also gave me my first real introduction to law when I was about 16. She knew I was thinking of studying it at university and so she suggested I spent a week at her law firm in Paisley for work experience. I was introduced to all the departments and was then asked to deliver some court documents. The kindly lawyer must have known what he was doing when he said I should ask the clerk at the court what was happening while I was there. I walked along the street clutching my documents and handed them over at the desk. The clerk told me there was an assault case being heard in one court and he ushered me into where the reporters sat. I pulled out my notebook and readied myself to take notes. I'm not sure if I thought I would fit in better, but I studiously wrote throughout the hearing. When the witnesses were finished for the day I ran back to the firm ready to explain why I hadn't been learning about photocopying or whatever else work experience students usually did. The lawyer just nodded throughout as I breathlessly recounted the day. "Is the case finished?" the solicitor asked. I shook my head. "Well, you'd better go back tomorrow and find out what happened." I spent the entire week in the court and loved every minute of the theatrical drama of the criminal case. I may not have learned much about what a solicitor does, but it helped convince me I had an attraction to the court aspect of law.

I enjoyed my schooldays. In primary school I learned that I had a decent memory, I could recite poetry, and I was good at sports, including the little-used ability to throw a beanbag a long way. I was competitive, I had little skill in singing although I loved music, I had a lot of friends, but was never the coolest in the gang. It was a safe environment to learn and develop and will always remember the fun in all the classrooms from Mrs Livingstone to Mrs Waudby. Two of our teachers, Miss Chisholm and Mrs Caldwell, sometimes worked in the theatre and had an absolute passion for the stage. They would be at the helm for each school show, and every year new costumes and songs would be created.

The first time I realized that I was tall was when I was the only one in my class to be an Emerald City person in the production of *The Wizard of Oz* while all the others of my age were munchkins. One summer I worked backstage in the Glasgow Theatre Royal's production of *Calamity Jane*. I absolutely loved the excitement of running on to the stage in the blackness to change the set, sensing the presence of thousands of people out there in the dark. I hero-worshipped the "stars" of the stage, although I didn't want those roles for myself. Working behind the scenes interested and attracted me far more than being on the stage. I had had my inability to sing firmly drummed into me by the school choir mistress when she allowed everyone in my year to be in the choir except for me and Lorna. We were excluded from practice and had to do other activities instead. I've never had confidence in my singing from that day on. I can see now the incredible power that positive encouragement or negative reinforcement has to affect a young mind at that stage of development. My big sister, Sarah, showed more promise than me, and while we both took clarinet lessons my attempts at the singing part of learning music were dire in contrast to Sarah. She was cast one year as Mrs Bumble in *Oliver!* and as a Pearly Queen in *Mary Poppins*, both singing roles, while I remained somewhere at the back of the chorus hidden from view.

My lack of talent in the choir didn't diminish my love for music. Mum always had the radio on or music playing, and Sarah and I were brought up with the early rock and roll music or the Beatles, Neil Diamond, Dusty Springfield, Elvis Presley, Simon and Garfunkel, Billy Joel and Abba. In the car we'd listen to *Evita*, *Jesus Christ Superstar* and *Joseph and the Amazing Technicolor Dreamcoat*, Sarah and I in the back seat arguing over which role we were going to play. One of my earliest memories of musicals was when I was tiny, sitting in front of the TV as my mum watched *West Side Story*. I was too young to really follow the story but loved the colour and music and movement of the dance. It all seemed to be going so well until Tony was shot and Maria lay on the floor holding him singing, "There's a place for us …" I turned with tears in my eyes to see mum sobbing behind me on the sofa. I still get emotional hearing that song. My first experience of a feature film at the cinema involved more crying as mum took Sarah and me along to see *ET* at the local Rio cinema. I remember the point where it looks as if ET is dying and there was a small voice behind us asking between sobs, "Mummy, is he dead?" There was a pause and then between even more sobs the mum wailed, "I don't know."

CHAPTER 2

In my last year of primary school I came second in the school sports award. My big sister yet again had shown more promise than me, having won it the previous year. I was disappointed with my second place, and seeing the title won by Jenny, who was a brilliant athlete who also always played "centre" in the netball team. The disappointment was very internal, as I didn't openly want to be at the forefront of things, but I knew deep inside that I wanted to win. The competitive spirit was always there but often loudest inside my own mind. Growing up, however, Sarah saw a lot of it. I benefited hugely from having a big sister who I could go along to things with. When she joined the swimming club, life-saving, badminton, tennis or the ski club, I went along at the same time or as soon as I could. It didn't feel scary going to new things because my big sister was there. And then, once there, I felt I should be as good as she was; the age difference didn't factor into my thinking. I struggled to keep up with Sarah but it never occurred to me for a second that I shouldn't compete against her. Mum said it started the minute my eyes could focus: they clamped onto Sarah whom obviously I felt had had the unfair advantage of being born a year before me so could, all by herself, move about, reach things, hold things, eat things. I seemingly watched with awe and as soon as I possibly could I was attempting to copy her in all things.

Sarah had the challenging role of playing the big sister while also having a strong competitive gene herself. She would hate beating me and seeing her little sister upset, but she also harboured a deep desire to win herself. As the younger sibling I had no qualms about simply wanting to finish on top. I really don't know where that drive came from, but sometimes when I watch my dad play cards or see my mum at work I witness the competitive instinct and the dedication that probably helped me to become what I am. Sarah has always played the role of protector to me and even now defends and looks after me whenever necessary. She has never shown one iota of jealousy about anything I've achieved and has been nothing but supportive in everything I've done. Of course she also gleefully beats me in squash or running when she wants to, but we have always had an incredible bond and have rarely disagreed in any way.

When I was younger I could sometimes be a bad loser, unsure of how to cope with the frustration of not achieving what I wanted. I hated letting myself down, and when I started playing more team games

I hated the prospect of letting others down. I do, however, think that losing is a crucial part of development, and it is often through losing that we learn how to be better, stronger and tougher and find out what is important to us. Everyone I know who has achieved great things in their lives can also talk about failures or disappointments along the way and they agree that this, in part, is what has helped them to be great. Taking risks, daring to try, not being afraid to make mistakes, learning from setbacks have been some of the vital steps on the way to some of the world's biggest inventions, discoveries, accomplishments and successes.

I learned other valuable lessons in school as I grew up. I had a close-knit group of friends when I moved on to the local senior school, Bearsden Academy. They were a great bunch of girls to hang out with, and together we embraced our teenage years of boyfriends, exams, nightclubs and trips away from home. We were inseperable as a group but at some point that became a problem for me as I had started to do more things outside of the group. One night there was some party or other that I didn't go to, and the next day they were all talking about it and I couldn't join in as I hadn't been part of the fun. There was a distinctly cool attitude and an even colder shoulder. It happened more than once: I had agreed to go on holiday with them and had saved up and spent my money on the deposit. Finally things got to the point where I woke up and decided I didn't want to go on the holiday. It was so far along now that I wouldn't get my deposit back; in fact I would have to pay the rest of the money whether I went on the holiday or not. I remember having a chat with my mum and being upset that, money aside, realistically this might be the end of the friendship. My mum is the most wonderful counsel and, far from mollycoddling me, reassured me that it would all be OK, especially if I learned from this. Learned how important my own voice was and that I shouldn't go along with things just because it was what the group wanted. In the end gran also stepped in to save me by giving me the money to pay off the holiday, while I took a shaky step towards adulthood.

Most of my young life, however, was not as complicated. I spent some wonderful weeks away at the outdoor activities residential centre in Garelochhead. There I fell in love with windsurfing, skiing, climbing, abseiling, even pot-holing. We had a fun dormitory room where everyone giggled away into the night and the next day drowsily awoke to learn how to tie knots and then launch ourselves off a cliff. Julie Forrest and I had some crazy trips on to the loch, trying to master the art of windsurfing, Julie with her pink sail and me with my bigger blue sail thanks to being a bit taller. As most beginners discover, travelling in one direction was fine, but turning and changing direction was a challenge. One memorable day Julie ended up speeding towards a lovely luxury yacht, and when she realized she couldn't stop or turn she did the first thing that came into her mind, which was to grab the handrail on the side of the boat, letting go of her sail. I convulsed with laughter as she hung at full stretch with her arms above her, clinging on for dear life to the side of the yacht.

At school my backstage work continued as the school productions were yet again a highlight of the school year. Mrs Thomson, our language teacher, was another teacher who had a flair for the dramatic and embraced her role as director. Our physics teacher, Mrs Montgomery, was the backstage director and I became her understudy, at first organizing tea along with Jacqui and eventually being entrusted with my own clipboard and script. We did *Oklahoma!* and *Guys and Dolls* amongst others and I loved them. The productions were taken seriously enough by the staff that by my final years I could easily get out of French or physics by reminding Mrs Thomson or Mrs Montgomery that I had something urgent to do as I waved my clipboard importantly. Unfortunately the school shows achieved the wrong kind of fame a year after I left, when news headlines were made by a 32-year-old ex-pupil who went back to the school pretending to be 16 again and starred in the musical *South Pacific*.

Personally I have never felt the need to go back and try school again, although I really did enjoy the time I had there. Like many pupils I loved the subjects where I liked the teachers. Mrs Ogg reinforced my lifelong love of stories in English class, and Mrs Nicol, recently back from a new film studies course, opened up the world of Hitchcock to us. As part of my love of reading and writing I joined the editorial board of the school magazine, although the most memorable thing from that time was when we were all reprimanded for making the magazine too "edgy" and potentially offensive.

I loved sport at school and tried everything we were given a chance to do. I played as much netball as possible, was thoroughly bruised from my enthusiastic attempts at volleyball, nearly killed our PE teachers Mrs Lindsay and Miss Greenshields with a discus during athletics, endured the endless running around the soggy paths of Kilmardinny Loch for cross-country, tried (and failed) to be as good as my sister at hockey and couldn't get enough of softball. I was suitably disastrous at dance and somewhere lurks an embarrassing film of me in a group re-creation of Michael Jackson's "Thriller" with our own bonus choreography. There was also a variety of lunchtime clubs run by parents and teachers, and one term I tried my hand at fencing. It was great to pull down the mask and brandish the sword in the way I'd seen it done in the swashbuckling pirate adventure films I'd watched with my dad. While the poor parent tried desperately to get us to practise the true form, which involves a more controlled use of the arms, wrists and body, we were all wildly slashing through the air personifying Zorro. But none of these sports hooked me in the way that one other did.

I had decided I would try the karate club. At the time I thought it would be good to know some self-defence and a few of my friends showed an interest in trying it too. Mr Davis was an art teacher and was a sixth dan black belt in Shotokan karate and ran an evening club out of school and a lunchtime club within school. I went along to the club at school as a white belt, unsure of what karate would be like.

I loved it immediately. It is a very physical discipline that involves tough and challenging training. I would leave class completely exhausted, knowing that the next morning my muscles would be aching in a satisfying way. But what I hadn't appreciated was the incredible mental and spiritual side to it. It is truly a martial art in that it is about flow and belief, trust and understanding, creativity and courage. The control I needed to learn over my body was unlike anything I had known, and I became more flexible both as far as my muscles were concerned and also in my thought processes. A key component of the training was respect, which had to be shown to the discipline itself, and also to the teachers and the higher belts. At the end of every session we kneeled, bowed and had a quiet moment of breathing and relaxation and clearing the mind. As I improved I learned power with control, speed through relaxation, pushing myself as hard as I could with discipline. It challenged and stretched me, and as I climbed the gradings and moved through the different coloured belts I faced nerves, fear and doubt and overcame them all.

I began to attend the evening classes too, and along with Gillian and Julie from school I made new friends and learned to trust my abilities. At the evening club I fought against grown-up black belts. I watched them, learned from them, admired them and idolized them. My time in karate helped me find my own feet and without a doubt contributed to me becoming more independent and to think for myself. I started reading about Bruce Lee and his training methods. Far more than just a martial arts expert who had made a few films, Bruce Lee was also a poet, philosopher, motivator, artist and soul-searcher. He was constantly on the search for further learning and believed that it isn't what happens in life that makes a difference between people, it is how people choose to react to those circumstances that will test the mettle of a life well lived. He thought worrying was a waste of energy and that life was too short for negative energy. And he wrote, "We are told that talent creates its own opportunities. But it sometimes seems that intense desire creates not only its own opportunities, but its own talents." When I got my black belt, Ken Davis, who had taught me from white belt to black, gave me his own very first black belt and to this day it's still possibly the thing I would rescue first in the event of a house fire.

Loving the classes away from school didn't prevent me from loving the classes within school. I studied hard and enjoyed pretty much all the subjects except for maths and maybe physics. I couldn't get to grips with the function and form of mathematics and was never shown the creative side of maths and how it can be used in strikingly different ways. Instead I sat at the scored and marked wooden desks and puzzled over algebra and equations.

Other than maths and struggling to find myself it was a pretty special childhood. I didn't have any major problems growing up, I loved my parents and always had my big sister for company, who would push me, protect me and encourage me. It took a while for me to realize that things weren't quite as idyllic for Sarah. When we were growing up Sarah was generally good at everything. She was brilliant at some things and got by in everything else. She has a very laid-back, generous, relaxed nature and always had friends and countless boyfriends. When Valentine's Day arrived the majority of cards that came through our door were for Sarah, and without fail all of the flowers were hers. Whereas my own relationships have not been as successful. For some reason my commitment to rowing and to studying has come easily; my ability to commit to long-term relationships has not had the same simplicity or success. I'm not sure why, but I hope it is a temporary thing.

Sarah did not always have things easy. Over many years she was to become a target. For no apparent reason the local bully, a blonde-haired, deceptively sweet, innocent looking, popular girl chose Sarah as one of her many victims. She made Sarah's life a misery on the walk to and from school and on any available opportunity in between. I didn't know for a long time, but at some point began to see it for myself. To Sarah's immense credit she didn't rise to the daily baiting or react in any physical way. But I saw her being beaten down by the verbal abuse and I hated it. Being the younger sister there was nothing I could really do without making the situation worse. Sarah would have hated me to try and step in to fix things. I occasionally wonder if this blonde bully grew up, perhaps had children of her own and then looked back with regret and acknowledged just what a bully she was, while seemingly smiling so sweetly to others. And the anger, the frustration, the sense of how unfair and cruel it was has never left me. It was possibly the beginning of my fierce awareness of justice and injustice.

That sense of justice began to shape what I wanted to do with my life. Alongside the reaction to what was happening in the real world, through the many books I read and the films and TV programmes I watched I was hooked by all things relating to law and order. Having been fascinated by the range of murder cases I'd watched with gran, I was now broadening my interest by making the transition from the mystery and detection stage to the courtroom. The trial process is a compelling narrative and has a theatricality all of its own. From *To Kill a Mockingbird* to *LA Law*, I was captivated by the speeches and the cross-examinations, the battle of wits between the prosecution and defence and the hope that justice would be done. When my mum and dad were out of the house I would borrow a briefcase and pretend to be arriving at court, placing my case on a table and then, copying what I had read or watched, I'd create my own speeches, always on the side of the righteous and always speaking profound truths. Or so I believed. Like Atticus Finch or Grace Van Owen I would cleverly corner the accused or the lying witness with my questions and leave the jury in no doubt about the right thing to do.

For a while I wanted to work in film or television, or to write, so that I could continue to create the crime dramas of my own imagination. The last year of school I spent a wonderful summer working in a cinema in Sauchiehall Street as an usher. With my torch in one hand I would collect tickets, show people in and then sit watching for hours, not only the films but also the audience reaction. *Jurassic Park* was showing that summer, and I must have seen it literally hundreds of times. I witnessed the power of the medium to unite, move, terrify and entertain a huge audience as I saw collective laughter and leaping from seats. But part of me back then thought maybe doing a job for real would be better than just writing or creating stories, and I did like the idea of making some sort of difference in the world. Mum and dad were also more enthusiastic about my idea of a law degree than any of the other various suggestions I had come up with as I roamed around trying to find what my "non-boring" life would be. Whether or not I ever practised law, having the degree was a decent start in life, they concluded. I knew I wanted to study Scots law, and so I would have to choose between one of the big five Universities in Scotland. I agonized over the options. To choose Glasgow would mean staying at home, and much as I loved my family, for University I wanted to experience life away from home. Mum and dad enthusiastically agreed on that point. Aberdeen University has a fantastic legal reputation, but Sarah had just gone there to study English, and I didn't feel I should follow her north. Dundee and St Andrews were possibilities, but I decided Edinburgh would be the way to go. Edinburgh had the attraction of being famous for my obsessions of the time. It had the main law courts of Scotland and was also renowned for its book and film festivals.

Mum and I went over to Edinburgh for a visit so I could have a look around. The city is beautiful in its own right, and its gothic spires have inspired a range of authors from Walter Scott to Ian Rankin and Arthur Conan Doyle to J. K. Rowling. Arthur's Seat rises up in the middle of the city like a green sea monster, and the Castle looks down over its rocky ledge across the Princes Street Gardens to the museums, the stylish New Town area and beyond to the sea. Mum and I walked the streets and finally wandered through the arches of Old College, the law school. Old College is an impressive old building with a huge open space in between the high stone walls, behind which lie majestic lecture theatres and the law library. On top of the huge dome over the entrance stands the famous "Golden Boy", a statue of a naked youth holding the torch of knowledge. It was at once impressive and intimidating. I was convinced this was the place to be. That summer I achieved the marks I needed in my exams. A few months later my mum and dad loaded up their car with all my worldly possessions and we headed east.

As a safeguard, I had mum's great friend Maureen, who lived in Edinburgh, to contact in case of emergencies. I didn't need her help then, but Auntie Mo has been a constant source of support for me ever since. Her warm and generous spirit is matched by her love of chocolate and she is the fun and witty presence at every family celebration. Mum and Auntie Mo had shared a flat together when young and they were bonded by many things, including their sense of humour and love of music. Sarah and I have always been impressed by the fact that Auntie Mo saw the late, great Freddie Mercury live.

When it was time for me to leave home, rather than giving Polonius's speech from *Hamlet* – "neither a borrower nor a lender be … to thine own self be true" – mum and dad gave me their own version. I don't remember the details but I do remember it was about taking opportunities, seeking new experiences, enjoying myself and, importantly, *not* walking across the Meadows at night. I gravely nodded, agreeing with their words even though I really didn't know what or where the Meadows really were. I was excited at the thought of University. I had loved my visits up to see Sarah at her halls of residence in Aberdeen. I remember thinking how grown-up and cool she was as she offered me tea and a cheese sandwich for breakfast. To prepare the meal she leaned out of her window and unhooked the plastic bag that hung outside from the window in place of a fridge. In the bag was milk for the tea and the student delight of cheese slices. I couldn't wait to be living this life for myself.

I moved into Pollock Halls in Edinburgh and was in Lee House – appropriate, I thought, as I still had a Bruce Lee fascination and was looking forward to joining the karate club at University. I was also interested in finding out about drama after my school experience with backstage work. How different it would all turn out to be.

Fresher's Week was my first experience of all that the University had to offer. There was an enormous fair where every University club and society was on show trying to attract new members. I meandered through endless halls and rooms gathering information on pastimes and hobbies that I didn't even know existed. I signed up to the juggling club, learned what ultimate Frisbee was and became very enthusiastic about the trampolining club. I had a tentative look at the drama club, but the level of professionalism was intimidating and far from my memories of school. In the main sports hall I gathered a vast array of flyers detailing new outdoor pursuits I could lose myself in every weekend. The options were endless. Towards the end of the day I decided it was time to head back towards the halls of residence. I was on my own by this point and wondered if there was anyone I could walk back with. It was my first year after all, and the insecurity of fitting in to a new place was the undercurrent. I spotted a girl who lived near me at the halls and asked if she was heading back soon. "Just one more club to visit and I'm finished," she said.

While waiting I casually leafed through my information about skiing, sailing, climbing, abseiling and, of course, karate. I glanced up to see which club she was waiting for and it was the Boat Club. I looked back down, uninterested. At one point a girl came over from the Boat Club asking if I wanted to hear about rowing. I shook my head, explaining that I was just waiting for a friend. She tried again, suggesting it might be something I would like and should consider. Again I tried to say I didn't want to know. She went back to the stand, picked up a piece of paper, hesitated momentarily, then quickly walked back to me. "Look, here's some information, we have a meeting on Thursday night, come along if you're free. No commitment, but we'll be going for a drink afterwards. I think you could be really good, you have the right height and build. Just have a think about it." I went back to the halls, stuck the paper on my pinboard and didn't think about it again.

The first night out in Edinburgh there was an overwhelming choice of parties all over the city. Bars, restaurants, the University unions, pubs and clubs were all crammed with fresh-faced new students intent on experiencing all there was on offer. The late summer night air was filled with music, laughter, boisterous shouting, drunken singing and the occasional siren cutting through the fun. There were two other girls,

Kirsten and Kerry, who were from my old school and had come to Edinburgh to study too. Kirsten had a big brother and we were invited to his flat party. The party was full of final-year students repeatedly slurring at us about how lucky we were to be starting out and these were going to be "the best years of your lives". The three of us were a little unconvinced by their bluster, but it was a fun night and many hours later we eventually left the party. I began to think that maybe they had been right about the best years when we found a friendly fish and chip shop still open at 4.15am. Merrily eating our chips covered in "salt 'n' sauce", we chatted away as we walked back to the halls through a beautiful big grassy area of Edinburgh. It was not until a few weeks later that I discovered that was the Meadows.

On the Thursday evening that week I was drawn to the Boat Club flyer that was stuck on my pinboard. Unsure but somehow intrigued, I crept into the back of the lecture hall where the Boat Club meeting was taking place. I stayed at the back, reluctant to commit any further. The club were looking for 16 novice women, and that evening 52 signed up. I still didn't feel sure I wanted to be part of this, but I could feel my competitive drive taking notice. I wasn't sure whether or not I wanted to row, but I knew instinctively I wanted to be one of those 16. I distinctly remember sitting in the boat for the first time and being asked to sit forward and square my blade. I remember thinking, "I don't know how to sit forward, I have no idea what a blade is, and is square really a verb?" Thankfully, although my skills in a boat may not have been groundbreaking, I did well enough in the various tests on the rowing machine and in the gym to be selected, and so joined the novice team.

That year was full of fun, challenging competition, great friends and the lovely time you can have when you don't know how good or bad you are in the relative scheme of things. We won many novice competitions, including our first race in Aberdeen on the River Dee. I remember our coach, Colin, telling us off for eating chocolate before the race. Then later he told us we rowed "like a bunch of handbags". I couldn't really picture what a bunch of handbags might look like but I guessed it wasn't a compliment.

We trained hard at the University gym at the Pleasance and after most evening training sessions we went to the nearby pub, the Maltings, to enjoy relaxed, entertaining chat. There was always some outrageous story being told about someone, and so frequent squawks of shock or denial burst through the low-level buzz of conversation. The time after training was precious, and was something I'd also loved when I attended the evening karate club back in Glasgow. I had joined the Edinburgh University karate club when I arrived, but I only attended the first few classes. Apparently the Sensei who was usually in charge of the club wasn't there and another student took the class. I was aware instantly of a certain resentment that there I was, a fresher and yet a black belt. Although I tried hard, the atmosphere just wasn't the same as the wonderful clubs I had been part of in Glasgow, and I felt I'd found the same camaraderie and fun in the rowing club instead.

In my second year I went through the usual trials, and in contrast to the previous year this time I knew I wanted to be in a boat and the best boat possible. I was more confident and it was with much more excitement that I bustled into the packed lecture hall with the other athletes to hear about the selection for the year. As with the novice selection, the senior team were wanting 16 women, four boats of four. As we sat chattering away the noise gradually quietened down when Andy, who made the selection decisions, stood to read out the selected crew lists. He read each four out in order. I hadn't made the first boat, but there was a core of four athletes, Jo, Nicola, Caroline and Kate, who stood ahead of and apart from the rest of us, so I wasn't too surprised not to make it into the first boat. As the names were called out I was a little bit surprised not to make the second boat. And I was very surprised and a little outraged not to be chosen for the third boat.

It was then with complete shock that I took in the fact that I hadn't even made it into the fourth and final boat. I sat with my heart thudding in my chest and disbelief flowing through me. I didn't know what to say or what to do. However, there was more to come. Andy went on to read out names for a fifth boat that they had decided to put together, designed for people who had showed willing but had no real ability. We weren't expected to go anywhere. And that was me.

I left the meeting in a state of frustration, anger, disappointment and upset. Alone I stormed through the dark streets of Edinburgh, unsure of where I was going or what to do with myself. I didn't want to talk to anyone or see anyone. I ended up back near the halls of residence, but I passed the shadows of the buildings and looked up into the night sky and towards the dark outline of Arthur's Seat. Without thinking I adjusted my course and walked through the gates of the park and on to the path that led along the crags to the peak of Arthur's Seat. I couldn't see the path under my feet and I stumbled and slipped my way up to the top, climbing up the last bit on all fours. At the top of the hill I had what I think of as my "Scarlett moment". Not in any way as glamorous or as eloquent as Vivien Leigh in *Gone with the Wind*, I nevertheless turned my tear-streaked face to the heavens and raged against the night sky. There was no blood-red backdrop of Tara burning in flames behind me, but I had the same idea of railing to the world that I would never put myself in that position again. That position where I felt too confident and possibly even complacent and had completely overrated my abilities. Where I could be humiliated and upset by my own actions. I swore I would never be deselected again. Frankly I *did* give a damn.

I realized that this sport was something I cared about deeply and something I wanted to prove to be good at. I accepted that I didn't have all the answers, all the knowledge, or all the skills yet to be good. And I was prepared to start from the beginning again. I learned from the coaches, the other athletes, the experts. I climbed my way back up. And throughout the hard work I laughed along with my crewmates in that bottom boat. We retained our sense of humour and I remember a shining moment when Krystyna, the Captain of the Boat Club, coached us. She was the second female Club Captain after the famous Dot Blackie, and we adored Krystyna. She led with style and grace. As we were mainly ignored, the fact that the iconic Captain said she'd come and have a look at our rowing was a source of great excitement, and nervousness. She might hate us and our rowing. She ran alongside us (which shows how slow we must have been going) and shocked us all by being positive. She praised the things we were doing well, and without giving us the false impression that we were fantastic, she said enough to give us confidence and be proud of ourselves. It took probably an hour out of her day and she'll never know what an incredible impact it made.

The following year it was suggested by a local coach, Hamish, that while my physical skills were improving and impressive, my boat skills were still lacking and the only way to get them right was to spend more time in a boat. And ideally in a small boat. Most of the time at University was spent in fours or eights, and Hamish decided the pair was the boat that would teach me the most. Nicola and Jo, the two top girls at the University, were tasked with taking me under their wing, and they took turns, one coaching and one rowing with me. Nicola, who had a background in GB junior rowing, was a fiery redhead unafraid to offer her opinion and who spent her university time fuelled by massive bowls of Frosties. Jo was on her second degree, studying to be a vet, and had the confidence and assurance that come with age. Together their patience, gentle teasing, encouragement and sense of fun guided me forward, and by the end of my third year I was a pretty decent rower. To this day they are both still my great friends and I am the proud godmother of two of their children. Jo and I raced the pair and together we won women's Henley, the National Championships and then selection to row for Scotland at the Home Countries event. It was the summer of the Atlanta Olympics, and I remember that while we raced our final at Strathclyde Park, at exactly the same moment Steve Redgrave and Matthew Pinsent were winning their Olympic final on the other side of the Atlantic. I was aware during our race that the Olympic commentary was being played out over the tannoy rather than the commentary on our own race.

Later that summer the non-Olympic World Championships came to Strathclyde Park. A reduced event from the normal World Championships, it hosted all the events that weren't in the Olympic programme. Becky, another great friend from the rowing team, and I volunteered to help and we were given the role of medal carriers. Wearing long tartan skirts we had to carry out the medals on the cushioned trays for presentation to the athletes. As we were waiting in between the races for our big role, one of the women who were presenting the medals struck up a conversation with us. She was Anita DeFrantz, a former US Olympic rower who was now a member of the International Olympic Committee. She asked if we rowed, and when we said we were part of the University team she looked down at the medals and then back at us with a benevolent smile. "Maybe if you work really hard and get really good, maybe one day you can win one of these." It seemed highly appropriate that when I won my first World Championship medal exactly a year later it was Anita who presented me with the medal. At the time she didn't recognize me as the young girl in the long flowing tartan skirt whom she had encouraged the previous year.

As the Spice Girls were preparing to take Britain by storm that summer, I began thinking of a holiday. Magda, my good friend and the popular cox of the University eight who would later produce a lovely daughter for me to be godmother to, had wanted to go on holiday too and one day we met with Cherry, another rower, for a hot chocolate and to discuss where to go. Magda was a geographer and so had a healthy grasp of the world. But we were severely limited by money. Our other requirement was that it was somewhere "a bit different". We spread out the holiday brochures across the table and pored over the glossy pictures. We had two weeks and the world was our oyster, as long as that oyster was quite cheap. As we dismissed some options, the choices narrowed. One favourite was Iceland. It was different and affordable, we thought. The pictures were stunning. Leaning back with a steaming hot chocolate in hand, Cherry wisely nodded, "Yep, that's the place for you." Magda and I looked at each other and nodded enthusiastically. We were bound for Reykjavik. The guidebook we bought advised us to prepare for "Scotland in summer", with "maybe a few layers". It had been a beautiful warm summer and so we optimistically planned our two-week camping trip in the wilds of Iceland. I said I'd organize the tent, Magda took on the cooking implements and soon we were flying north.

When we climbed off the plane and on to the waiting bus to Reykjavik, I looked around thinking people were a little overdressed. There were two other groups on the bus, a team of geologists and a small number of army and marine personnel. They were all wearing huge boots, thick outdoor kit, gaiters and waterproofs and I almost felt sorry for them as I sat in my denim cut-off shorts with a fleece casually tied around my waist. A few hours later I realized they were in a far better state of preparation than Magda and I. As the sun went down, the temperature plummeted and the rain started. And it didn't stop for ten days. My dismal failure in clothes preparation was matched only by Magda's attention to detail with regard to cooking equipment. She had managed to pack the camping stove and a pan, but hadn't thought of plates or bowls or any form of cutlery. Thankfully she realized this while we were flying to Iceland and so we managed to eat with Air Iceland cutlery for the fortnight.

We also vastly underestimated the price of everything in Iceland, and had a horrible realization when we spent half of our budget on the round-the-island bus ticket. Unable to pay for much more, we survived for two weeks on one slice of cheap white bread with jam for breakfast, two slices of bread with jam for lunch, and half a packet of "Yum yum chicken noodles" for supper every day. We were hungry, tired, moody, cold and soaked through for most of the trip, but Iceland didn't disappoint. It is a country of stunning natural beauty, and while every day may have presented challenges for us, it also brought us beautiful views, breathtaking geysers, vast glaciers, volcano craters and an incredible variety of landscapes. And although we often couldn't afford the hot showers at the campsites, the burning natural hot springs became our saviour, offering us a way to stay clean and warm for free.

Perhaps it was through surviving that ordeal, or maybe it would always have happened, but I returned for my last year at Edinburgh University feeling anything was possible. I took on the role of Boat Club Captain, following in the footsteps of Dot, Krystyna and Jo. I would be sitting my final law exams that year and also going for British trials. I learned to drive the minibus and was soon filling it with students and attaching the 30 foot long trailer, complete with tens of thousands of pounds' worth of boats, and heading over to Glasgow, up to Aberdeen and Inverness, down to Newcastle and Nottingham and then London for various races. On my first trip to London, in the days before satnav, we got completely lost, and I remember driving the massive bus and trailer into a very narrow dead-end suburban road. Undaunted we unhitched the trailer, pushed it back out on to the main road, stopping traffic, and headed off in search of a river.

The minibuses were an old breed and we used to drive on to the long uphill road out of Inverness at about 20mph, with cars speeding up behind us flashing at our dangerous progress. On one memorable journey to London we had just pulled back on to the motorway after stopping at a service station when one of the guys, who had been lying sleeping on the back seats, groggily sat up, looked out of the back window and asked where the trailer was. We looked round to see … nothing. Jo, who was driving, slammed on the brakes and, without hesitating, pulled on to the hard shoulder, threw the bus into reverse and we arrived at speed back at the services, where just on the edge of the road we found our trailer full of boats which had disconnected itself after our apparent failure to attach it properly after the break. Another trip was even worse. We were on an A road south of Edinburgh, early in the morning, with thankfully little traffic around, when the trailer started to snake behind us, moving heavily from one side to the other. The usual response is to accelerate slightly and so pull the trailer back into line. Unfortunately there was damage to the connecting pin, and as we accelerated the pin snapped and the whole minibus watched in stunned silence as our trailer suddenly shot past the right-hand windows, overtaking us on the wrong side of the road and finally coming to a stop after hitting the grass embankment on the other side of the road. Luckily we all survived those minibus years.

In my year as Captain I relied heavily on my fantastic Committee and also the experts at the Sports Union. Irene McTernan was the secretary and had been since time began. My first few experiences of walking in through the heavy dark wooden door completely terrified me as I peered around, to be met by Irene's raised eyebrows under her styled white hair. The more I grew to know Irene the more I realized she was the constant, the rock, the reason why the University's sport was such a success. She had seen it all before, many times over, and nothing would be new or a shock to her. I stopped being surprised when I walked in through the door and Irene would answer my question before I had the chance to ask it.

With the sporting side of my life flourishing, I had to be sure my academic studies didn't falter. Although I was excited by all that might happen in rowing, it was just as important to me that I finished my law degree and graduated. By my honours year I was studying the subjects I had the most interest in, the majority of which were in private law, the subjects about people, about individuals, about stories. I had never been gripped by commercial law, company law or tax law, despite the riches they might have promised. Instead I soaked up the less financially rewarding but, for me, eminently more fascinating and stimulating criminal law, family law and medical jurisprudence. Two of my lecturers for medical jurisprudence and criminal law were Professor Ken Mason and Professor Alexander McCall Smith. They were both renowned within law and still exuded a childlike fresh enthusiasm for their subjects, despite carrying impressive titles and awards alongside their names that recognized long and distinguished careers. Alexander McCall Smith went on to even greater fame as the writer of the No.1 Ladies' Detective Agency series, but to us he was the friendly, funny, slightly bumbling, crinkly-eyed Professor who loved posing a challenge to us and watching us find the answers. He adored his work and was proud of his students. It was undoubtedly their infectious enthusiasm that inspired me to go on to Glasgow University to study a Masters in medical law and medical ethics under the respected and leading expert, Professor Sheila McLean. My Masters was a part-time course to allow me to row seriously, but during my undergraduate years I was still juggling a full-time degree course and a desire to see how far I could take my rowing career.

Just before the Christmas break I was sitting on the ergo, having finished a training session, when Hamish came up behind me. He very casually dropped into the conversation that he had been thinking that Jo and I should try for British selection. I nearly fell off my seat. I had to check with him that he wasn't joking. It was a ridiculous idea. It was still only a few months after the Olympics after all, and to try to compete against the Olympic squad would be to enter a very different league from anything I had done before. Hamish left me, having planted the seed, knowing only too well that the seed was bound to grow.

The following Easter Jo and I made the trip down to Henley-on-Thames, where the national open trials were to be held. As we put the boat on the water ready for the race, there was a shout from along the bank, "Oi, Jocks!" I looked along and saw one of the GB boatmen gesturing at us. "You might want to put the boat in the right way." We had put the boat in the wrong way, against the stream, breaking the circulation pattern, a cardinal rule of rowing. The boatman, Russ Thatcher, laughed at us kindly and in his strong East London accent talked us through what we should do as he slapped us on the back and wished us luck. I would always be "Jock" to Russ throughout the rest of my career. The trial went well and we made an impact with our result. Walking along the path by the river later on, we saw some of the GB team ahead of us. Jo and I nudged each other as we recognized the Edinburgh University legend, Dot Blackie. This was the closest we had ever got to her in real life and it was exciting to be so close to one of our heroes. As we walked behind the group she was in, Dot leaned back and over her shoulder said nonchalantly, "Well done, Edinburgh," and then returned to her conversation. Jo and I nudged each other even more. Dot had talked to us. And even more than that, she knew who we were!

We were invited on our first international rowing camp and journeyed out to Hazewinkel, Belgium. Jo and I shared a room with two of the regular team members, one of them being Miriam Batten, the oldest and most experienced and successful of the women's team. We unpacked and it didn't take me long to open the small wooden cupboard at the end of the bunk bed and put in my University lycra and three cotton t-shirts emblazoned with a variety of slogans and cartoon characters that defined University crews. Sitting on my bed I watched in awe as Miriam continued to lift kit out of her apparently bottomless bag. It was like watching Mary Poppins, and I wouldn't have been surprised if a hatstand had magically appeared from the depths. When she was finally finished, my mouth hung open as I counted the enormous array of kit Miriam had brought. She had packed enough for a fresh training outfit every session, which meant she wouldn't have to worry about trying to wash and dry kit in the small restrictive cabins we were staying in. It wasn't the fact that she packed so much kit, it was more the fact that she seemed to own endless amounts. Here was someone who had been rewarded every year with another national team lycra. Little did I think then that a few months later, after that small but well-meaning fib that began my career, Cesca and I would start gathering our own kit collection in earnest, and be heading for international racing.

CHAPTER

3

DECISIONS, DISCORD
AND DONUTS

After the end of the glorious racing summer of 1997, when we landed back at Heathrow Airport I had a connecting flight up to Aberdeen. I remember being surprised at how sad I was that the summer had to end and I had to say goodbye to teammates whom I now considered good friends. I felt I had become part of a big family, a family full of crazy, quirky, charismatic, driven, hilarious, loving people. And I didn't want to say goodbye.

The night we won the medal in Aiguebelette I experienced my first Worlds party. They are generally a highlight in the rowing calendar – one night of the year when every athlete relaxes, the season is officially over and all the different nations get together to celebrate. And it usually produces enough stories to last for years.

We had started with champagne at our hotel and the nine of us having a meal together in various degrees of sobriety. Then we went on to the main party where Sue, Alex, Lisa and I danced the night away, interrupted by the odd water pistol fight courtesy of Rachel. We all finally made it back to the hotel and a few of us including Matthew Pinsent ended up chatting through the night until breakfast at 4.45am. I still couldn't quite believe I was sharing stories and laughing with Matthew, who just 12 months ago I had been watching from afar as he won Gold at the Olympic Games. The lack of sleep was painful, but it was worth staying up as there were a number of people who missed breakfast and subsequently the bus trip to the airport, and they weren't just athletes. Famously the chief men's coach and the head physio were among the missing numbers and had to chase behind in a taxi in order to catch the flight.

The following year we saw an illustration of how Maggie has achieved legendary status in the British Rowing office. Maggie is the Team Manager's right-hand woman and is generally behind the scenes sorting out problems around the clock. Nothing appears to stress her and she fixes everything with the minimum of fuss. At the next Worlds party one of the girls from the eight was missing the following morning when everyone was getting on to the airport bus. Rachel ran up to Maggie to explain the situation. Trying not to land the missing member in trouble, Rachel stuttered, "Well, I think she was with a guy, but I'm not sure where they went or when she might have got back or what his name was or …" and trailed off, aware she was possibly making things worse. Maggie, without any hint of concern, merely looked up from her clipboard to ask Rachel, "OK, which country?" The hotel where the Casanova was staying was quickly located and soon the missing squad member was hastily making her way to the airport. No fuss, no panic, just a healthy dose of shame. Moments like that are why Maggie is worth her weight in gold.

So after my first experience of work and play with the squad it was hard to say goodbye to this crazy new family. But I did feel I'd be back and I wouldn't let myself wallow in melancholy too long. Sitting in the plane on the tarmac at Heathrow I wrote: "I've just realized that I have to let go of my daydreaming, of my idealizing of the last month. It was fantastic, something I'll never forget, and I'm already impatient to get my photos back. But I can't live in the past. Remember it, of course. Talk about it and enjoy it, relive it – but don't long for it, don't ignore the present to live in the past. There are a lot more great things to come.

Look forward to them. Be glad of the experience you've gained and the friendships you've made. They'll just get better and stronger as time goes on. This is just the beginning. And what a beginning. The future is certainly bright."

And to some extent I was right. But what I couldn't predict was just how different the next 12 months were going to be.

I had an invitation from the squad to train permanently in Marlow, but I was also doing a Masters degree in Glasgow and I wasn't prepared to give that up to move south yet. All the main trials until April would be in singles, and so I had the perfect opportunity to learn to scull, compete in the trials and do my degree. Hamish was happy to coach me, and between us we knew the level of training it would take to be competitive with the other squad members. I knew that by effectively staying outside the system I would have to prove myself at every trial in order to be considered for the summer racing. Otherwise I had made it too easy for them not to select me.

I still felt I had a good relationship with the others on the team and I would regularly speak to the girls I had raced with in the summer before. But the true pleasure of being part of the British team is being a member of a group every day that supports, encourages, teases and pushes you in equal measures. It was a harder world up in the Edinburgh winter, where I did most sessions on my own without any of the squad camaraderie.

I was lucky to have Hamish coach me through this time. He had a stable and secure manner about him. Rarely did he get upset or show stress. He had a clear plan of what we had to do and he believed it was possible. As far as I was aware he never knew limits, and felt there was a way to make anything possible. He was a numbers man and so the goals didn't appear to be fantasy based, but based on simple hard facts, making them seem so very real and achievable. I've always been someone who enjoys challenging the impossible, who loves dreams, who is a sucker for a great speech, empowering words, challenging thoughts. But sometimes to match the big picture concept you need someone who will be able to share those goals and yet bring with them a sense of why it is possible and the detail of how, thereby making it even more realistic. Hamish did that for me in 1998.

Every morning I'd meet Hamish at the Union Canal in Edinburgh.

It's a narrow bit of water, about 1,500m long with a few handy bends in it. There's also the matter of tight stone bridges to steer through and the canal is only one boat wide, so if more than one boat is on the water the other needs to pull in to the side. But it's generally sheltered, so gets fantastic flat conditions, has a towpath right beside it for up-close coaching, and the narrowness of it means it is the best teacher for steering. When I became more proficient I could judge the bridges so finely at full speed that I could skim one side of the blades along the stone walls to create sparks. But generally not when Hamish was watching.

Hamish had a wonderful interested mind. I distinctly remember him always turning to the obituary section of the newspaper. I thought what a miserable thing it was to be interested in until one day he explained. "They only write obituaries about interesting people. People who have done something with their lives." And from then on I saw things differently. I realized that there was so much to learn from others and not just others in my own specialist area, but people from all areas of life. Hamish used to regularly arrive with cuttings from the business section of the paper, from the arts, from finance, from travel; there was nowhere that didn't hold an interest for him, and this bigger thinking was infectious. It is very easy to get limited thinking with a narrow vision when you've worked in an area for a long time. I was grateful that he always stressed the importance of balancing rowing with allowing time for friends and family and for a career outside rowing. I have always strived to keep that balance and feel my life is richer because of it. I will always thank Hamish for being the kind of coach who was still able to think outside the box and for using the whole world as a source of inspiration. Sadly, however, not every day was filled with such exciting thinking. Many of them were just long, tiring, relentlessly repetitive days.

I'd meet Hamish in the pitch black long before anyone else had come down to train. The weather didn't affect the training other than making it a bit more enjoyable or a bit harder. Some mornings were beautiful with the promise of a stunning sunrise later in the day. Some were utterly freezing, and I would stand there stamping my feet, with my hands tucked into my armpits, while Hamish told me what we would be doing and flakes of snow danced around us in the air. Those days usually meant I would have to break through the layer of ice on the canal to reach the water. Sometimes a bitter wind would be blowing and I could hardly hear Hamish as the icy air whipped around our faces. The worst was when the rain had started early and in earnest. When you are soaked before the training even begins you know it's going to be a tough day.

In the gloom we'd exchange a few words, I'd get the boat on the water and start off up the canal as he got his bike together and cycled after me. Hamish is a man of few words but uses those words carefully. The majority of the training session would be in silence other than the splash of the blades, my heavy breathing and occasionally the terrifying sound of beating wings if the swans were feeling unsettled. Hamish would interrupt only to add the odd bit of technical advice or gentle encouragement, or to give me the speed I was hitting or needed to hit.

My favourite bit of the day would be the break after the first session. I would be glad to have finished the hard physical session and wearily climb into Hamish's car. We would then drive to his mum's house in Edinburgh. Pots of tea were always being made along with hot fresh toast and marmalade. I don't even like marmalade but for some reason that's the only place I would eat it, in front of the fire with Hamish's mum. She was always on my side, and the days when I looked particularly exhausted she would look at Hamish accusingly. I remember one day it started to pour with rain just before we were due to head back to the canal and Hamish's mum asked what we would do now. Smiling and with my eyebrows raised I looked up at Hamish. How would he answer that? I was dry and cosy now and I quite liked the thought of getting the kettle back on and settling in front of daytime TV. Hamish looked to his mum without any change of expression. He just shrugged and said, "Back to the canal for another session." His mum looked shocked. "But it's raining." Hamish looked out of the window. "Oh yes, it is. Hope you haven't got washing out." Ten minutes later, I left the warmth and with hunched shoulders stepped out into the downpour.

The rain doesn't stop training, neither does snow, hail, wind or sleet. The only thing that would stop us being on the water is if the water had turned to such thick ice that it was unbreakable. Or occasionally the wind might get so strong the water got unrowable; then we would move indoors. But generally any weather goes and the only thing to consider is how many layers of kit are needed before venturing out.

CHAPTER 3

That winter was a tough experience in self-motivation. Hamish was brilliant in planning my training so I knew what I needed to do every day. And every morning he would be there at the canal to coach me and take me through the first session. But then he would need to go to his own work. He was working full time then, and although he had a young family at home he sacrificed mornings at home to be with me before anyone else was awake. Then he would head off to work and leave me to another water session and then a gym session.

Those sessions were mentally the hardest. The first session was nasty as it was such an early start to get up for, but easier for knowing I had someone there at the boathouse meeting me. The other sessions were alone and I had to keep reminding myself of how badly I wanted to do it and how I had felt in Aiguebelette when I realized in the summer that you would give anything for some more training time. The aim was to be the fastest sculler in Britain. It was a tough goal, as I didn't know how to scull until I began to learn after Aiguebelette. And I'd be taking on Guin Batten, the British single sculler from the Atlanta Olympics, her sister Miriam and Gillian, who had just won the silver in the double scull at the World Championships, and everyone else on the team. It might have seemed an impossible dream, but then so did flying in an aeroplane or walking on the moon or sending emails by phone once upon a time. Dreams are always worth having because that's how we move forward.

The time was made a little easier by not having to face the challenge alone. Although only I could do the physical work necessary, it was helped by the enthusiastic support of the people around me. I trained from St Andrew Boat Club on the canal and everyone seemed to know what I was doing and why. The occasional word of encouragement from the club members or from the university could help to ease the exhaustion. Mike Morrice was one who gave so much more than verbal encouragement. He bought a brand new Empacher single for the club, the boat of choice for most of the GB team, but with the understanding only I would use it. Mike's generous gesture made sure, as far as equipment was concerned, I could compete on equal terms and I was determined not to waste the opportunity he was giving me. Dave Patterson, a constant reassuring presence in the Pleasance gym, made sure I was ruthless in my mental preparation. Mike Haggerty, the main rowing correspondent for the Scottish press, and a FISA umpire himself, knew the challenge I faced and offered all the support he could. Along with the rest of his family, Mike was then, and remains now, a loyal ally always putting available work or media coverage my way, anything that might help. His love of rowing is matched by his enthusiasm to help and his willingness to use any of his wide network of connections for a good cause. My "team" behind the scenes was an unplanned group of individuals willing me on. I felt a growing responsibility and confidence.

When April rolled around I met with everyone at Nottingham, where the trials were to take place. There was only one result I was interested in and I got it. I won the British national trials for the first time and only a few months after learning to scull. It was a massive achievement for both myself and also for Hamish and all he believed in. Even knowing I hadn't managed to take the scalps of all the big names didn't diminish my pride. Gillian and Miriam were both withdrawn from trials with medical exemptions. Guin raced despite experiencing the recent trauma of losing her mother, so in all reality was probably not at her best. But still I had taken on everyone who was there and I had won.

I was now able to compete at the World Cup events as the British single sculler. There was, however, a reluctance to allow that to happen. It was decided that Guin would also race the World Cups, and after the first two there would be a decision on what would happen next. It was my first ever World Cup racing and to do it as a novice sculler was a big deal. Perhaps the selectors weren't willing to hand over such a big role to such a new athlete, or perhaps they genuinely wanted to be sure they had the right person in the boat. Either way Guin and I raced against each other and the rest of the world in Belgium and then in Germany. In both World Cups I learned so much and gained so much, but in both Guin beat me. She would now take back the British single title and I would – well, I didn't know. There had been no Plan B.

There then followed a period that will not go down as my favourite time. It was weeks of agonizing dilemma, having to choose between going back into the squad and joining the eights group or staying out and improving my sculling. Mike Spracklen and I had a few calls over that time, and he was mainly supportive. We are both strong personalities, however, and just as I didn't want to go back on everything I had achieved so far, he didn't want to have to ask me to come down to be in the group. One of our calls seemed to end with an ultimatum – I could come down and join the eights group if I could tell him honestly that that was the boat I would be in at the Sydney Olympics, but if I was considering anything else then he wanted to give the seat to another athlete who was aiming for that boat. I told him honestly that I didn't know what boat I'd be aiming for at Sydney, but having only just learned to scull it had opened up more options. So that was that: if I wouldn't definitely join the eight for the Olympics, then I wouldn't join them for the 1998 World Championships. At the end of the call I hung up feeling a little shaky. I hadn't made a decision, but the options were now very clear.

I continued to agonize over what to do. And I felt this could be a major decision point for me. Whenever decisions are stuck in front of you it always feels like a huge moment, and yet somehow looking back you think it might well have worked out either way. Books have been written about the fact that people overestimate the impact of almost every life event. There are studies on just how well we can adapt to things, so much so that whatever happens we can generally make it work for us and find a way to be happy. We are at our unhappiest when struggling to make a decision or, if it's been made, when we then think we could go back and change it. One of the potential issues with the modern world is just how many choices we have, and this can often prove debilitating and paralysing. The best course of action seems to be to make a decision (hopefully the "right" choice, but even a wrong choice is usually better than none at all), move forward and use the natural human ability to make it work for you. Back then I didn't read such books and studies and so I stayed lost in my hell of indecision.

The safest route was going back with the squad, keeping up my international racing experience and spending time with the team. The riskier road, and the one less travelled, was staying away even longer. The risk, the unusual route has always been an attraction to me, and so I considered it a genuine option. I spoke to a few people. Hamish said I should go with instinct. My friend Sharon, who was a great training partner and wise counsel, said I had to decide not which was the bigger risk but which risk was the one I was more willing to take. I talked to Rachel about working away from the team, and she said she wouldn't advise anyone to work outside of the squad, "But you're tough and I think you can make it." Lastly I spoke to my mum. My mum is always the first or last person I'll talk to in a crisis, often both the first and last. She said it was a scary choice and she didn't think she could do it, but that it was right for me.

I made my choice, had two gins and phoned David Tanner. I said I felt the best decision for my long-term improvement was to train through the summer, get my sculling as good as it could be and then see what the next year would hold. It might not be so good short term, but it would be better for me long term, and long term meant the Olympic Games. I also didn't want to feel I was trapped into only being considered for one boat as Mike had suggested. David was OK about things but told me he would have decided differently. He was generous in implying he would have liked me to be in the team, but made it clear it would do well without me. I went out, bought a road bike, came back and phoned Mike. I told him that I thought it was the right decision, as I felt I couldn't honestly say I would definitely be aiming for his eight in two years' time. He was also surprisingly OK about it, although disappointed, and as I hung up I felt the welcome relief of a decision finally made and a sense of having taken the future into my hands. It still wasn't clear whether or not it was the right decision, but I had made it and I would live with it. And now there was even more of an incentive to make the training work for me. All of the doubts and concerns would make me train harder.

Shortly afterwards the effects of my decision became clearer. The offer of a new boat and support down south disappeared, my funding was vastly reduced, and I felt the full force of the British Rowing Team's disappointment. I wasn't now a member of the national team and so couldn't access the privileges that came with that. Thankfully the Scottish Sports Council in the form of a wonderful Australian woman called Diedre stepped in to assure me there was support and help there whenever I might need it. The hardest thing was knowing I wouldn't be part of the squad for the summer. That I wouldn't be spending time in the company of those wonderful friends I had made the year before. Missing out on being in the British team just 12 months after experiencing such a wonderful time in Aiguebelette was very painful, but it also taught me a lot of life lessons.

I still had doubts, based on possibly having made the wrong decision and the wrong enemies. Deep down, however, I knew that I had been honest with them and with myself, and that if I was as good as I wanted to be then I would race my way back into the squad. I would also stop wallowing in thoughts about what I could be doing and make sure I made the most I could of the summer ahead. Rather than going on the Italian training camps and to the World Championships in Cologne I instead raced at the National Championships in Nottingham and the Home Countries at Strathclyde Park in Glasgow. I won the National Championships in my single and went home to Aberdeen to give gran the little shield I was given along with the title. Gran had it on her wall from that day until the day she died, she was so proud of that title. I trebled up at the Home Countries, experiencing the single, double and quad, and loved every minute of the racing.

Away from rowing I filled my time with other fantastic things. I experienced the surreal delights of the Edinburgh Festival, witnessing the endlessly amazing creative and entertaining things people can come up with. I also made a wonderful trip with three great friends to Kenya and Tanzania. There we went on my first safari and we climbed Mount Kilimanjaro. Camping in the Massai Mara and waking up to the sounds of the wild, not knowing what spectacular show nature would be putting on that day, was thrilling. Standing on top of the highest mountain in Africa surrounded by breathtaking ice fields as the blood-red sun broke through the dark morning sky was a special, soul-enhancing moment. It was an awe-inspiring holiday and gave me a welcome fresh perspective. It would become the first of many trips to that magnificent continent where I would recharge batteries and ponder my life under those vast African skies.

Over in a grey and wet Cologne the men's four won again, Gillian and Miriam made history by winning the first ever World Championship gold for a British women's crew, and Dot and Cath put Aiguebelette firmly behind them by winning an impressive silver medal. The women's eight finished a disappointing 8th.

I stayed on in Edinburgh and finished my Masters degree. The next set of final trials were once again in Nottingham and this time I didn't win. I met with Mike Spracklen and we had a pleasant but frank discussion over the options. His line was simple. "Katherine, on Monday there will be a quad training in Marlow. It will be the quad trying to win selection for the Olympic Games. The other three athletes, the boat, the equipment and the coach will all be there on Monday morning. If you are there you'll be in it. If you're not then you won't." He couldn't have made it any clearer and it was the right thing for him to do. I drove back to Edinburgh with Hamish the next day and it was obvious what my decision would be. There was to be no agonizing this year. As I dropped him off in Livingston he collected everything out of my car. And I mean everything. Even the old brown pair of shoes that had been in my battered estate car for what felt like forever. In his matter-of-fact, practical way he asked for the money that I owed him, and to me it felt like a divorce.

We stood by the car awkwardly and I really didn't want things to end like this. He asked if I was heading off or if I wanted a cup of tea. Given the choice of driving away on that note or the tea, I chose tea. We chatted about a few things, discussed what a great team we'd been, how good it all was, and then with a hug and a few tears from me I was driving away. I was taken aback by how unexpectedly and abruptly the end had come. I asked what training I should do and he replied, "Oh, steady state stuff, up to you." That's when I knew it was over.

I had the weekend to see friends, pack up all my belongings and move. My sister Sarah came down from Aberdeen to help, and we hired a white van, loaded everything I owned into the back of it and headed south. It was such a quick departure that I had many friends phoning me up the following week from Edinburgh asking if I wanted to meet for a drink, have a coffee or go to the cinema. I had to let them know that I was now living down near London. I was concerned about moving from a student flat to the south-east of England where everything was a lot more expensive. Mike had been great and arranged a three-month rental agreement, at a very favourable rate compared to other rentals in the area, at Bisham Abbey where the National Sports Centre is. I was nervous but also excited as Sarah and I drove along the impressive driveway and up to the striking thirteenth-century abbey, once the home of Henry VIII and Elizabeth I. This was to be my new life.

And although the separation from my life in Edinburgh was hard, I loved my new life. I had the most wonderful big room at the top of the tower in Bisham Abbey. The abbey itself is a beautiful old building, right on the edge of a quiet part of the Thames and surrounded by green fields. My room had a top window that opened as a fire escape and I would climb out of it, down a few metal stairs, and lie on a flat bit of roof that trapped the sun and had a view out over the river and the fields beyond. The staff at the abbey were wonderful, welcoming and friendly, and I learned to play a bit of tennis with Steve, who was in charge of the grounds, and a couple who looked after the LTA kids. Bernie in the kitchen always kept me food if I missed mealtimes and Nikki would make sure I had everything I needed. I originally moved into Bisham for three months and would finally move out over ten years later.

Although I had rowed at Longridge before with Francesca in the pair and had had the odd weekend trip there, it was a different game turning up from now on every day in my single with a huge group of competitive athletes. At the back of everyone's mind was the knowledge, a bit like musical chairs, that at the end of the day there were more athletes than available places in the team and when the music stopped not everyone would be getting a seat in the squad. The room where we all met was plain, in fact it was less than plain. There were no trophies on display, no certificates, awards or anything to suggest this was a national training base. Instead there were pictures of kids trying to cross rivers and grinning excitedly around campfires. We met at the Longridge Scout Camp, and whereas now it's a vibrant, modern, busy place with new buildings, not too long ago, though warm and dry, it was also full of caked-in mud, with wellies strewn around all corners of the room and various bits of kit lying on radiators.

When I moved down south I experienced that awkward first-day-at-a-new-school feeling where everyone else knows what to do, when to move, where to be, and what to say. Or more crucially what not to say. First thing in the morning, especially in the depths of winter, Longridge was a dark, quiet place. There would be the odd muttering or murmuring between two people, but generally the laughter and noise and boisterousness would be left until after the first training session was safely completed and the tea and toast could flow.

Mike would sit in a corner, and while there was a semblance of stretching being done, or perhaps video from the previous training being shown for technique reasons, most people were in their own world. At some point Mike would raise himself up and talk through the training session we had ahead. In his flat, monotone voice he would list the periods of work, the required intensity and the rate. The work would take the form of seemingly interesting sessions involving "castles" and "pyramids", which was deceptive as it simply meant the work would be varied throughout the session. There would be heavy sighing, deep intakes of breaths and the occasional audible groan from various parts of the room – but rarely was there any complaining. To complain would be to draw not only the attention of the Chief Coach, but with it invariably a sarcastic remark about your commitment, your ability to cope or your mental toughness.

As Mike finished I thought everyone was still in their own world, but I was wrong. At some point in his monologue there must have been the suggestion, the hint, the understanding that it was time to go. And when he did finish with "Is that clear?" I looked up to see if there were any questions and instead witnessed the tail end of the squad squeezing out of the door with elbows, shoulders and legs mixed, overlapping and pushing to escape. I glanced back at Mike to see him looking at me with a raised eyebrow and the hint of a smile at the edge of his mouth. Like a tough teacher watching the new kid in class, he was mildly amused, waiting to see what I would do. I grabbed my wellies, hopping on one leg as I tried to cram my foot and accompanying thick sock into the cold rubber. Without a glance behind me I hopped, tripped and fell my way to the cold dark air outside and entered a world of chaos.

People were literally running to their boats. Oars were being gathered in one hand, single sculls shouldered and held with the other, and then somewhere between an ungainly run and a march they headed to the edge of the water. There were more athletes than space on the landing stages and apparently no one wanted to be last. Not even the thick slippery mud stopped people in the rush to get out, although it did raise the heart rate; with hands full and thousands of pounds' worth of boat on your shoulder, one slip could be very costly. "What's going on?" I asked Rachel. "Just get your boat and get out there," she replied breathlessly without pausing in her sprint to the water. It was clear as soon as I managed to get boated.

There was a similar amount of frenzied activity on the water – although there was a period of "warming up", the whole ethos of training was competition. The first leg of the session was a paddle of roughly 5km to the Cookham Bridge. This 5km was designed in theory to warm you up both physically and technically. There is an array of technical exercises – square blade paddling, changing slide lengths, pauses, feathering. Exercises that a few years ago would have sounded like a different language to me now held magical meaning. But not at this point. The warm-up became a race to get to the bridge anywhere but last. At some point Mike would be taking to the water in his custom-made launch and generally athletes tried to have the first part of the morning to themselves. Once the gaze of the coach fell upon you and the megaphone was raised to his mouth, an athlete could be in for words of wisdom or words of criticism, and it wasn't always predictable how long the focus would be. It was expected and often valued, but if the first 20 minutes of the morning could be protected then the race to the bottom of the river was worth it.

I did notice that Miriam was one of the few not looking panicked. Incredibly capable and rightly confident in her own ability, Miriam emerged from around the island behind me and serenely paddled down the river. She was a world away from the chaos in front of her and seemed oblivious of the Darwinian need to survive and stay ahead that everyone else was experiencing. I couldn't understand why one of our best scullers was happy to be warming up in the worst water, water that had been churned up by the desperate blades and boats ahead. As we huddled masses gathered at the bridge it made sense why she would be staying away from the group. All too late. The rowers were in an unruly cluster by the bridge, trying to turn their boats, but blades were overlapping and there was not enough room for everyone. Top layers of kit were trickily being removed. That's one of the biggest tests of the winter months – balancing a skinny, unstable boat with a spare hand and your knees while trying to unzip top layers and pull things over your head. Invariably someone would have the heart-stopping moment when the balance would go, the boat would lurch sideways and a wild grab for the blades would be just enough to stabilize it again. And all of this was being done under the pressure of time. Water bottles were snatched up for a few mouthfuls of freezing sports drink and then it was time to begin. Whatever had been planned for the day began at the bridge, and at least the next hour and a half would be filled with pushing physical limits.

Sometimes we were set off in "waves", meaning small groups; and in that strange mix of reassuring support but also steely competitiveness, every session was a chance to prove yourself, although sometimes at the expense of others. Other times we were set off in one big group, and that was where Miriam's graceful arrival at the back of the group paid off. Away from the mêlée, she could spin her boat and then with the reversal in direction she was first to race back up to the island, clear of the chaos and in the best water. Often Mike would make the better athletes start at the back of the group, giving them a harder challenge but the chance to prove themselves. This was where Miriam's experience proved invaluable. Her skill at negotiating the river was second to none and she used her knowledge to reap every advantage, tucking in out of the stream at just the right point in the bend to avoid battling a raging torrent that more inexperienced people like me found themselves in.

The longer I trained at Longridge the more I learned what a friend the river itself can be once you got to know it. The Thames has her own way about her, and although some corners would seduce you with their welcoming calm they held still water that would only slow boats down. The idea was to use the fast-flowing water to your advantage when going with the stream and then get well out of it when it was against you. The more experienced athletes knew these lessons through years of trial and error, the new arrivals learned the hard way and usually spent frustrating weeks at the mercy of the water. There was an area known as the "travelator" where, if the stream was at full force, poor unsuspecting athletes could get stuck seemingly for ever in a tortuous treadmill of being unable to move forward against the water. Mike would generally carve through the group keen to focus on the best athletes leading the charge. The weaker athletes caught at the back would be subjected to the rolling wash of his launch and face a tougher challenge making up ground.

It was an apprenticeship in tenacity and toughness, and that was how Mike operated. Mike had arrived in 1997 and became the first full-time paid coach for the women's team. His job was to create a professional set-up for the women and he succeeded in that. Under his leadership we had the first British women's World Champions and Olympic medallists. He transformed the team into a hard-working, full-time, competitive group of athletes who could win medals regularly on the international stage. Mike pushed us harder in training than we ever thought possible and as a result we began to excel on the water and in the gym. But the journey wasn't easy or comfortable. Mike had the outward appearance of friendly grandfather figure, along with quite a dark twinkle in his eye. One of his gifts was knowing just what buttons to push with people, and he took much pleasure from pushing them often. A favourite method of control was asking, "What would a true champion do?" It was used to devastating effect on anyone he felt needed to be pushed, reeled in or challenged.

I remember being on the river once when Mike decided to do an exercise which involved counting how many strokes in a row we could take with our blades off the water. In rowing, once the blades have come out of the water, they are carried back above the water before being put back in to take the next stroke. Ideally the blades remain off the water and therefore have a clear uninterrupted return through the air, and it is the fastest way to move. However, in a small unsteady boat that is being pushed around on a river in full flow the task becomes a little more challenging. It's never been one of my strongest suits even in flat conditions and Mike knew that. As we set off, my heart dropped as I saw Mike and his launch taking a slow but deliberate path towards me. He would drive his launch like a carnivorous animal who had seen his prey but was in no rush to make the final kill. The humiliation and the threat were all part of the thrill.

I was trying desperately to get my blades off the water, but my instability coupled with the unpredictable flow of the water meant my boat was dipping from side to side, with the result that my blades were touching the water on alternate sides with each dip. Mike's calm but steely gaze was on me and it was only making me worse. Slowly he raised the megaphone to his mouth. "Let's see what you can do then, Katherine. Shall I count?" It was a rhetorical question and I knew I was in for an unpleasant session. "One ... One ... One ..." Each stroke I was catching the blades again, so Mike wasn't getting past one in his counting. "One ... Tw – oh no, still one. I thought for a second you might manage another one but clearly I overestimated you. One ... One ... Oh dear, this isn't going well for you, is it?" This went on for a while and then he would look over my shoulder and across the river through his megaphone we'd all hear, "That's much better, Gillian. That's what a true champion would do. Well done. OK then, Katherine, let's see what you can do. One ..."

You learned to take the bad days and longed for the good day. So much of our time in training is spent on the things we do wrong that it's easy to get very disheartened. Most days can feel like constant criticism, being told why we're not good enough and how much better it needs to be. This is inevitable as we need to improve continuously to be competitive, but there must also be an awareness of the toll it can take mentally. Negativity added to exhaustion and stress can spiral downwards into dangerous territory. That's why athletes, even intelligent, mature, wise athletes, still find they crave the occasional positive bit of encouragement from a coach. Some coaches give that positive reinforcement a lot more easily than others. Mike generally withheld it, saving it for maximum effect, and so the days when he did give you praise were the days that you felt invincible. And although somewhere inside yourself you might hate that desperate need for praise, we all experienced it.

Everyone handled the training in different ways. One morning we were doing some work at a specific rate of 22 strokes per minute. We have a "stroke coach" in our boats. A little computer that can tell us strokes per minute, speed, time etc. That day we were aiming for 22 strokes per minute. Mike was pottering along behind us in his launch carefully looking out over the whole group to see if anything stood out in any way. And to him it did. He put his hand on his accelerator and manoeuvred his way over to where Guin was sculling. He raised the megaphone and said loudly, "Guin, 23." Usually at this point the athlete in question would drop the rate back to where they should be and hopefully become invisible once again within the group. But Guin was made of sterner stuff than most athletes. Mike cast his eye over the others and through the megaphone came: "Dot, 22, good. Miriam 22, well done. Gillian, 21 and a half, excellent." He then turned his attention back to Guin and his voice took on an edge as we all heard: "Guin, 23 and a half." There was an imperceptible collective intake of breath as the rest of the squad seemed to huddle together as far away as possible from where Guin and Mike were having their showdown. We wanted to see what would happen but not be close enough to be caught in the crossfire.

Mike's flat voice rose in volume and anger as he said, "Guin, 24 … Guin, 25 … Is that what you need to do to compete, is it, Guin? Cheat? Guin 26 and a half …" Neither was willing to back down and as Guin's rate continued to rise she began shouting at Mike too. He couldn't hear, or acted as if he didn't, and moved the launch so close as to be almost over the top of Guin's boat. "Guin 27. Guin, is that what a true champion would do?" But his words were having no effect that day, other than driving Guin further into extreme sculling. They were eye to eye and the fury in them both was rising. There could be no winner in this game. They had both passed the point where they felt they could back down without losing face. Eventually it ended with both of them thinking they had made a point and probably both believing they had the upper hand. And the rest of the outing continued. These crazy moments were part of a normal training day.

Out on the water the quad I was put into consisted of Sarah Winckless, Lisa and Guin. Lisa I knew well from the time we had spent together in the eight. Sarah I had met the previous year, and once met she is never forgotten. She is larger than life, and before I joined the squad her entertaining drinking tales had taken on mythical status, as had some of her mornings after. She was a warm, friendly, loud presence and had come from Cambridge University where she had been the biggest of fishes. There was an adjustment period when she first joined the squad.

There has always been the feeling in the squad that you earn your place and no one should arrive with any unearned rights. It can make for a harsh beginning if people arrive with a lot of confidence, but on balance it's a healthy way for it to be. Everyone is welcomed as long as due respect is shown.

Sarah was someone who simply wanted to be in the middle of things and was incredibly sociable. She was always up for anything and soon she became a trusted friend and loyal ally in the various situations we found ourselves in. And we found ourselves in many.

Guin had spent most of her career in the single scull and wasn't used to being in a crew. She was going to stroke the quad, and that coupled with her international experience meant she would take the leadership role. Lisa, who also had had great international experience, would sit in the bow and make the calls, guiding and steering us as best she could. Sarah and I would sit in the middle, adding the power and trying not to mess up. Louise would be coaching us, the only female coach in international British Rowing.

We had a huge goal in sight, the World Championships in Canada, where we could qualify for the Sydney Olympics. In rowing there are two chances to qualify: at the preceding year's World Championships or at the Olympic qualifying regatta held a few months before the Games. The former was preferable, as it then left a full year to focus on the Olympic Games rather than trying to peak twice in a short space of time to qualify for and then race at the Olympics. We would have to come within the top seven in the world to qualify. With the athletes we had this should have been simple, but as I learned the hard way a crew is far more than just the sum of its individuals.

The tensions, insecurities and problems in communication meant that time and time again we created obstacles for ourselves and came very close to self-destruction. Here were four intelligent, driven, self-aware people and yet conversations could be edgy, personal, defensive. And although we had a clear goal to be aiming for, somehow that wasn't enough to get us through the difficulties we were having. Guin had very high standards for herself and the boat and, whereas in the single she and her coach would sort it out between them, here she had three people behind her who seemed to be part of the problem rather than the solution. The pressure was on, and rather than it bringing us together it was pulling us collectively and independently apart.

It wasn't all bad and we did manage some fantastic outings and even had fun along the way. When it was good it was very good, but the inconsistencies meant we just never knew when and why those good patches would come. It was bad news for a crew to be unaware of why it was performing the way it was. It could lead to doubt and tension. Rather than feeling every moment was important and an opportunity to move forward, many of the days were simply endured.

Our last bit of racing before the World Championships showed the cracks. We were able to operate at a high standard but the problems we had would stop us from being real contenders. It was Lucerne, the beautiful Swiss lake where some of the best international rowing happens annually. In the inspiring surroundings we had our worst race to date. There was a strong tailwind – which is when record times can be set – but rather than being able to seize that opportunity we raced with blades all over the place, no settled rhythm, the boat chaotically rocking around, and in the midst of this Lisa caught a crab. We (eventually) crossed the line behind everyone else and Lisa unleashed her frustration at Guin, saying that Guin looking round caused the crab. Ideally in a racing situation only one or two people have the job to look around, and with us that was Lisa's job. She didn't need and didn't want anyone else needlessly taking on that role. Guin said nothing, so we warmed down in furious and uncomfortable silence.

Eventually it calmed down and we looked towards the final. To reach the final we had to make it through the repechage. We had put ourselves into a tough position and with only two qualifying slots from five we were facing the realistic chance of not making it to the A Final. But thankfully in the repechage we were a different crew from the heat and for most of the race we were within a second of the leading Ukraine crew. Then Denmark pushed through to take the lead and we were second, ahead of Ukraine. We were into the dying metres of the race, Lisa called for "ten", and at the end of that ten Guin started looking around for the finish line. As she looked around Guin caught her blade and stopped, Sarah screamed at her to go, we crashed across the line in complete disorder, level with Ukraine. I looked over and saw the bow girl from Ukraine level with me, which meant we were one seat ahead. I turned and smiled at Lisa, but then looked forward to see Sarah punching the water in despair thinking we had missed the final. Guin was hanging her head saying nothing. The Ukrainians looked over at us blankly and shrugged their shoulders. They didn't know the result either but didn't seem to be going into an emotional meltdown. Lisa and I snapped at each other in the warm-down and then we were told we had indeed secured second place and were through to the final. We ended up fifth in the final and just about still talking to each other.

We weren't the only boat cracking up. We next moved to Canada for the pre-Worlds training camp and there was one particularly memorable outing in Welland, a long canal where our training camp was based. We were on our way back to the landing stage and from a fair distance away we all could hear a strange and unusual sound. I frowned, trying to work out what it could be. Maybe some unusual Canadian wildlife we hadn't yet encountered. I knew there were bears, but would they really be near to a man-made canal? There was indeed a wildness to the noise, something raw, but also something vaguely familiar. It was only when we got closer that we realized what it was. It was Dot.

I knew of Dot long before I ever met her. Dot Blackie was the biggest name at Edinburgh University Boat Club. Her picture was on the walls and the stories of when she was Captain were infamous. She was the first ever female Captain and made sure that for the first time the women's team had a fair run at things. The most famous story was about how she finally got so fed up with people being late for training that one day as she drove the minibus from the University to training she didn't stop and wait to collect anyone. If they weren't there at the end of their roads as instructed she simply drove on. That day she arrived at training with just a handful of athletes and many more standing confused at the ends of various roads around the city. It only happened once.

Dot always had a very strong sense of justice, and if she had been born in another time she would have been marching with placards, handcuffing herself to the railings and stirring things up with Emmeline Pankhurst. She was never afraid to stick her head up and argue for what she felt was right and would leap to the defence of anyone in need. Her long dark plait would swing with more and more intensity, in time with her growing enthusiasm for a cause. She was a formidable presence, but if she was on your side you felt safe and supported. And also entertained. Because along with the serious side Dot had a wonderful, childlike sense of fun.

In Canada one night after a great day out we didn't feel quite ready yet to go back to the residences. Just before turning into where we were staying Louise swung the steering wheel around and we careered over the grass and away, ending up at the Donut Diner. There the challenge was to see how many donut holes could be fitted into a mouth. I watched in awe as Dot seemed to dislocate her jaw to fit more donut holes in. I felt like I was watching a wildlife documentary as she appeared to defy all known principles of human anatomy. I swear there were kids moving closer to their parents in that diner. If I hero-worshipped Dot before, well she had just gone into a whole new stratosphere. True, this superpower was probably more impressive to watch than useful in any practical way, but that night in Canada the practicalities weren't important. This was a challenge and Dot was winning it in style. Until we realized she couldn't actually breathe. Or move her jaw. Thankfully the donuts finally gave way and Dot could move her jaws just enough to start chewing. And breathing. It would have been an awful way to lose a member of the team.

But the day on the water with the wierd sound wasn't one of those fun days. As we drew closer Louise's eyes widened as she realized what was happening. "OK then, I think we should just do another lap of the course." We turned the boat in silent but unanimous agreement and rowed away from the showdown. Dot had finally snapped. For the time we had been in Canada the pair and the double had been sharing a car to get to and from training. After what had felt to Dot like many changes to fit in with what the double wanted, there had been one change too many. Dot decided to let her feelings be known. So she unleashed her fury on Gillian and the noise that we had heard from the other end of the course was Dot explaining in full voice just how unfair the current set-up was, how their training was equally important and this close to racing no one should be messing each other about. When we tentatively arrived back on to dry land later the storm had blown through and everyone was probably better off for knowing true feelings. But it was also a lesson: if potentially difficult conversations about what might upset each other were not had ahead of time, then it was liable to come out when the pressure grip started to tighten.

When it came to racing there weren't fantastic results that summer. For the four of us in the quad although we had started off aiming for medals the crucial thing was to finish in the top seven places, which would mean we had secured the quad's place at the Olympics. We began the event well enough with a decent heat, but then we missed the chance of a place in the final with a lacklustre repechage, and now we were at a crucial stage. The six boats in the final had won automatic qualification for the Olympic Games and there was only one place remaining. The winner of the B Final would take the last slot. The only problem was that the Belarussians were also in the B Final, we had not beaten them all season and so far we weren't giving any impression that there was magic waiting to happen. With backs firmly against the wall we met one last time to try to put things right.

What we couldn't afford was another result like our repechage. To be outclassed is one thing, but to race without the feel of attack or fight or determination is a soul-destroying and infuriating experience. The signs had been there. The night before our repechage we had a meeting with Louise. The four of us had agreed the time and the place, but when we gathered we didn't have Guin. It was the night before a crucial race and suddenly our meeting wasn't looking good. As it turned out, Guin had tried to meet with Louise earlier and when that hadn't happened she had decided there was no point in having the crew meeting. We raced the next day without cohesion and without the team ethic that underpins a great crew. Instead of the innate trust that should have been there, there was doubt. We sat in the back of the boathouse after the race with everyone in various stages of exhaustion and exasperation. No one had gained anything and we were in danger of losing a lot more.

The morning of the B Final was inauspicious. We were up before anyone else in the hotel and shuffled silently out to the minibus where Louise was sitting in the driver's seat trying to gauge our mood. The mood was sullen and weary. We drove to the course in the pitch black of night and then weren't allowed on the water as it was too dark and too early. The B Final was being rowed before any of the other finals and there was nobody about. It felt like everyone shared our mood of just not wanting to be there. We got on to the ergos instead and Louise had to drive the minibus up next to us with the headlights on so we could see what we were doing.

As the light finally improved we got ourselves ready for the race. We boated and I knew that we had never been ahead of the Belarussians, so if we were ahead of them by halfway we would win. I was nervous, not about the race but about not knowing how we would race. It makes such a difference when you have the luxury of being in a boat where you know what will happen. This boat always held its own surprises, and that makes a crucially important race like this one even more tense. We sat on the start and I just hoped we would be able to produce something more than the underwhelming feel of the repechage. And within two strokes I knew we would. The boat felt like a different being. Guin was leading it with the bit between her teeth and her racing head on. We were ahead of the Belarussians already and pulling away. I grinned with masochistic pleasure, knowing that here was a race we would be able to hurt in at last. I shouted with the sheer pleasure of feeling we were racing again, that we were going to do justice to our abilities at last. We blazed our way to the finish and in front of a crowd of maybe seven people we crossed the line first and secured the important Sydney berth. We celebrated as if we had crossed the Olympic line in front of thousands. The few early risers were probably taken aback by such emotion, but it felt like we had dragged ourselves through hell to get that tiny bit of success.

That last weekend in Canada with the team was a memorable one. We had finished our racing early and it had been a poor display from the women's side. Our quad had scraped the last place to qualify for the Olympics, at least salvaging something out of a potentially disastrous year. The pair and the double had done better by finishing in the A Final and qualifying their boats but they were also out of the medals, so it was disappointing for them. I was back at the hotel when Gillian came looking for someone to lead astray. Gillian had a great sense of fun and wanted company. I was a willing target. "All right, hen?" she asked in her Glaswegian twang. I nodded. "Fancy going out for a drink?" It was early and I hadn't eaten, but then neither had she. So I felt it was OK. We headed to the end of the racing lake where there was a single street that seemed to make up St Catherines. We found a wonderful bar with a pool table, a large dancing area and plenty of friendly folk leaning back against the long bar-top chatting. I can't remember if there was straw on the floor but there should have been, it had that sort of a feel.

Slowly the place filled and more people joined in. We were playing pool when a couple of women came in and stood with us at the pool table. We played against them and thought we were doing OK, so they suggested we add a bit of money to make it more exciting. As competitive athletes we jumped at the chance, allowing our love of a challenge and the beer we were drinking to make the decision for us. With dollar bills stacked to one side we were soon looking on in dismay as they completely took our game apart. By the end they were kind enough to say they wouldn't take our money. They did this professionally and decided we were too nice and too soft to be left broke. So they moved on to more deserving targets. This place was full of good people, I decided, as I watched the pool sharks from afar.

I went to get some fresh air and found a row of gleaming motorbikes lined up outside the bar. I was looking over them with an impressed air when one of the owners came over. "Do you like bikes?" he asked. "I do," I replied but added, "although I know nothing about them." "Ever been on a Harley?" "Nope," I said. "Well, do you wanna have a go?" "Oh yes, please," I grinned, forgetting my new laid-back persona. A few minutes later I had my arms around this stranger's waist as we sped along the dark forest roads. It was wonderful and exhilarating and only for a brief second did I think this might not be the brightest of ideas. Ah well, too late, I thought, and held on a little tighter. I remember looking overhead at the stars and thinking life was very, very good.

We finally returned to the bar and as I swung my leg off the bike I thanked the man for letting me experience the ride. It had felt like just moments, but we had actually been gone a long time. I turned to see Sarah standing with hands on her hips and anger in her eyes. "Where the hell have you been?" she demanded. "I was on a Harley!" I exclaimed with a big smile, feeling that was enough of an explanation. I then had a mini lecture on how dangerous, how irresponsible, how stupid, how thoughtless my behaviour had been. "But it was amazing" was all I could come back with – and "He was a real gentleman." The poor guy was standing behind us during the tirade, and when Sarah threw an accusing look at him he simply shrugged and offered her a ride. She looked exasperated and told him the very thought was absolutely ridiculous. And impractical. She was wearing a skirt for goodness sake. A few minutes later I was wearing Sarah's skirt, she was wearing my jeans and was disappearing off into the night on the back of a Harley. It might have been an insane season but, boy, I did love Canada.

CHAPTER 4

BREAKTHROUGH IN SYDNEY

It was sunny and hot but not oppressive. Some days on a rowing lake the heat can feel like an enemy, like extra opposition. On a training day the heat might be welcomed. More than once I've sat in a boat discussing the finer points of technique, each member of the crew unusually attempting to pinpoint something intangible – a dead giveaway of an unspoken pact between the rowers to steal an extra bit of rest and recovery and enjoy the summer sunshine, while the coach hopefully believes his athletes are finally finding a deeper understanding of this complex sport. But on a race day the heat can become a problem, leaving dry mouths, uncomfortable breathing, sweaty hands, an extra feeling of fatigue and lethargy. On the water there is no escape, especially on the startline, where it is often quiet and still and no cooling breeze exists to give you a respite from the baking sun.

But in Sydney there was a comfortable heat. The much predicted and feared gale-force winds had not arrived and the lake was like glass. The weather wasn't the problem. It was my first Olympic final and I had no idea what to expect. It was a race, like others I had done before in that it was over 2,000m in a six-lane final and the first across the line would win. But it was also a race unlike any other race I had done. It meant everything to every athlete in the line-up: no matter what country, which athletes, what background, however long or short their respective journeys, it is always the Olympic final that people want to win. And when the gun goes there is no stopping, no half-time, no time-out discussions, just one flat-out, lung-bursting, leg-pumping adrenaline rush from start to finish. Well, to be fair there is a bit more finesse than that, but I was very aware we had one shot at this.

I sat on the startline sucking in deep breaths and trying to calm my racing pulse. I was the youngest and least experienced in the crew and I felt a huge (self-imposed) pressure not to let the others down. I may have been the greenest in the boat but I was determined not to be the weak link. I looked down at my feet, I leaned over and checked that the locks holding my blades in were fastened tight. I was going to be strong, reliable, I was going into battle for and with my crewmates and I was willing to go to any dark place necessary. I would do whatever was asked of me and give all I had to give. More than I ever had before. Why wouldn't you? It was the Olympic final, with a lifetime to recover if necessary. There would be no training tomorrow, nothing to hold back for or save myself for. I looked up and over the shoulders of Miriam who sat in front of me. I felt fired up, ready. And it was at that point that I saw a ridiculously huge camera swing very slowly from the boat in the lane next to us to our boat. It was the biggest camera I had ever seen in my life. I knew that TV screens at the finish end of the lake and TVs all around the world would be showing that shot and a commentator would be reading out our names. And from nowhere I heard in my head the words of a friend, who just before we left for Australia had said, "I think about a billion people watch the Olympics worldwide." My pulse rate soared.

TOP LEFT: Mum with Sarah and I on our first day at the zoo. Apparently rather than looking at the lions I was more interested in perfecting my "race face".

TOP RIGHT: Sarah and me wearing one of gran's many inventive creations. No curtains were safe!

MIDDLE LEFT: Even from a young age and with a dodgy haircut I loved collecting medals and ribbons.

MIDDLE RIGHT: Gran and grandad and I at Aberdeen beach. Learning about unconditional love. And how to survive in very cold temperatures.

ABOVE: Dad and I at the top of a Munro on the west coast of Scotland. One of many mountains I would tackle in my life.

LEFT: My proudest athletic achievement at school – gaining my black belt in karate. (I wasn't usually allowed to practise on the school desks.)

OPPOSITE TOP LEFT: My first "international" race. Lagan Head in Northern Ireland with Edinburgh University.

OPPOSITE TOP RIGHT: 1994 Edinburgh University Boat Club Women's Squad. I'm in the back row with the rest of the unloved "fifth boat".

LEFT: 1996 Women's Head of the River Race, and a few months after the release of the *Braveheart* film. Inspiration can come from many sources.

TOP: Celebrations with Edinburgh University Boat Club at the Sports Union Dinner.

ABOVE: : Jo and I winning Women's Henley in 1996. It was my first major summer of success and the smiles say it all.

TOP LEFT: Winning Under-23s with Cesca in the pair and Hamish coaching. My first GB vest and first gold medal on the world's stage.

TOP RIGHT: Aiguebelette 1997. By wining the first medal for a British women's eight we proved "Girl Power" was truly alive and kicking in the 1990s.

ABOVE: Mike and Annie Spracklen with (from left to right) Miriam Batten, me, Lisa Eyre, Sarah Winckless, Dot Blackie. Guin Batten, Sarah Birch, Cath Bishop, Gillian Lindsay. The super-eight put together to win Henley Royal Regatta.

RIGHT: Dot's embrace at Sydney showing the generosity and selflessness that sport can sometimes display.

ABOVE: The first ever Olympic medal for British women's rowing. Another pioneering first and a moment that would change everything.

BELOW: Two happy athletes. The closing ceremony in Sydney where Steve Redgrave won his historic fifth gold Olympic medal and ended his Olympic career and I was just starting.

LEFT: Milan World Championships 2003. Winning the coxless pair with Cath and becoming a World Champion for the first time despite all the odds stacked against us that year. A very proud and special moment.

BELOW: Racing against the Romanian Olympic champions at the Athens 2004 Olympic Games.

BOTTOM: The Athens silver medals complete with those becoming olive wreaths.

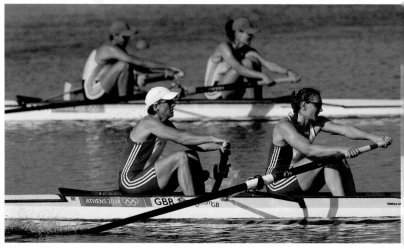

ABOVE: Poznan 2006 World Cup. We are on a mission to Beijing and every race would matter.

TOP RIGHT: The Grainger girls at Buckingham Palace. Mum, Sarah and I on our way to my first investiture.

RIGHT: Heartbreak for Elliot and Tom and many other loyal fans as we are beaten in front of a home crowd at Dorney in 2006.

BELOW: Dorney World Championships 2006. Watching the Russian flag rise and listening to the Russian national anthem while the pain of defeat burned. We didn't know at this point that the Russian boat would be disqualified for taking illegal drugs.

ABOVE: Beijing Olympics 2008, the moment was here and we meant business.

LEFT: The podium in Beijing 2008. A complete contrast to the feeling in Sydney 2000. Same coloured medal, wildly different emotions.

BELOW: Edinburgh proudly welcomed home the Scottish Olympic medallists. It was a great day for everyone although the widest smiles and the greatest respect was rightfully reserved for Chris Hoy's magical treble.

The Olympic year had started well with an early training camp in Australia. For many of us, including myself, it was our first experience of Australia, and what a fantastic time we had. Compared to our usual training this felt like the closest we would ever come to a holiday camp; the training was still hard, but there were also some sessions on the beach thrown in for good measure. No matter where we went for our camps or how far away, Mike always worried about "Day 5 syndrome". In his mind five days after arriving somewhere our body would struggle the most. Whether or not it was true, it allowed us some recovery sessions in which to play Frisbee on the beach. That was when I met Daley Thompson for the first time. He is a good friend of Cath Bishop's and so came to join us one day on the Gold Coast. Daley is a larger-than-life character and when you meet him you realize how he won the incredible gold medals in the decathlon in 1980 and again in 1984. He is without a doubt one of the most competitive people I have ever met and I sometimes think I must have met most of them.

He joined us for a game of Frisbee and although it had been competitive before, he managed to raise it to a whole new level. There was no "getting to know you" phase with Daley. The first contact I had with him was when I was holding the Frisbee and suddenly felt a massive force hit me squarely in the back. I was instantly felled and pinned to the sand with the weight of him on top of me. I turned my head, spitting out sand as I did so, and rather than any apology I got his wicked grin and "Come on then" as he leapt up and chased off towards another target. He has an infectious energy and enthusiasm and does everything with a ridiculously cheeky attitude that means he can get away with most things. He didn't join us for the harder and less exciting ergo sessions, but even they felt manageable to us because we were in Australia and it was where the Olympics would be and everything had an exciting purpose. Soon, however, those days in the sun were over and we returned to Britain for the winter and the chance to compete for a trip back to Australia with the Olympic team.

Two days after our return from the camp it was back to the training on the river at Longridge. Mike decided the way to go was a 13km time trial in singles. It was hard enough on any given day, but shortly after returning from Australia with jet lag, a huge time difference and the difficult change from dry heat to damp fog, it was always going to be a challenge. Only a few of us made it to the start of the training session and even fewer made it to the end. I was feeling fairly pleased with myself when I finally crossed the finish line, having stuck it out and completed the course. But within seconds I wished I hadn't. The finish line was a few hundred metres from the landing stage and as my boat crossed the line I hung my head and body over my blades, trying to steady my breathing. As I did that I tried to lift my hands off the blades but realized that I couldn't. I was confused as to why they seemed stuck to my blades, but as I slowly forced my fingers to uncurl I understood. The stickiness was coming from a mix of skin, blood and nasty stuff that was covering my palms. I looked down in horror at what used to be my hands. They were a mess of raw red flesh. I still had to get back to the landing stage – and the only way was to put my throbbing hands back on to the blade handles and paddle in.

I don't remember how I carried my boat and blades off the water, but I do remember sitting in the Longridge kitchen about 15 minutes later. The kitchen was where we all met in between sessions and was usually a hive of activity and noise. People would be making absolutely enormous urns of tea with tea-leaves from ancient, battered silver pots. Someone else would be at the toaster churning out plate after plate of hot and often charred toast to the hungry masses, while butter and jam were tracked down and thrown on to the centre of the table and fought over. Alison Mowbray would normally be in front of the stove, whipping up enough porridge to feed the whole country, and when everyone was happy and seated there would be a wonderful excited buzz of conversations flowing and falling over each other and the odd shriek of laughter or gasp of horror as a story was recounted from that morning or years ago. There was often a trip to the local bakery, and then there would be a scrum to reach the iced buns. The atmosphere could be altered distinctly, however, if there were any selection issues or personality clashes involving people in the room. Then there would be a more sullen, awkward feel and the fight for the iced bun would take on a darker edge.

The morning of my ripped hands, however, I was the quiet one. Louise sat next to me and asked if I wanted a mug of tea. Wrapping your hands around a cosy bit of china, usually chipped, stained and with some strange cartoon or advert on it, was a reassuring, even essential part of the morning ritual. I said yes to Louise but as she pushed the mug towards me I realized I couldn't open my hands to hold the mug. I had been sitting with them closed and they had fused shut again due to the nasty liquid seeping out of the open wounds. There was a general understanding in the squad that you didn't admit to injuries if you could help it. Mike could see that as a weakness and nobody wanted to be given that label. Louise looked at me and asked what was wrong. I said I'd hurt my hands that morning during the timed piece. She asked if they had blistered and I nodded, wondering if that was an accurate description of it. When I tried to show her she didn't hesitate but sent me off to the local GP.

I sat in the waiting room holding my hands shut, with bits of tissue paper around them. I was in a corner trying to avoid attention, as people might have been somewhat horrified by my appearance. When I was finally called through, the doctor asked how he could help me. I said I was sent to him to see if he could help my hands before they picked up an infection. As I unfolded them he took one glance and said in a mildly scolding tone, 'Or because you do have an infection.' I smiled weakly.

One of the more surreal moments that winter was when we were all asked to Mike's house for a Christmas lunch. Mike was married to Annie, who kept herself busy at the local amateur dramatic society and was a happy, vivacious, outgoing presence everywhere she went. It was a lovely thought to get us all together for an end-of-year lunch, although I was a little unsure of how the day would go as we rarely socialized as a large group. I arrived a little nervously, somehow feeling like I was having dinner with our boss and unsure of the social etiquette of it all. Others were not as shy about it, because as Mike opened the door we were greeted with the sound of Miriam on the karaoke machine. It was before lunch and Gillian, Guin and Miriam were relaxing with a spot of singing. Soon the food was ready and as we sat down to eat there was the promise of more singing and games after the meal. Unfortunately I had to leave as soon as we'd finished eating as I had a flight to catch up to Edinburgh and I wasn't willing to risk missing it in the Christmas traffic. Sarah, Dot and Cath had offered to take me to the airport, with the sad result that none of us ever did get the chance to try that Christmas karaoke.

Finally the exhausting winter days passed and as the days started to lengthen we could begin thinking about the summer. The summer of the Sydney Olympics. The trials would be crucial and this time we would be racing in crew boats for selection. Dot and Cath were favourites to win the pairs racing, and there were three boats that were going to be fighting it out in the doubles racing. I was partnered with Sarah, Gillian was with Frances Houghton, and the Batten sisters Guin and Miriam would be racing together. It was the first time in the past couple of years that Gillian and Miriam wouldn't be racing together in the double. The plan for the sculling race was to see the margins at the finish and if two of the boats were close in speed we would form a quad as the priority. If one boat won comfortably then we would have the double as the lead boat.

There were two races – one a time trial, whereby the boats race individually one after another against the clock, the other side by side, head to head. Sarah and I won the time trial and although Louise called our sculling "agricultural" we had taken first blood. The key race would be the side by side final and in a thrilling race with not much to split the crews Gillian and Frances beat us by 0.8 seconds. Sarah and I were desperately disappointed but at least we had laid down a marker. Guin and Miriam would now race Gillian and Frances and see what the margin there would be. Although winning would obviously have been preferable, Sarah and I were in a strong position. It looked for the moment as if we would be in a quad with Gillian and Frances as the margin was so close. With one race to be done either the Battens would beat Gillian and Frances and take the top double slot or they would lose and take the double as the second slot. The only complication would be if they came closer to Gillian and Frances than we had. What happened was none of the above. Gillian and Frances won convincingly over the Battens. And Gillian and Frances said they wanted to be the double.

So Guin, Miriam, Sarah and I became the quad. It was a slight concern going back to the boat that was so similar to the 1999 quad after the difficulties we had experienced. But we had the Olympics to think about and that was a sobering focus. There was a brief moment when Mike toyed with the idea of putting his top eight athletes – the quad, double and pair, into an eight and sending that to qualify for the Olympics. The idea had its attractions as we had raced as that combination at Henley Royal Regatta and demolished the opposition. Racing in that eight was one of the most memorable experiences of my career; it was packed with passion and drive and determination and skill and power. Cath stroked it with a focus I had never seen and when she bellowed for "more power" during the race the boat willingly responded, eager to give her everything she demanded and more. She was as inspiring as she was physically impressive. To race the eight, however, would be risking three boats to get one result and would also cause untold devastation for the existing British eight that was trying to qualify for the Games. So eventually the idea went away and we returned to our own boats.

The summer season was underway and actually the quad was going very well. We still had ups and downs along the way, but generally we were competing well internationally and moving forward all the time. The double, meanwhile, were having a slightly more inconsistent season.

An unfortunate and unforeseen incident changed the course for all of us. Sarah came in from an outing with a very sore side and soon she had the news we all feared. She had a rib stress fracture. It would take her, and us, out of the last World Cup in Lucerne before the Olympics. She was devastated but there was nothing to be done except allow her the time to recover, and the three of us would continue training in her absence. That was until the double went to Lucerne and finished out of the medals.

Mike mentioned that either Gillian or Frances could sub into the quad, but he thought it would likely be Gillian as she was the faster of the two and she would make the quad quicker. A few days later the bomb was dropped. Mike had a meeting with us all over the tea break and told us about his plans to strengthen the quad as a result of Sarah's injury and that Gillian was the person for it. That began the arguments – from Sarah that she was ready to come back in, from Mike saying she had too much technical work to make up, and Frances arguing that she should be considered too as she was as good as anyone, and that all seats should be looked at, not just Sarah's. There was a lot of shouting and tears and Mike, in exasperation, said he would go back to the original quad and double, but we must know that was not a decision based on merit, rather an emotional decision. There was silence. We went out in the original quad line-up.

The next morning, however, Mike had changed his mind again and Gillian would be in the quad after all. By now everyone was getting uptight and stressed by the changing situation and there seemed no clarity moving forward. Mike himself wasn't happy about the decisions he was having to make. Two days later in the break he led us all to the concrete steps leading down to the water at Longridge, where the hot sun was beating down, and chaos descended. Mike went back to the beginning of how this year had all begun. Sarah and Frances took notes throughout the meeting and every so often Mike would stop himself to look at them both and drily asked if he was talking too fast. At one point Sarah stopped writing and again Mike asked if he was going too fast. Sarah replied she would start taking notes when he started to say something relevant. The atmosphere was charged.

Mike challenged both Sarah and Frances and then sat listening as the suggestion was raised that if we were now seriously considering the quad to be the top boat then we should put the top four people in it, putting everyone under threat, especially Guin and Miriam who hadn't performed well in the trialling. Frances repeatedly pointed out that if we were going to trial for Sarah's seat then all seats should be tested. The arguments went round and round in circles, and finally Miriam said we could either get four of us into the boat, based on at least three of the current squad, and make it work and move forward taking the best chance we had, or we could take five steps back, start again and never reach the end because we would run out of time.

The discussion was getting increasingly heated as the temperature and the tension mounted. Everyone was aware that crucial Olympic places were at risk and that the decision made here would decide the chances at the Olympic Games. Ultimately Mike said there would be a trial for Sarah's seat but that was the only trial to be done because we didn't have enough time to start again. It was now only weeks before the Olympics and there was a quad up and running, so one seat could be tested, brought about by the injury, but he wasn't prepared to start from the very beginning all over again.

Selection is always an interesting area. Although much is made of trials and tests, there has always been a bit of space for the coach to use his own judgement when final decisions are made. It may be harder to justify but there is an appreciation that a good and experienced coach can use what he sees every day in training to help him make some of the tougher decisions.

We duly had the trial and Sarah, Frances and Gillian all raced. Gillian won, and so it was decided she would join the quad and Sarah and Frances would become the double. On the training side the professionalism held strong with everyone taking to training in their new boats. Off the water, however, personal damage had been done and would never be healed. The atmosphere was always tense whenever all of us were together and it couldn't even be eased by the balancing presence of Dot and Cath, who were training elsewhere and experiencing their own difficulties. And so, with this in the air, we flew out to Australia to complete our Olympic preparations.

We had a British Olympic Association camp before moving into the Village. It gave us some time to adjust to the effects that flying to the other side of the world would have on us. I enjoyed being in Australia, although things took a while to settle down. When we were in the crew things were moving forward, but outside of the training sessions and meetings I still enjoyed spending time with Sarah who happily was on speaking terms with me, if not the others. It was great to catch up with Lisa, who was back stroking the eight, and it was fantastic to have Dot and Cath back in close proximity. I didn't want my time with other members of the squad to have an impact on my crew. I knew as the Olympics were getting closer there would be a ratcheting up of the sensitivities on all sides. I wanted to reassure Gillian, Miriam and Guin that I enjoyed spending my time with them but also found it good to catch up with some of the others in the team.

Thankfully around that time we had access to Kirsten Barnes, a psychologist who had previously been a member of the Canadian Olympic rowing team. She was a welcome presence, being fun, friendly, open, reassuring, patient, wise – and just happened to be a double Olympic Champion too. She allowed our conversations to be out in the open and in our first session made two important points. Firstly, it was crucial that as a crew we were there for each other during the training sessions and the racing, and we had to have trust in each other that that was the case. But it was OK, and indeed healthy, to feel we could spend time apart and not feel we had to be artificially close the whole time. And the second thing was to be yourself. She said it was a risk to try to be anything else now, as being ourselves was what had got us here. Kirsten's chats were great for defusing the sensitive and emotional situations we kept finding ourselves in and for reassuring us that we were doing OK as we were. She also talked to us about our commitment to the crew and what we brought to it. I was to speak up when I had something to say, stay quiet when I didn't, and lighten the mood whenever I could.

Just as we were finding positives between the four of us, trouble came from a fifth member of the team. One day we were looking at video with Mike and he paused the video on me. Rather than talking about my technique he said my waistline could be better. Miriam laughed, thinking it was a joke, but he became very serious, telling us that I couldn't rock over with my body as well as the others because of my figure and that the boat was a millimetre further under the water because of me. My humiliation was complete. Everyone sat in silence. Thankfully afterwards the others were all very supportive. Miriam held me back to say I should ignore him and not to worry, Guin said they all needed my power and not to do anything stupid, and Gillian reassured me back in our room that I was fine. I was still so upset and frustrated and embarrassed. It was about two weeks before racing, and any serious change in my weight would potentially jeopardize my performance, but I was now uncomfortably self-conscious.

Despite all the chaos, when we came together as a team to race over 2,000m as a rehearsal for the fast approaching Olympic racing, we managed to finish top of everyone in percentages, including the men's four with Steve, Matt, Tim and James, so the stress behind the scenes at least didn't seem to be slowing us down too much.

We moved into the Olympic Village on 12 September and that night I wrote my diary by the light of the Olympic Stadium. I was sharing a room with Gillian and she was asleep, but I was too excited. I'd had no idea what an Olympic Village would be like, but was taken aback by just how like a village it was – there were streets and buses and shops and a post office and rows of apartment blocks. Every team stays together, so the British team were together in the Blue Starfish area. Because the

Village covered a huge area, parts of it were named after marine animals so we could find our way about a little more easily. What obviously makes it different from other villages is who it is populated by, and I hadn't been prepared to be in the vicinity of thousands of athletes and so many sporting heroes and famous faces.

But the wonderful thing is that in the Village that's just seen as normal, so you walk about in your brightly coloured national sports kit greeting fellow athletes from all around the world as if it was the most natural thing in the world. I vividly remember walking through the main street and seeing a guy swaggering towards me that I knew. He had a confident gait and a wide smile as he approached. I said, "Hey, good to see you," and he nodded smiling and said, "Hey, how you doing?" and then walked on. A few steps later I realized I didn't actually know him personally but recognized him because he was Maurice Greene – the 100m Olympic Champion. Moments like this kept happening and it was surreal but wonderful. There is a fantastic mutual respect that exists in the Village because everyone has earned their place to be there by being great at what they do.

The Opening Ceremony was a massive highlight for me. There is always the talk of whether or not such a late and tiring evening will have a negative effect on performance, and our men's eight, for example, chose not to march as they wanted to focus solely on their racing. It worked for them, as a week later they went on to make a special bit of history by winning the gold in the fastest rowing event of them all. I don't even remember there being any discussion for us about whether or not we would march. As we walked into the stadium behind the giant figure of Matthew Pinsent waving the oversized Union Jack as the figurehead of the British Olympic Team, I was so glad that we did. Before we got to that point, however, we were taken to the holding area in the gymnastics stadium next door to the main stadium. I was stunned to see everyone in one place, with all the different countries seated around the arena, and I began to appreciate the enormous scale of what we were doing.

Suddenly after a long wait we were being told to gather, and in theory we were supposed to stand in our rows according to height order, but soon the walk, march and mild gallop turned into an excited rush as the massive doors ahead opened into the stadium. I remember seeing the first few brightly lit rows of packed seats, and as we walked towards the doors we looked up and up as the rows stretched endlessly into the sky and disappeared in the towering bright lights of the stadium. I squinted up into the biggest stadium ever built, a packed-out 110,000-seater. The noise was deafening and the sight was stunning with flags covering all parts of the stadium. Flash bulbs constantly lit up the crowd and the athletes, while there was a continuous roar from the crowds as they cheered and sang and waved on the athletes who were looking around at each other and the impressive stadium with excited smiles. However hard I'd tried to imagine what it would be like, nothing could have prepared me for the reality of entering that stadium. Pride fills your chest until it's almost impossible to breathe. The marching part was over too quickly, but as we gathered in the middle a vast flag was released and it flowed down and over the athletes like water and we were underneath it, passing it over our heads with our hands, united by this one symbol.

It was soon time for the flame to arrive and the cauldron to be lit. It is always a secret who will light the cauldron and how they would do it. My strongest memory before Sydney was of the Barcelona Olympics, when a lone archer fired a flaming arrow up into the night sky and as it dropped into the cauldron the Olympic flame ignited and the huge bowl of fire lit up the stadium. Every time it is different and unique to those Games. Sydney marked 100 years of women competing in the Games, and so the final leg of the torch relay, that had been all across Australia, including under water along the Great Barrier Reef, was to be carried in a relay for one lap of the stadium by past Australian female Olympic champions. The last relay exchange would be to hand the flame to Cathy Freeman, who would light the cauldron.

Cathy Freeman was a popular choice for the big moment. She would have the expectation of the nation on her shoulders when about ten days later she would be back in the same stadium for the 400m final, attempting to be the first aboriginal to win a gold medal for Australia. As the flame was passed to her she ran up the stairs to a platform above us all and then walked across water. Literally. She lowered her torch to the edge of the water and a ring of fire ignited around her. The flames licked the edges of the water and as Cathy stood there with torch held aloft the fire slowly rose above her head and up to the giant cauldron at the top of the stadium.

The flame was probably the biggest moment for me. When it was lit in the Opening Ceremony I realized for the next two weeks while that fire blazed above the stadium we would be witness to and part of the greatest sporting events in history. The Opening Ceremony is a place of hope and opportunity and excitement, as no one knows who or what will bring those historic moments, but we knew there would undoubtedly be some. The sense of being part of something rare and something special was almost overwhelming, and with the speeches, the flags, the countries and the crowds I finally recognized why this global event with its history, its culture and its values is raised up and beyond mere racing and competition. It is something that helps to define the human spirit, the spirit that will overcome obstacles, refuse to believe in limits and reach outwards and upwards relentlessly. It represents dreams and hard work and shows people pushing themselves to new heights – to win or lose, but never to fail. Because the valour of the attempt, the work taken to get to the startline meant for those individuals they could never fail. By daring to live their dreams they could potentially lose a competition, but they would never be seen as failures.

I consider myself very fortunate to have been in the Olympic Stadium when Cathy Freeman arrived for her final. Talking to Denise Lewis and Jonathan Edwards, who had competed in the athletics stadium at that time, it was clear something special was happening. Everyone knew it, from the packed crowd to the fellow athletes on the track, and to the officials. The sense of anticipation was electric, and when 110,000 people fall to a hushed nervous chatter as a woman simply walks on to the track to warm up, you know there's history in the making. The crowd livened up again as there were triple jumps to watch and other events happening, but as the 400m runners finished their warm-up and walked to their blocks you could have heard a pin drop, and I held my breath because it seemed selfish to be trying to breathe at that moment. Cathy was in a world of her own, apparently oblivious to the crowd, and slowly she lifted her hands to pull up the green and gold hood she was wearing. As she lowered to her blocks her sleek profile dominated the massive TV screens all around the stadium.

My heart was pounding in my chest as I witnessed what performing under pressure really meant. The gun was raised and the trigger being pulled released everyone from their hypnotic trance. The stadium erupted in a deafening roar, the lights of a hundred thousand cameras followed the runners around the track in a Mexican wave light show as Cathy Freeman led the other runners home. There could only be one winner that day and there was. Cathy's closest rival Marie-Jose Perec had left the Olympics a few days previously under odd circumstances and it appeared to clear the way for the result everyone wanted to see. But Cathy Freeman still had to prepare, walk into that stadium alone and perform under the greatest of expectation. It was a masterclass in delivery.

Another historic moment happened at our own venue. The day before our final the attention of the world was drawn to the Penrith Rowing Lake to see if Steve Redgrave could win a fifth consecutive gold medal. Within the team everyone felt it would happen despite the constant press speculation as to whether Steve could still perform at the top while being 38 and struggling with colitis and diabetes. But anyone who had trained anywhere near Steve knew that he was different from anyone else and his desire, his pride and his sheer force of will combined with his phenomenal strength and boat-moving ability would do everything required. And additionally he was not taking the challenge on alone. Alongside him he had arguably the most physiologically powerful man in the world in the form of Matthew Pinsent, perhaps the most skilled talent in the form of Tim Foster and almost certainly the most driven, hungry and committed force of nature in the form of James Cracknell. Overseeing the four of them was the steady, reliable and masterful hand of Jurgen Grobler. To us they were a force that couldn't be beaten. Even though they had lost at the most recent World Cup regatta in Lucerne, to us they were heroes and they were winners. And on 24 September they proved that to the rest of the world.

As far as our own racing was going, we were on track. On track for what, I wasn't sure, to be honest, but we had made it to the final. In the heats we finished with the fourth fastest time. The Germans dominated, leading by about 2 seconds over Ukraine in their heat. The Russians beat us by over 3 seconds in our heat and their winning time was considerably slower than the Germans'. So for the final the Germans looked easy favourites to win again (they had won this event in every Olympics and all but one World Championship), with Ukraine and Russia behind.

The night before our final we moved out of the Village and into a house near the lake, so we wouldn't have any traffic concerns in the morning. I was nervous, although not uncontrollably so. I was really looking forward to it. I felt this was an opportunity to be seized and I felt incredibly lucky to be in that position. We had a fantastic meeting that evening. It was the four of us, Mike and the British Rowing psychologist, Chris Shambrook. After we talked through the logistics of the day we began talking about the actual race itself and Chris asked what it meant to each of us. It was a masterstroke from Chris. In the short time we had together we had mainly focused on how to make it work and the logistics and the detail. Now we tapped into the emotion.

Each one of us was incredibly honest about why the race was important and how much it meant to us. Everyone had personal reasons behind their motivation and we were open with each other about that. And we discussed how it is always possible to dig a little deeper than you think and find more. That's why if something goes wrong in a race you can actually get a surge in speed with the burst of adrenaline, or why 90-year-olds can lift a car if their grandchild is underneath it. There is this other layer that humans can tap into and we can go into more pain than seems to be possible and still survive. Bringing it back to the specifics of our crew, Gillian talked confidently to us, telling us why we were good and why she wanted to race with us. To Miriam she credited her single speed, to Guin she recalled the years of experience and coming fifth in the single at the last Olympics. And to me she said I was an ergo queen, I had been great in the doubles trial and then she simply looked to the others and back at me and said, "She's got it." Whatever it was she thought I had, I wanted to use it that very night, not have to wait until the morning.

I said I thought this crew had the chance to make history, and despite all of our differences and difficulties we were the four to do it. We might have to step into the darkness to get it, but if we did come out the other side it might just be golden. Mike said this might well be the best chance any of us would ever get. Chris talked about us needing "rhythm and soul". And he was right. We had to hit the rhythm, it is crucial in rowing, allowing you to apply maximum power and speed while not interrupting the flow of the boat or the water and allowing as much recovery as possible between each explosive stroke. We had to hit the right rhythm and have the belief in our soul that by working the process the result would take care of itself.

We finished the meeting raring to go but also bonded on a far greater level than ever before. We were prepared to do everything for each other. Sleep wasn't an option after the adrenaline-fuelled meeting and so we watched the 100m women's final on TV. I remember being hugely impressed by how much the winner was enjoying the event even before she raced. She didn't seem weighed down by expectation, she was even smiling at the start and won by a huge margin. Very sadly that woman was Marion Jones, who a few years later was publicly stripped of her gold medal and others, having been proved to be a drugs cheat. Her tears as she went to prison would not make up for the respect and love the world had given her when they thought she was naturally the fastest woman on the planet.

As we put the lights off I wrote in my diary: "Now I'm living for 9.30am. That's all I'm thinking about. How lucky I am to really test myself, to push myself to my extremes, to rise above normality and mundane days. To finish knowing I could do nothing more. Now I see why people talk about that more than the medals. It's a personal thing – not with the Russians or Germans or Ukraines. But with me. This is why the years of work are done, why they're worthwhile in the cold and dark and exhaustion. To get here, to take this chance. No dread. No wishing it was over. Almost the opposite, wanting this time to last for longer. The anticipation. The opportunity. The possibilities. Once every four years, and less than that for some. And all too soon it will be over. I'm ready. We're ready. Is the world ready?"

And there I was on the startline, trying not to look at the biggest camera I had ever seen in my life. Deep breathing. Attack the darkness, don't be afraid of the pain. Want it for six minutes – let's see how the opposition likes it. And we were off. I know for the first 250m I had a mantra in my head, "Don't mess up, don't mess up" – exactly what every psychologist would tell you not to do, but I just needed to get that part of the race over, eight blades whipping through the air and around the body at the highest rate, and I looked forward to surviving it and getting into the meat of the race. Guin was giving us feedback on where we were and Gillian was shouting the technical focus and changes we needed. Miriam and I were silent except for our forced breathing for most of the race and the odd low-key word of reassurance or encouragement from me to her. Until we entered the last 500m. At this point there were crowds on both sides of the lake, the noise was swelling and exploding around us. I wasn't sure where the other crews were but I didn't care, I just wanted us to get everything possible out of ourselves in the last minute we had. By then all four of us were shouting and screaming and yelling and I have no real idea what we were communicating other than heart and soul and passion and we burst across the line in a blaze of unplanned energy and emotion. I knew we had stayed ahead of Ukraine, which had been our main focus and meant we were in the medals. There was mass celebration – we had just made our own little bit of history by winning a bronze medal and being the first women's crew ever to win an Olympic medal for Britain.

We made it over to the landing stages and got out to hug and congratulate each other and anyone who happened to be nearby. The Russians and Germans were also happy, so hugs and smiles all round. Kathrin Boron, the most successful female sculler ever and who had won the double scull gold the day before, happened to be there so she came and joined in the hugs. It was crazy. And then an official came up to tell us there would be a delay for the medals because of the photo finish. I had no idea the Russians had pushed the Germans that close, I thought. But no, it turned out the photo was between us and the Russians. And my first reaction was honestly, "Oh, no need for that. I'm over the moon with a medal, I don't mind what colour it comes in." The happy, innocent days when the colour of the medal meant nothing to me. How times would change. It took them about 12 minutes to decide the result and I went from not caring, to thinking what a shame, imagine if we had managed to pull off the silver, to thinking I'll actually be a bit disappointed if it's not silver now. All in the space of 12 minutes. That is how fast expectations and standards can change. Meanwhile, Gillian knew it had been close as part of her role was to be aware of the boats around us, so in the waiting time she had more expectation of the silver result.

Shortly a piece of paper was brought over and slowly opened in front of us. With hearts still pounding we tried to make sense of the small writing and numbers. Gillian looked straight at the second name on the results and reacted instantly. We had beaten the Russians by 8 hundredths of a second. There was even more jubilant celebration. It was like winning twice and I honestly couldn't have found a way to be any happier if we had won gold. I am grinning like an absolute fool in the photos of us on the podium and it reminds me of just how wonderful a silver medal can be. When we stood there, next to the overjoyed Germans and the now underwhelmed Russians, I thought the trees somehow looked greener, the sky bluer and the sun brighter. Everything was bathed in a wonderful Technicolor effect and life was wonderful. From the podium we rowed over to the other side and there I managed to find and embrace my mum and dad, who both seemed in a state of happy shock. My mum was in tears. I don't know what they had expected with their first experience of watching the Olympics but probably not this. They were surrounded by friends they had made in the past couple of hours as parents from all over the world empathized and helped each other through the torture of support.

The first athlete I saw there was Dot. She gave me the biggest hug and it meant the world to me, knowing that just 24 hours earlier her own dream had fallen apart as she and Cath finished ninth in the pair. To have had the strength of character to come over and find me to congratulate me for my wonderful result in the wake of her own devastating disappointment showed a courage and compassion that I don't think I possess myself.

A few people stand out to me as showing that same humbling response. Back at the Village, Lisa was another who sought me out to say congratulations in spite of her own disappointment.

But perhaps the most impressive act came from the person I admired most in the team. The morning after our race I found myself alone in our apartment. Miriam was with her husband, Gillian was off seeing her boyfriend, Guin was out somewhere and I was at somewhat of a loose end. Every detail is planned leading up to the race – everything from what time you get up, to where and what you'll have for breakfast, to what time of bus, to how long it takes to walk to the bus, to the bus trip, to the session, to rest times to meeting times to psychology and physiotherapy sessions; every detail is considered and discussed and noted. Not one moment of effort is wasted on thinking of the hours or days after the race. And suddenly you find yourself in this unknown world called "after the Olympics". So I was sitting in our apartment, gazing out of the huge window that looked across to the stadium and the flame that was burning brightly, with nothing to do, nowhere to be, no one to meet and suddenly no drive behind anything to be done that day. Cath walked in and asked how I was doing.

I said I wasn't sure what to do or where to be. I was lost. She looked at me for a split second and then said, "Right then, let's head over to the stadium." She took me out for the day and we sat in the sunshine of the stadium with beers in hand, talking and laughing and witnessing fantastic track and field events unfolding before us. Cath had suffered the same awful year that Dot had. They went from silver medallists two years before sadly to an unstoppable slide into disappointment at the greatest sporting show on earth. Cath had proved herself time and time again, on the water, in the trials, and she also held the British and World record on the rowing machine. But there was no Olympic prize to show for all the effort. Her frustration and disillusionment must have been enormous, and yet here she was looking after me, the Olympic medallist, and making sure I was OK.

Although it had been in one respect the most successful Olympic result ever for the women's team, it wasn't a universal success. While the quad won the silver medal, no other women's boat made the final. Alison Mowbray admittedly did a great job in the single by qualifying it and then racing it, but finished tenth. Sarah and Frances ninth. And the eight came seventh. Relationships were fractured, athletes resentful and a large proportion of the team were left disenchanted – and although that wonderful silver medal was rightly celebrated, behind the scenes there was a sense of "But at what cost?"

CHAPTER

5

ALL CHANGE

The Closing Ceremony in Sydney was another extraordinary experience. Whereas at the Opening Ceremony there were discussions about whether or not attendance would be conducive to performance, now the performances were over. Whether successful or disappointing, the competition part of the Games was finished for everyone and there was one last major night of celebration to be enjoyed by all. From the experience of the previous two weeks we knew Sydney was ready to put on a show. As with most major events there had been a negative build-up to the Games, with concerns over traffic congestion and the invasion of hundreds and thousands of people adding to an already busy city. Australians had been told to either support the Olympics or leave Sydney, and as a result the city was a wonderful feel-good, excited, enthusiastic place. The biggest, and most popular, rumour of the Closing Ceremony was that Kylie Minogue would be appearing in a thong. The idea of the universally loved popstar singing to the stadium in a tiny pair of pants had everyone talking. When the moment finally came, hearts were broken all over the stadium as Kylie made her entrance riding on a giant thong – which is what the Australians call flip-flops or sandals. Kylie appeared in a vibrant pink headdress and joined other Australian celebrities who paraded around the stadium on giant floats while beach lifeguards and giant shrimps on bicycles danced around them. It was a magically surreal way to end the greatest show on earth.

There were the usual sombre speeches from dignitaries, but in the centre of the stadium there was too much noise to hear the serious stuff and the partying continued while the Olympics was brought to a close. It was only later we heard that Juan Antonio Samaranch, the IOC President, pronounced the Sydney Games "the best Games ever" to a deafening roar of approval from the fans in the stadium. I didn't have time to think about how the flame would be extinguished, but in a stunning display fighter jets screamed overhead and at the moment they passed over the cauldron the fire went out and as we looked up the leading plane had fire trailing behind it, looking as if it had picked up the flame and was taking it back to Athens, where it would wait for another four years to once again light up the world.

I gave the space-age-style silver and blue box that housed my medal to Dot, who was flying straight home, and I left the comfort of the Village to explore Australia. I stayed with a family in Sydney who were volunteers at the Games and had contacted me as they were friends with the grandparents of a university friend. It was a tenuous link and yet they welcomed me in as one of the family and I saw Sydney through the eyes of locals rather than a sporting tourist. I then went to Ayers Rock, learned to dive in Cairns and spent a week on a diving boat on the outer Great Barrier Reef, sailed around the Whitsunday Islands and did a wreck dive in Townsville, where I experienced a whole new magical underwater world. I then met up with a university friend in Melbourne, where the rain never stopped, and finally returned to Sydney to soak up the harbour one last time. In Sydney Harbour I visited one of the islands with a fascinating historical background and had been chatting to a tour guide while we waited for the giant ferry to come and collect us. Eventually the guide asked what I was doing in Sydney, and although for most of the trip I had deliberately avoided

Olympic subjects (it was great to become anonymous and something other than an athlete for a short time), if I was asked directly then I never lied. So the tour guide found out I was an Olympic medallist and as the massive shadow of the ferry enveloped us the tour guide shouted up from the jetty saying, "You've got an Olympic medallist on board, drive safe!" As I climbed aboard, one of the guys who worked on the ferry leaned down the stairs to say the captain wanted to see me. I nervously entered his cabin and was stunned by the best view in town as we effortlessly slid towards the city – the Sydney Harbour Bridge was to our right still displaying the temporary Olympic rings, the Opera House was to our left, and the towering buildings of the city shone above us in the glittering sunlight.

As I squinted into the metallic blinding light the captain shook me by the hand and slapped me on the back in congratulations. He smiled and asked if I wanted a go. "Of what?" I asked. "Of the wheel." I hesitated momentarily, unsure if he was joking or not, and then stepped forward nodding. When would I get this chance again? I took the wheel and manoeuvred the huge craft towards where the captain was pointing. He nodded and smiled and chatted as we cruised through the water. As we drew closer to the harbour I noticed the gap we were aiming for was not very big at all, and surrounded by milling people either on their way to or from work and also tourists taking photos of everything around them. That was a lot of people to wipe out in one inexperienced move. Luckily at the last minute the captain suggested he should "park it" and I willingly stepped aside to watch him skilfully control the engines to allow the ferry to dock.

The post-Olympic weeks were full of surreal moments like that. I arrived home from my Australian adventure to the biggest pile of mail I had ever seen and envelopes with "Downing Street", "Office of the Prime Minister", "Buckingham Palace" and "Westminster" stamped on them. I had missed many of the parties but there were others still to happen that I did manage to attend. It was a part of the Olympics that I didn't know existed, the ongoing celebrations when people all over the country wanted to be part of the huge success we had experienced over in Sydney.

After spending time at home seeing friends and families it was time to return to Longridge for the new year to begin. The beginning of an

Olympic cycle is always an interesting time. There are new faces joining the team, old faces missing, new plans and visions and a need to avoid the feeling of "here we go again". It did feel different. At the top end Steve Redgrave had retired for good this time and would no longer be the ever-present figurehead of the team. Tim Foster also left, along with most of the gold medal winning men's eight. On the women's side Dot, Miriam and Gillian all retired. And Mike Spracklen left to coach in Canada. There would be a very different look and feel to the team aiming for the Athens Olympics.

Marty Aitken would be taking over as the chief coach for women and lightweights. An enthusiastic, out-going Australian, he spoke quickly and he had an incredible ability to brush anything off – everything was water off a duck's back to Marty. He was good fun and always seemed full of energy and ideas. He had come from a very successful time as head coach of the Swiss rowing team overseeing multiple World and Olympic records. As a top cyclist and skier in his own athletic career, he took us to try cross-country skiing on a training camp in Sarnen, a very cold part of Switzerland where Swiss German is spoken. Marty spoke in a wonderful half Swiss half English language dominated by his Australian accent and his confidence. He could have some crazy ideas but his enthusiasm and utter self-belief were endearing. Nothing was impossible.

The trips to Sarnen were challenging. The camp was designed as a mixture of cross-country skiing and rowing. The skiing itself had its hilarious moments. We were given skis, the briefest of instructions and then we were sent off to the classic tracks. For our first session we gathered just outside a beautiful deep green forest where the snow had settled on top of the trees in a classic Christmas card fashion. The tracks disappeared into the forest and looked strikingly romantic. We were sent off one at a time and I gazed around at the view, enjoying breathing in the fresh crisp air waiting for my turn. My head whipped around as a brief scream broke the mountain silence. Marty cheerily called, "OK, next one." I stared, confused. What had just happened? The next nervous-looking athlete pushed off and headed towards the now somewhat more threatening woods. I waited. As they disappeared around the corner there was another scream and then silence. What on earth was happening in the woods and why was no one stopping us from going in there? One by one the team vanished into the darkness, and each time there was a scream or a muffled shout, and often a vague thud or crashing sound of branches.

My turn came and I felt I had no option but to lift my poles, plant them into the soft snow on either side of the tracks and advance towards the trees. This was part of being an athlete, following instructions even if occasionally they seemed to make no sense. As the path dipped away and my skis picked up speed I entered the darkness and saw shapes everywhere in front of me. There was a steep bend and this is where things had gone wrong. Being inexperienced cross-country skiers but unafraid of a bit of speed we had all entered the bend too fast, couldn't corner and ended up in various bushes, trees or across the tracks. There had been no time to clear out of the way before the next athlete was sent in, so suddenly the choice was either to crash into nearby bits of greenery or try to stay in the tracks and ski up and over fellow team members, thereby launching yourself in a new and unplanned direction. It was some of the craziest training we had attempted. By the end of the camp, however, we had massive respect for cross-country skiers as the endless hours on the tracks pushed us to our physical limits.

Unfortunately, going somewhere that was good for skiing meant going somewhere that was absolutely freezing for rowing. We went out on the lake and it was often minus ten degrees. Ice formed on the boat, on the riggers and on us as we trained. It was beautiful but perishing. One day Cath and I were out in the pair and freezing fog surrounded us so that we couldn't see further than a few metres. I squinted into the fog as my eyes tried to find something to focus on, but there was nothing, so it was a strange sensation of looking but not seeing anything at all. It was also eerily quiet, making it the most surreal experience. Finally we had to row a few strokes at a time, turning around to make sure we weren't about to hit anything, until we found the shore, and then we inched our way around the shore until we found the boathouse. The other problem was that there was never enough hot water, and the final bit of training across the lake increased in intensity as the subtext was the race to the hot showers before they ran cold. There was not much in the way of entertainment in Sarnen, and the place we were staying didn't cater, so we had to walk into town for every meal. One of the regular meals was watery salty soup. It tasted of salty water. Sometimes with bread added in. Cath and I stashed necessary sweets in the "safe" in our room – it was meant for valuables, but by this point sugar was a valuable so any sweets or chocolate we could find were fiercely protected there.

The news was that in January of 2001 a new women's coach would be joining the team to work under Marty. He was also from Australia. His name was Paul Thompson and Marty had known him for years. He had a very good reputation, having coached the Australian women's pair to gold in Atlanta in 1996 and silver in Sydney 2000. Cath and I were excited, as we had ideas on the pair and here was arguably one of the best women's pairs coaches in the world. We met in January when Paul arrived ahead of his wife and young son. He set up home in Shiplake, near Oxford, and had a few weeks to settle in before his family followed him. Early on the rules were laid down. He would be our coach and not our friend. He had to keep his distance so that he could make tough decisions. Thommo's statement of not wanting to be friends was well intentioned but turned out to be inaccurate. I think we evolved together over the years. His knowledge and skill were superb from the beginning, but as we became used to each other's company and characters, our understanding deepened and our faith in each other grew. In time he would have the power to inspire, to guide, to enhance, to share. And we did become friends. After the London Olympics, Anna and I had some lovely relaxed meals with Thommo and his wife, Dr Alison McGregor, with generally the three of us good-naturedly teasing Thommo about something. But the earlier years were undoubtedly tough, and to some extent I wish I could have known then how good our relationship would become to have possibly avoided the trickier times. That wasn't to say we would have avoided all "disagreements", and over the years those heated discussions became valuable. We didn't disagree on many things, but when we did it was generally an area worth thrashing out between us and our relationship wasn't damaged by it.

From the very beginning Thommo had a technical eye that was truly world class. He can look at a boat and know instantly where the problems are and have a range of possible solutions. This attention to detail never wavered and over the years was further enhanced by an increasing openness and willingness to try new techniques or exercises that could help the overall performance. Thommo has always had a great vision for his crews and the team. From when he arrived the standards were high and he considered winning crucial because success did justice to the world-class ingredients that were gathered. He didn't only use his athletes as sounding boards, but turned to the experts around him and challenged the strength and conditioning coaches, the physiologists, the physiotherapists, the nutritionists, the psychologists to come up with something different and new that would help our performance. With coaching it must be tempting to stick to tried and tested methods that have succeeded in the past, but to Thommo's great credit he was willing continually to look further and keep ideas fresh. Sometimes the experiments would lead to dead ends, but usually they were worth the detour. Very similar to an athlete never feeling they are fit or strong or technical enough, Thommo doesn't sit back and feel his job is ever complete. There are always new routes to explore and new standards to find.

In our first international race in Ghent, we lost the first day of racing and were strongly told off by a disappointed Thommo about how badly we had raced. We were determined to be more aggressive the second day, and I remember throwing the race plan out of the window and just shouting different focuses every ten strokes down the course. Poor Cath wouldn't have had a clue what was going on, but she is a natural racer and will respond and fight until she has nothing left to give, never questioning and never faltering. It was an unconventional way to race, but we had the "whatever it takes" mentality and with no experience together to rely on we went with instinct and a simple, in-the-moment focus. The natural trust we had between us helped and we won the race. Thommo was pleased if a little unsure of just what sort of crew he had in front of him.

The next World Cup we raced was in Seville and we were out of the medals with about 500m to go. Thommo had been following the race but peeled off at that point, disappointed at our performance. He missed our sprint for the line that brought us into the medals, and it was Marty with a grin and a laugh who told us, "Nah, Thommo gave up on you guys and went off to watch another race."

Despite our lack of winter training and our inconsistent racing we were still ambitious about what might be possible in our pair. It's hard to explain but it was the first boat I had been in that had both the amazing power and strength and yet the lightness of skill and technique to create a thrilling speed and rhythm with ease. We didn't have it all the time but there were enough glimpses of it to have Cath and me excited. This was the first time I was in a boat that felt as if it could genuinely be the best boat in the world. It had magic.

Cath and I preferred wooden handles for our blades and we would often be found sitting in a quiet area by the rowing lake with sandpaper or file in hand carefully smoothing or roughing and shaping our handles to just the perfect contours. I used to love the smell of sawdust that fell from the wooden handles and enjoyed being lost in the craftsmanship of sculpting the perfect handle. It was an individual task and preference as the handle was an extension of ourselves. We would sit in quiet contemplation enjoying each other's company while lost in the care and attention of the job in hand.

We raced the World Championships in Lucerne that summer and made it into the final, although we were one of the last boats to qualify for it so we raced in an outside lane. It was the lane closest to the warm-up and warm-down area and also the crowds – in some ways it is the trickiest lane in Lucerne, but we saw it as a positive to be in our own area of focus and possibly under the radar as far as the other crews were concerned. We raced hard and fast from the start and were in a leading position early on. However, as the race progressed the lack of training began to show. As the other crews attacked we tried everything to respond but I felt as if my muscles were trying to move through treacle – I couldn't fire my legs in the way I should and everything felt sticky and slow. It is the most painful thing mentally and physically when you know you have to respond and yet there is nothing you can physically do. We finished in a disappointing fifth place, made worse by being overtaken by the Australians at the very end. Being beaten by his own country would have been the final embarrassment for Thommo. We also raced the eight and finished fifth there too. In our first season together the best we could say so far was that there was "potential". To Thommo's credit he took Cath and me out for a drink on one of the boats that sat at the edge of Lake Lucerne. Together we put the racing behind us for a night and relaxed in each other's company.

There was no exotic diving or sailing holiday that summer. In fact as it turned out there was no foreign holiday at all. I was due to fly to New York in the late summer of 2001, but unfortunately other things were destined to happen to the city that never sleeps. As terrorists in hijacked planes destroyed the Twin Towers in the most dramatic fashion and many lives were lost, all trips to New York were postponed. It was a chilling reminder of just how fragile human life is. I remember driving back south from Aberdeen in September listening to the debate rage across the airwaves about what it all meant for a world that now seemed a little more unsteady than it had a few weeks previously.

In our own small way Cath and I were also considering what our future would hold. I hadn't realized just how different our views would be until I met her that evening. On my drive south I had a call from Cath asking me to come to her house to talk through things; she would have some wine ready for me when I arrived. In between hearing about ongoing terrorist fears I thought about what Cath and I needed to do to truly bring out our very real potential. If life was such a fragile thing then it was there to be enjoyed, lived, celebrated, and pushed to the maximum. Everything possible should be wrung from it.

I felt lucky that we had such a fantastic project ahead of us and wanted to make the most of it. As in every job there were so many areas that we could look at and find ways to improve. A full training year would be a good start. And then there was technique, nutrition, strength and conditioning, psychology, physiology – you name it, we could improve it. In a way the feeling that we had endless areas to work on and improve was very exciting to me. Of course it meant there was a challenge ahead, but wasn't that what made every day interesting? I parked outside Cath's house and arrived with my head spilling over with ideas. I couldn't wait to get going.

We hugged and sat down opposite each other and Cath poured the wine. I looked up, ready to share our ideas and plans. I was not only excited about the things I had thought of but also excited to hear what Cath had come up with. We hadn't spoken over the holidays about the future, allowing ourselves to fully enjoy the short break. Cath was then, and still is, one of the most intelligent, driven and capable people I know and I wanted to hear her ideas about where we would go next.

She would have been thinking more deeply and widely and would likely be able to come up with things I hadn't even considered.

Nothing prepared me for what she had come up with. As my mind buzzed with science-based concepts, physical challenges and mental pathways, Cath placed her wine glass on the table in front of us and levelled her gaze. Looking directly at me she said the last thing I was expecting. "I'm going to join the Foreign Office."

I froze, unsure of what exactly that meant. My mind raced, struggling to grasp which part of our rowing that specific thing would benefit, but thought it must be something I hadn't thought about. I was still processing such a left-field statement when Cath looked at me sadly and said, "I've had it with rowing, I can't go on any more." I blinked. My brain couldn't get on track. It didn't make sense with where I had been in my own thoughts. I managed a profound "Oh, OK." I was shaking. Cath came over and gave me a long and strong hug. "I'm so sorry. But I just have to do this. It's the right thing for me." The warmth in her voice but also the certainty broke the spell for me. I physically sunk in her arms and we both cried. It was the end of the vision and dream we had had and it wasn't the way either of us had imagined. We finished off the bottle of wine and got going on another. I wanted to toast her new life and also I wanted to numb my own disappointment.

The four-year plan I had built had come crashing down around me and now lay shattered at my feet. There was nothing I could do to change that or fix it. That dream was over. As the realization sank in over the next few days it became more painful as it became more real. Cath had suffered a very painful defeat in Sydney and one that had been made infinitely worse by the few years leading up to that point. She desperately needed a positive experience in rowing and our fifth-place finish in Lucerne was never going to be enough. The possibility of future potential wasn't enough either. She had applied to the Department of Sport, Media and Culture for some work, but then had a call from the Foreign Office, who had been impressed by her multilingual CV. They gave her an offer, and an opportunity, that she couldn't refuse. It was the chance of a relevant, challenging, varied job where she would be valued and given responsibilities, where she could make a real difference. In contrast, more endless hours in the gym and going up and down the river with no guarantee of any good outcome seemed a poor option.

So with mixed emotions I moved forward. On one hand I was pleased for Cath and proud of the decision she had made to move on to something new. She is an impressive individual who deserved more than being lost in her own hell of disappointment. But I wanted to be part of a positive new project for her and I wanted to share it with her. And so my overwhelming feeling was a heavy heart and a lack of energy to come up with a new and exciting challenge.

I met up with Thommo to find out what the new plan was to be. He was also sad to see Cath leave the team. There was no obvious option but for me to once again join the sculling team and we would see how the boats would form depending on the winter months and spring trials. When spring came, there was the prospect of an exciting new quad with Sarah Winckless, Alison Mowbray and Rebecca Romero. We were the second women's boat behind the lead double of Fran Houghton and Debbie Flood. We were quite a mix of a crew. Sarah has always been the loudest, most extrovert member of any boat and this year was no different. Becs had a brooding intensity when it came to training; she was always hard on herself and could appear sullen until her face broke into a wide smile that lit the place up and her unexpected laughter transformed any situation. Al is a natural introvert but always willing to talk and make sure people are getting on with each other. She has an ability to take any criticism or negative result in her stride and not let it send her off balance. Despite not having the more common physical gifts of pure strength and ergo ability, Al made the most of her technical skills and her boat-moving ability to get very impressive results. She is an excellent example of using your strengths and not focusing on any perceived weaknesses. She had raced in the single in Sydney and was now back playing in the crew boats. The funniest thing was her lack of spatial awareness, so marked that we would often wonder who would be next to be whacked on the head or the back by her oars as she carried them to the water. She was a delightful one-woman Laurel and Hardy without realizing it.

At the World Championships that summer the most memorable bit of racing we did was quite possibly in the repechage, but it had nothing to do with our racing ability. We were leading the race comfortably until in the last few hundred metres suddenly it felt as if we had hit something, the boat lurched and our bodies were thrown forward at the sudden decrease in speed. I remember trying to put my blades in the water but finding resistance. I looked down to see an oar alongside the boat. It didn't make sense. Becs was trying to row in front of me, Sarah was shouting behind and I looked up through the confusion to see the backs of the crews behind us fast approaching. The repechage is a do-or-die race; if you don't make it through to the final then the Championships are over. We scrambled and dragged the boat across the line and managed to qualify. About an hour later as we sat in front of the media to discuss the race we knew they would ask what had happened as the almost-disaster had been directly in front of the grandstands. I still wasn't sure what exactly happened, other than that Al had caught a crab, her blade had spun out of her hand and stuck parallel to the boat, she couldn't reach it to bring it back without us stopping the boat, and hence our ungainly finish.

The question came as expected. "So, girls, what happened at the end there?" The one thing you don't want to do is hang any teammate out to dry, and so there was a collective intake of breath as we thought of what to say. It wasn't necessary, however, as Al spoke up. "I hit a fish." I summoned all of my control to keep my face neutral and not react. I was somewhere between "What the hell???" and laughing uncontrollably, but to the press I simply smiled as I looked from Al to the gathered dictaphones and back again. Al didn't elaborate, as if it was the most normal thing in the world to say. The other three of us had nothing to add; it was the first we had heard of this turn of events and we really didn't feel it was the time to discuss it. So we nodded sagely and moved on. I haven't heard it being used before or since, but the "I hit a fish" defence is available to all should the moment ever arise.

In the final the best we could manage was fifth place. Another disappointment. On a weekend that saw Matthew Pinsent and James Cracknell smash the men's pair record and set a time that would last for ten years, the best that the women's team managed was a fourth place. And it wasn't good enough any more. The Sydney Games had proved British women could compete with the best in the world and stand on the podium, and that was the new mentality. We were there to compete at the top and it was disappointing for everyone to be falling just short. Thommo hadn't made the move to Britain from his success in Australia for this; I hadn't continued after Sydney to get worse results; and the rest of the team didn't spend hours every day pushing themselves to their limit in order to just make a final. Something had to change.

There was a great change ahead for me. During the year I had kept in touch with Cath as she took up her new role in Westminster, the seat of the UK Government, and we would meet regularly to exchange stories. Naturally her side of the conversation always seemed a little more exciting as she mentioned war zones and warring politicians and developing countries and the expanding European Union and the future of democracy and various fascinating subjects. My contribution of how many hours we had spent in the gym or on the rowing machine didn't seem to me to be able to hold much interest. But Cath was interested. And I knew the natural competitor in her was still intrigued. No one had stepped in to fill the pairs event and there was a sense of an unfinished job and unfulfilled ambition. One lovely sunny day we agreed to take a pair out from Marlow Rowing Club just for old times' sake and we paddled up the river enjoying the fresh air and the relaxed company. Our conversation varied from the current storyline in the soap operas Cath watched to what was happening in The Hague. This was how it was with Cath: she could bring her fierce intelligence to any area of discussion and was equally at home talking about the state of international relations and giving her informed opinion on that morning's chat shows. We even threw in a bit of racing work just for fun. And it was fun. And fast. I smiled to myself, thinking the magic was still there.

A few weeks later Cath announced her return to international competition. I was thrilled. The game was on again. But it wasn't as simple as Cath rejoining the fold. She had to prove herself. The first hoop to be jumped through would be the long-distance trial at Boston, Lincolnshire. The October assessment was designed for new people wanting to break into the squad as the existing international team were exempt from the early trial. As Cath hadn't been part of the World Championship team she had to compete in her single there. As a surprise and to show solidarity I timed my drive back south to coincide with her trial at Boston. Her face lit up as she recognized a familiar face among the fresh-faced nervous excitable wannabe athletes around her. As soon as Cath had mentioned coming back, the two of us started making plans to resurrect the pair and this time do it justice, but the powers that be had other ideas. As far as the management was concerned we had tried and failed in that project and there was no assumption that the best way forward was together.

That opposition made for one of the toughest winters I ever had to endure. The challenges and obstacles set in our path were endless. The team manager, head coach and even our own coach all decided it was a bad idea and not a plan that should be supported. It was down to the two of us to constantly reassure each other that we knew something that they couldn't – that by knowing just how good our boat could feel, we owed it to ourselves, to each other, to the boat and to the team to prove we really could be the best in the world. At this point no one else believed it. The popular concept was that I should return to sculling, where I had won my Olympic medal, and Cath should prove herself in the single and then they could make a decision where to put her.

Decisions, as ever, would be made after the final British trials that took place in Hazewinkel, Belgium. The Hazewinkel trials were the stuff of legend where battles were fought, won and lost. Where old egos were destroyed and new heroes were unearthed. Where pride was challenged and points were proved. It was always some of the toughest competition, increasingly so as the British team became stronger and stronger and internal trials reached an international level of performance. It was here that Cath and I would be tested in our singles. We drove to the trials together, along with Sarah in her old Renault 4, the entire car shaking as she pushed it to the maximum on the German autobahns. At the trials I can't even remember where I finished, somewhere around fifth at a guess. Cath didn't make the final and raced against Guin in the B Final and lost to her. As Cath came off the water she was just relieved that her testing in the single scull was over. She hated the single boat, and although on a good day she could move it very well she was always uncomfortable if there was as much as a ripple on the water, and so she just considered it a necessary evil to get her into the crew boat part of the year.

The B Final was the last race, and aware that Sarah and I were finished, Cath came off the water quickly, caught up with us, and we left the highly tense and stressful location as fast as we could. We were all set to win the race to the ferry but wanted to stop for food first. While we were in the Drive Thru queue at McDonalds, Cath's phone went. It was Thommo. She waited until we had got our food and then listened to the message. It was a short and sharp message informing Cath that as she hadn't yet spoken to him he assumed she was still at the course as she would not have left without speaking to him first. He was still at the course and would wait to see her. We all looked at each other in horror. Options? We had to go back. It was agreed. The slightly euphoric adrenaline high we had experienced for having survived trials drained out of us as we drove back towards the course. I didn't know if it was imagination or if the clouds really were getting darker and more threatening above us.

Cath found Thommo in front of the boathouse and his face was as thunderous as the sky. In front of the other coaches and athletes who were still packing up boats and trailers he proceeded to shout at her. He was furious about her attitude to the racing, before the competition, in the warm-down, in the speed she had left, in the lack of respect he felt she had shown him. In front of the lake Thommo unleashed his frustration, publicly stripping this strong, intelligent, articulate woman of her dignity, leaving her shaken and speechless. It was a quiet journey home.

The next stage of the trials process was crew formation at Dorney Lake. The top women's boats would again be the double and the quad. This time the double would be Debbie and Becs. The quad would be Sarah, Al, Fran and one other. That "other" would be either Elise or myself. At this point Cath was on gardening leave. I had spoken to Thommo and still said my choice for the summer was to be in a pair with Cath. But it wasn't my choice and he told me that he had worked with World Champions before and he didn't think she had what it took to be a World Champion. I disagreed. I didn't often disagree with Thommo so there had to be a good reason in my mind. Perhaps I couldn't prove on paper why, but I knew on instinct, from experience, from some unknown certainty that Cath and I should race the pair again.

CHAPTER 5

The Dorney trial happened and I lost to Elise. She would now take the final place in the quad and the sculling boats were confirmed. I climbed back into my car and drove to Cath's house experiencing an unusual emotion: relief at having not won. I rang Cath's doorbell and waited. She opened the door and looked at me in expectation. "I lost." She didn't say anything. I looked at Cath steadily: "Ready to make plans?" We sat and planned our mission. It would be tough, we would have to win people over, but we were getting a chance to do what we had always believed in through a long dark winter. It was in our hands now although there was still a long road ahead and we would stand or fall by our results.

Our first meeting with Thommo was as we might have predicted. We were excited and determined at the prospect of officially going out in our pair and training for the World Cups and then the World Championships. The challenge was on and we loved the prospect. Thommo walked in and sat down in front of us. His fury was visible and we shuffled uncomfortably in front of him. After a period of silence he said slowly, "Well then, you've got what you wanted." It wasn't said in a tone that encouraged enthusiastic agreement. We were quiet. He leaned forward and told us in no uncertain terms how tough we would need to be to do this. My heart was pounding. He was right. It has been our dream, but that didn't mean it would come easily. In fact the opposite; the hard work was just beginning. And I also knew we needed Thommo on the journey. His skill, knowledge and expertise would be vital and we needed to move past this temporary hostility. The silence rang out in the Longridge kitchen. There was nothing to add or to say. Luckily somewhere deep inside of me a small voice defiantly said 'BRING IT ON.' Because I knew just how tough we could be. All three of us, united, could be the toughest the world had seen.

The good thing was that we soon moved on from the challenging winter. Ultimately we were united by a very clear common goal, creating the fastest pair in the world. Thommo might not have liked the route we took to get there, but he did have a passionate, determined and committed couple of athletes in front of him. We were there every day delivering everything that he asked of us, and we respected his knowledge and trusted his sharp technical eye as to how a pair should move. As the days went by we combined Cath's unnerving ability to push herself harder every session with Thommo's unstinting attention to detail and not letting us get away with even the slightest thing and my enthusiasm for a project which I loved getting up for every day. Thommo undoubtedly brought a new level of technical expertise to our rowing and he kept introducing new exercises that tested every element of balance and timing. He wanted us to master the complexity of the small boat. He knew that if we felt we had complete control of the boat beneath us then more would be possible.

Away from the boat we also looked at new ways to train and try things. Cath and I worked separately with a new physio, Ashleigh Wallace, whom we asked to push and test our skills off the water but if possible relate it to how we would need to be on the water. We weren't sure what exactly we were asking for, but Ashleigh rose to the challenge and soon we were wobbling on Swiss balls, throwing medicine balls, balancing with wooden poles and trying things on one foot and with eyes closed. It was like trying to harness the Force under the guidance of a strict Jedi Master. The sessions were incredibly hard and crazily imaginative but hugely enjoyable and it felt great to be developing skills in a whole new area. Ash was positive and encouraging about our progress and gave us the confidence to try more elaborate things than we would have thought possible for rowing athletes. Soon we looked forward to dealing with any conditions on the water as the usual nervousness and hesitancy that rough water can bring simply brought a chance to test our new skills. Thommo wanted us to feel we had absolute ownership over our boat, and soon it became second nature to us. The focus wasn't just on the major muscle groups, but the small muscles that connect and control everything. By getting all the details to the top level we were opening up a whole new range of possibilities and ready for whatever faced us.

CHAPTER 6

THROUGH THE PAIN

And soon the racing season was upon us. We had only a few weeks from the chat in the Longridge kitchen to the first World Cup regatta, but it was enough time to make an impact. We raced and medalled in the three World Cups and by that time had convinced people that the pair was the right boat for us to be in. With no obstacles other than the opposition we had two camps left in the summer to prepare for the World Championships. Our final camp in Varese was superb, we once again had moments when our boat flew unlike anything I had ever seen or felt. It was at its best when it felt natural, it felt easy, it responded to our every move. And the control we had worked so hard on was there. We loved doing above-pace bursts of speed – short bits of work that was faster than we would be required to do for the majority of the race.

As the World Championships in Milan approached we kept working on every detail we could. Thommo had us doing a lot of exercises at the front of the boat – when your knees are bent and your back extended over your knees. Work that would get our precision better for how we

121

would put the blade into the water, but work that was also testing for our backs. One day while we were out paddling I felt a painful twinge in my back. It wasn't anything I had experienced before and I put it out of my mind. I checked with a physio later who had a look but wasn't concerned. The preparation continued and soon we moved to Milan.

Our arrival in Milan, however, did not mark the end of our challenges. As we arrived Thommo heard that his grandmother in Australia had passed away. He was far from home and unable to do much. We focused on the competition ahead and although our preparation had been great our first race was far from it. We finished behind and off the pace, displaying none of the excellence that we had showed at the training camp. Thommo met us off the water and demanded to know what had happened. When we couldn't answer he sent us off to get changed, saying he didn't want to see us again until we had answers. We were desperately disappointed ourselves and at a loss as to our sudden drop in form. The next night a storm blew up and the boat above ours blew off and put a hole straight through the bottom of our boat. Everything was unravelling.

The next challenge was our semi-final. The year before the Olympics is often the most competitive World Championships as there are Olympic places up for grabs. In the pairs event if you make the final then you guarantee a boat place at the Olympic Games. So making it through the semi-final was crucial to us. Thommo asked us to write down on a piece of paper what we would do in the semi-final. It was only for our own reading, we didn't need to tell each other. Despite all that was going wrong around us I wrote that we would beat the Canadians. It was bold, as they were the favourites on our side of the draw and we hadn't beaten them at that point. But now was the time to be bold. I put my little scrap of paper into my kitbag as we left for the course.

The warm-up to the semi-final was going well until in one instant I felt more pain than I had ever experienced in my life. It was a shocking, sudden, agonizing stab of pain in my back and I had no idea what had happened. We had to stop the boat anyway by coincidence as there was a race coming past and etiquette demands that warming-up crews allow the race to pass without creating any disturbance in the water. I was confused and in shock and sat breathing heavily. I didn't say anything to Cath, probably because I didn't know what to say. I had no idea what had just happened and what might happen next. I was in the bow seat giving the calls so I suggested we row towards the start, nice and relaxed and easy and not overdoing anything. We could try a warm-up start in our lane. There was pain every time I took a stroke but not as awful as the initial agony. I was nervous about what would happen when we started; we had always been very explosive and fast out of the blocks and I knew it would test my back. I survived the practice start and we went back to the startline to begin the race for real. I was still confused. I had no idea what had happened or what might be happening as we sat there awaiting the starter's orders.

I sat forward and closed my eyes, putting myself in the lap of the gods. I couldn't risk pulling out of the race, in case it was a minor problem and I would in effect be needlessly ending our best chance to claim an Olympic slot. We had come through too much to turn back now. And if I ever had to prove myself then this was the moment. I would commit to the race with everything I had and not stop until the finish line or something terrifyingly worse forced me to stop. With a heart pounding even more than normal I waited for the gun. That mix of adrenaline, fear and doubt forced me to focus intently on every stroke in a way I never had before. I had to row as well as I could to protect my back. We raced out hard and fast, we settled into our strong familiar rhythm and soon started moving through the field. I wasn't aware of pain as adrenaline flooded my body and my mind was focused only on the job in hand. We were level with, then ahead of the Canadians and then had everyone in our wake. Behind us there were three crews level and battling desperately for the two remaining Olympic places; by getting out front and ahead we had secured the first one and put ourselves out of danger. Although their battling brought them closer to us, we had enough of a lead to not slip into a nervous style of rowing and we raced as we knew we could. Crossing the line was a wonderful moment and I had forgotten about the earlier pain.

Even climbing out of the boat and walking around seemed to be fine, so I relaxed and enjoyed our win. One race left, the World Championship final, and a chance to race the best in the business, the Romanian pair. The Romanians were unbeaten so far this Olympic cycle and were reigning Olympic and World Champions as well as world record holders. They had an aura about them and were the pair that beat Thommo's crew in the Sydney Olympics. Even he talked about them with a sense of awe. We were here to test ourselves against the best, but for Cath and me there was a different test. It was more a test of just how fast we could make our boat go. That was the challenge we had set ourselves. It wasn't about being World Champions or beating specific crews, it was about seeing how fast we could go. It was our goal, our focus, our aim. And so the racing was less result based than I had ever experienced and more process focused.

When we got back to the hotel I went to see one of the physios to try to explain what I had experienced in the warm-up. It was strange trying to describe it, especially in the aftermath of the great win we had just had. It didn't seem possible to have been in so much agony and yet be able to race hard and fast. I couldn't understand it myself, but I knew I hadn't imagined it and I knew that to be in that much pain wasn't normal. The physio looked at my movement and decided I should be taped up. As she was taping my back Cath came in with a worried look on her face. "Not to worry you but we're supposed to be in a meeting." I checked my watch. Dammit, I was late, not by much but enough for Thommo to notice. Cath said, "It's OK, do what you need to do but just to warn you he's not in a good mood." The physio smiled and said, "Don't worry, I'll come and explain." I grimaced inwardly, thinking she wasn't fully aware of the situation and stress she was about to walk into. Her innocent optimism was soon shot to pieces as Thommo's angry words cut through her explanations. He didn't want an injured athlete, he was frustrated that when the end was in sight we had had yet another setback and it was all completely outside his control. He raged at Cath, at Miles, at the physio and at me. He was frustrated at yet another setback out of his control. The timing was a disaster and it must have felt like the absolute last straw. No one knew what the implications were for the next crucial 36 hours, but things didn't look good.

The next day I was in agony, but once again didn't want Cath to be burdened by the pain I was in, as there was nothing she could do and with emotional implosions all around us there was enough going on. She knew her coach was stressed and her partner had some sort of injury; that was enough to be going on with. We were sharing a room, and whenever I had to get up I waited for Cath to be in the bathroom or to go outside, so I could literally roll off the edge of the bed, from where it was easier to get up than trying to straighten up from a horizontal position.

The night before the final we went to the course and a storm had blown up complete with gale-force winds. The course was closed and I was happy. I felt physically sick from pain and didn't want to be in a boat, even our wonderful pair. Unfortunately the rowing machine was the replacement choice. I didn't want to tell Thommo I couldn't face or risk that, so I climbed on to the machine, known to be not the best friend of backs, and gingerly lifted the handle. We didn't stay on them for long but I managed enough to reassure Thommo we had completed a session before our race. Cath was kind in not commenting on the poor scores I was displaying as Thommo paced around us, his mood matching the weather outside.

The morning of the final came and I rolled out of bed, longing to be on the water and doing what we came here to do. Although it was still uncomfortable to move, the pain was less and after everything else that was concerning and exhausting I just wanted to be racing. I saw the doctor and the physios in the morning and although they handed over a large dose of painkillers they reassured me that my back was now fine and everything had been done to make sure it would be OK now. I took their word for it and headed to the course thankful not to be thinking about my back or our issues, but thinking purely about the one remaining chance to let our boat fly. The problems had all been on dry land, and so when we pushed away from the landing stage Cath and I both felt a relief to be doing what we knew best. Somehow the physical movement of leaving land made us feel we were leaving everything stressful behind. On the water was where we were now most comfortable, most at home and most able to think about the simple things. The water felt like a respite; it was permission for a short while to think of nothing other than simplicity.

Cath and I had met often with Chris Shambrook, the team psychologist. He was only too aware of all the issues surrounding us and he did his best to keep the communication flowing. He is very experienced both within and outside sport and is creative at coming up with brilliant new ways of thinking about problems and bringing out top performances. When we met we talked mostly about not obsessing about the end result. To find out how fast we really could go we had to stay intently focused on each stroke we were on, as that was the only way to impact on the result – to make each stroke as good as it could be. We could use the opposition as a reference point but we wouldn't predict the outcome based on how we were doing at that particular point of the race. Chris described having a trampoline at the finish line turned on its side, so that any thought that jumped to the finish or the outcome was immediately bounced back to the present moment we were in, and once again what mattered was the stroke we were on at that point.

On the startline I repeated the mantra under my breath: "Trust the process, trust the process, trust the process." Everything we had worked for and against that year had come from an innate belief and trust in what we were doing. Now wasn't the time to change. When the gun went we leapt out fast, but not the fastest of the crews; although it was close, soon the Romanian pair moved ahead and settled into their easy, efficient rhythm that had seen them dominate every race. By halfway we were a considerable distance behind them and lying in fourth place. I remember looking around and noting the positions without having any emotional reaction to it. There was no panic or concern, it was not good or bad news, it was purely information. Our boat felt good and we had more moves to make as the race would unfold.

With 750m left of the race I started to call our changes in gear to move up towards the final sprint finish. The boat was smooth and responding well, and with 500m to go we had drawn level with Canada in third place. I called again for a change in power and rate and Cath applied the necessary increase in work while keeping the rhythm fluid. This was feeling great. I was loving it. Our boat felt unstoppable and like what I can only imagine a racehorse must feel like when it is in full flight. Our boat was like an animal and we just set it free. The rate increased, the work increased and throughout it all we were thinking solely about one stroke at a time. I glanced to my right and there were the Belarussians. We passed them easily, and then I couldn't quite believe it when I saw another boat. It was the Romanians and I had just enough time to tell Cath we were closing on the Romanians when we passed them. I didn't know why they were making it so easy for us – as we flew past them it felt as if they were in slow motion. There was no reaction from either of us as we were still concentrating on if and how our boat could go even faster; it had never been about beating any specific crews. The race was 2,000m and we wanted to know how fast our boat could go over that distance. We moved away from everyone as we sprinted at full stretch to the line, crossing to deafening roars from the crowds in the stadium.

I couldn't believe how great the race had felt and reached forward to grab Cath's shoulders. It was then that I saw the giant television screen that was showing the live pictures of us in the boat, and beneath our image were the words "Great Britain – World Champions". It was electric. We had actually done it, against the odds, against the obstacles and against the fastest pair the world had ever seen. Our hands were raised in celebration as we tried to let the moment sink in. We had to paddle across to where Martin Cross from Radio Five Live was waiting. He leaned across the water in a challenging position to hug us in the boat and as we all grinned at each other he asked the most wonderful question I could have imagined hearing. "So, girls, what does it feel like to be the best in the world at something?" Martin would know, as a previous Olympic champion. That's when it sunk in. On that day at that moment we were officially the best people on the planet at what we had just done. It was a sweet moment and it demonstrated just why the title of World Champion is so special.

As we waited for our medal ceremony we had time to watch the men's pairs final. We talked with Barbara Cassini, the businesswoman who was instrumental in the beginnings of the London 2012 Olympic bid. We were all overexcited about the gold medal as we gathered to watch Matthew and James. This was going to be more British success and another dominating win by this great pair, who had blown the opposition away in Seville the previous year. We stood in front of the crowd as the roars from the spectators prevented Cath and me being able to say anything to each other. When the boats approached we didn't need words – the look between us said it all. Matthew and James weren't winning, in fact they weren't even in the medals, they were trailing in fourth, a position neither athlete was used to. They would be devastated and it was bound to spark speculation about whether changes would be needed. The papers the next day commented on the fact that Great Britain won the pairs event – but not the pair people expected.

Happy and proud, Cath and I left Milan, and I headed off to Paris with my mum to explore another beautiful city. For the first couple of days it was wonderful. I was still smiling about the Milan success and now was amazed by finally seeing the enigmatic smile of the *Mona Lisa*, captivated by the impressive aura of Rodin's *The Thinker* and stunned by the scale and imagination of Monet's water lilies. We walked around the Louvre, climbed the Eiffel Tower, took in the view of and from the Sacré Coeur, were dwarfed by Notre Dame, relaxed in the parks along the Seine and watched the world go by from the outdoor coffee shops.

It was all going well until one night I was woken up simply by turning over in bed. My back had shooting pains, and at breakfast when I went to sit down I had to put my hands on my thighs to support the weight of my body and take it off my back. Although once again I tried not to show it, my mum is a master of observation and noticed immediately. I played it down, not wanting to spoil our trip. By the time I went back I knew things weren't quite right, but then again, as in Milan, it would ease off for a bit and become bearable.

I returned to Bisham a couple of weeks later and the pain had gone from my back. Before we went back to squad training I was running across the grass when Ash, the physio, saw me. "Are you limping?" she asked. I brushed it off. I hadn't been running for a while and I put it down to cramp in my calf muscle. Ash wasn't as easily put off. "Just do something for me, would you? Go up on to your toes." Thinking it was a bit of an odd request I did just that. Now what? I asked. OK, try on one foot. OK, no problem. Now the other. OK, oh, hang on a minute. I couldn't go on to the toes of my left foot. I thought it was extraordinary and hilarious. "Check this out, Ash, I actually can't go up on to my toes! That's crazy!" I was looking at my foot and trying, and I couldn't quite believe how I could lose power to my toes like that. What I didn't notice was how quiet Ash had gone or how grey-looking. She frowned at me for a while and then brightened up. "OK then, I think we should get you scanned soon and find out what's going on, eh?" I nodded and still tried to move my foot – it was fascinating, but at that point I found it entertaining more than anything else.

Soon afterwards Ash drove me to the BUPA hospital at Bushey. I was feeling happy, I was a World Champion and life was pretty good. I was a little concerned about having to go to the hospital but as I wasn't in any pain I didn't think it could be too bad. I had my first ever MRI scan and lay listening to the deafening pounding and thumping of the machine as the hospital tried to drown out the mildly disconcerting noise with a bit of Roy Orbison. As I lay there in my unflattering hospital gown, ironically listening to "Oh Pretty Woman", I didn't feel overly concerned about things. This was a new experience for me and it felt about time to find out what was happening with my back.

Ash had been talking to the radiologist while I was contemplating the top of the scanner that was just in front of my eyes. We left with a full sheet of the results. I had never seen a scan before, so was naïvely intrigued by the black-and-white pictures. As we headed back to Bisham, I was still chatting away about my MRI experience and once again oblivious to how quiet Ash had gone. At that point the radiologist phoned her to discuss the results. I sat turning the scan back to front and upside down and trying to figure out what I was looking at, as she gave monosyllabic answers. "Mmmm hhhh, yes, I did, yes, I know, that's correct. No. No, raced the final. Yes. Won. I know." I wasn't really listening and it was only later that Ash related the full conversation.

The radiologist and Ash saw what I couldn't see. One of the discs in my back hadn't just bulged, which sadly is a common problem in rowing. It had been blown apart, complete sequestration. The soft spongy stuff that lives in discs to keep them supple and moving had been compressed to the point where it had been forced out of the disc and was visible all the way up and down my spinal canal. The disc itself had effectively gone and the stuff was now compressing a nerve, hence the lack of power to one foot. When the radiologist talked to Ash he couldn't believe someone could have rowed on it, never mind raced or won. He was asking when I was booked in for surgery. My body had naturally started to lean to one side to avoid the pain, which came from the nerve impinging on the disc matter. When I had been taped in Milan my body had been forced back into the position where the nerve was affected most, hence the excruciating pain. So I knew what the problem was; now we had to plan for the future. It was about 11 months before the Athens Olympics.

The first step was to deal with how the news would affect everyone in our small team. Thommo had been aware of problems with my back since I had returned from holiday, but we now needed to talk about what would happen next. Thommo called a meeting with Cath, Miles Forbes-Thomas and me. Miles had played a crucial co-coaching role in the Milan World Championships with us and the other crews. Thommo explained to Miles and Cath what the situation was and might mean. He talked to us for an hour about the many challenges we would face on the way to the Olympics, including the media, the increased pressure from being World Champions and mainly the huge problem that my back would pose. He explained that the situation was far from good and we had to realize just how tough it was going to be. Heart pounding, I stared at the floor as Cath and I were hit with the sledgehammer of information. There was more to come. At the end he took me aside and told me that if surgery was recommended by the consultant I was due to meet, and I chose that course of action, then my Olympics would be over. And possibly my career.

A few hours later I met with Matt Stallard, also known as Matt the Knife on account of all the operations he has performed on athletes. Matt is an orthopaedic surgeon, father to an international rower, Tom, and an ex-rower himself. He began by asking me about the weeks leading up to the World Championships and the various signs I'd had. I tried to put together the order of what symptoms I had had when, and explained the level of pain I had been in. Then he asked me about the race itself, but this time not in relation to the injury. He wanted me to tell him about the last 250m of the race because "Well, were you just flying and keeping going or were you holding on? Because to me it looked as if you could just go on and on and I know what that feels like – like when you're windsurfing and you are just flying with the wind until you fall off and it's like Wow!" I smiled in spite of myself. I smiled because he understood what racing could be like, because he used the same words Cath had used to describe the feeling of "flying" in those last 250m. I smiled because his infectious enthusiasm reminded me of what I had lost sight of in all the pain and argument and stress. That rowing at the international level in a crew of the top quality was a wonderful child-like joy and privilege. Matt finished by saying, "I'd love to operate but right now there's no reason I can think of why I should do it." I was flattered that he wanted to be the one to cut me open but also relieved that he would wait until it was necessary before sharpening his scalpel.

The rehab continued. One morning I got up early to wave goodbye to

Cath, Al and Sarah, who were heading off to training camp while I, for the first time in my career, stayed behind to start climbing the mountain that is rehab. Being injured can be a terrifying time in an athlete's career. Any sense of control is gone, you start to doubt your body and lose trust in the movements you used to take for granted. You are isolated from the team and constantly aware of the work they are doing and that you are not. It can be a lonely, frustrating, depressing and dark place. It also feels like a rollercoaster, in that some days are positive steps forward and you begin to see the light, and then the next day can be a giant step backwards. There is uncertainty and no predictable path.

Considering how that could have felt, I count myself ridiculously lucky with the support I had at that time. It was the year the English Institute of Sport came to Bisham, and on site I had the most incredible team I could have wished for to work with. Ash would lead the physio and rehab, Dr Richard Budgett oversaw the medical side, while Jean Watson had the role of "athlete career adviser" at the time, which also meant she took on the challenging task of looking out for my general well-being, making cups of tea and letting me talk when she saw the darkness had descended. Whatever title Jean held, she was always the steady presence at Bisham, reassuring and helpful in any way possible to struggling athletes. Matt Robinson was inspiring in the gym, tough and gentle in equal measure, and rebuilt my physical confidence. Al Smith was the physiologist and was very patient at talking through options and various fitness tests along with irrepressible Craig Williams.

And the support was not just from the people on site. I walked into the gym (which was actually in an indoor tennis court due to renovations of a new super national sports centre) after the others had left for training camp, and next to many of the machines Cath had left inspirational messages: "You are a World Champion training to be an Olympic Champion", "This is a once in a life opportunity". She may have been dragging herself up hills on a bike over in Cyprus, but she made sure I knew her thoughts and support would be here with me. Both Cath and Sarah had given me a bag of little presents to open to keep me sane while I was left behind. It's small gestures like that that can mentally add so many positives to rehab.

Thommo kept in regular touch, wanting to know how much training I had done and when I thought I'd be back in a boat. He was keen to know how soon rehab would be over and when I'd be able to be in the squad once more. He undoubtedly wanted me fit and was worried, but I had all my energy and focus invested in the rehab and couldn't look too far ahead. Thommo was feeling out of the loop and he hated the loss of control he was experiencing, but I was using all my own energy to try to keep things positive as I rode my own emotional rollercoaster. I was due to have a meeting with another neurosurgeon, Chris Adams, and so left a message for Thommo letting him know that was the next step. He replied with a text from Cyprus: "Katherine. Thanks 4 msg. Good luck tomorrow. Hotel here has private beach, dive school, 3 pools, 5 bars and 7 restaurants to explore!! Take care, Paul." I felt very far from that world.

I was determined to focus on getting myself fit and strong and working with the rehab team to come up with challenging new ways to attack the problem. The feeling back at Bisham was upbeat, defiant and inspiring. So even on my low days there was someone there to step in and help. There were a few other girls on the team who had been left behind for various injuries, including Lisa and Ros, and we became a support group for each other and maintained a necessary sense of humour.

Thankfully I didn't feel isolated from the squad and I was able to work hard in the rehab environment. Sometimes a change of programme and scene can be very refreshing even if caused by something as worrying as an injury. But there were things I missed from not being with the squad. I missed Cath's company, but she was spending her days on a bike in Cyprus or in a boat and for a while we seemed to be on different paths. Cath did a brilliant job of being a constant reliable support while she must have been concerned about the unpredictable road ahead. We had long calls to each other while she was on camp, but the stressful environment she described didn't inspire me to be back with the squad.

I met with Chris Adams (the father of a son and daughter who rowed too) and after checking me over physically he sat me back down to "talk about things". He had a lovely gentle manner but looked very serious at this point. He told me that surgery was necessary to remove the disc, although that would mean three months out of the boat, and so he wanted to leave it for two more weeks as there was no harm in doing that. The biggest concern, however, was the nerve that was being crushed and stopping any function in my foot. If we let that continue too long the nerve could sever and die. And I might then have irreparable damage to my foot. If there was no significant improvement then it would definitely mean surgery and he repeated, "I'm sorry, I really am sorry." I tried not to react emotionally to his words and just stared intently at the sympathetic and concerned face of the surgeon in front of me. The third surgeon I saw agreed with the prognosis too.

From the sporting perspective the choice was: do we go for the operation now to allow the longest possible recovery time, or do we delay the chance of the operation, hoping that we could make improvements without the surgery but knowing that if no improvements happened it would definitely put at risk any chance of recovering in time? I thought it was a tricky decision. Ash didn't. She knew that surgery had its own risks, and also cutting through tissue and muscle could have unknown reactions. She discussed it with Dr Richard Budgett, the Chief Medical Officer for British Rowing, and they agreed to do everything to avoid surgery.

Whether because I didn't want to worry people, didn't want sympathy or didn't want it to be real, I sent very upbeat messages to Cath, Sarah and my mum and dad. I managed to train hard and luckily wasn't in any pain at all during this period, but as time went on I was getting increasingly exhausted in body and soul. I wanted to keep pushing myself as physically hard as I could – it was still the Olympic year after all – but in addition I was on edge, with the stress and uncertainty about what was going to happen and trying to keep in contact with all the various people who were involved in my training and rehab, and trying to keep my connection with the squad. Meanwhile the days were running out for my potential surgery.

There was no visible change despite being regularly treated with acupuncture and massage, and pushing myself in the gym. Ironically I was probably fitter and leaner than I had ever been as my body was forced to adapt to new training that it wasn't used to. Mentally I enjoyed having more responsibility for my training – rather than simply following the training programme provided, I could have input on what I should be doing, and I loved the challenge of new training I hadn't tried before. But we hadn't seen a change and that was a serious concern.

One day I was up in the makeshift gym talking to Ash and Ros. The girls were asking how Freda was doing. Sarah had nicknamed my lazy foot Freda – it's a technique to stop an injury appear threatening or scary by giving it a name. I said not much really and demonstrated by showing there wasn't any movement. Except this time there was. It was tiny, marginal, but my heel lifted a fraction off the floor. Everyone screamed and pointed. Ash grabbed me and we ran down to Richard Budgett, interrupting his discussions with a young doctor who was shadowing him. "Look at this, Richard!" I lifted my heel again, worried that it might not work again, but it did. His reaction was equally enthusiastic and I was embraced in a bear hug. "That's wonderful news!" I'll never forget the look of unimpressed surprise as the student doctor witnessed the celebrations for an international athlete managing to lift her heel slightly off the floor.

We had made the deadline by a day. But it meant surgery wouldn't be necessary and the race was now on for real. It was still going to be a long journey but we at least knew which road we were on. It was many weeks before I went back into a boat, but at least now Cath and I knew it would happen. By the new year I was in the boat and we were back where we wanted to be. The time out hadn't damaged our rowing but it had caused some damage to my relationship with Thommo. He felt I had cut him out of my rehab and I felt he hadn't given me the support I needed. We were probably both right to some extent. Meanwhile my absence hadn't strengthened Thommo and Cath's relationship and so we had tough times ahead. With hindsight it was a discussion we needed to have, but it never seemed to be the right time.

For the first and only time in my career I turned to independent help and talked to a counsellor who was recommended by the staff at the English Institute of Sport. She was a wonderful woman who let me sit and talk and listened as I opened up about my frustrations. I surprised myself at just how hurt I had been by the past few months, by the lack of support I had felt in certain areas and how my disappointment and fear of the injury had combined with the challenging communication to put me in an unhealthy place. However, being able to talk about it with someone who didn't judge, who didn't have an agenda and who genuinely seemed concerned for me, was a useful step forward. Slowly I began to feel that I wasn't mad and that I could deal with the inevitable problems ahead.

My first camp back with the squad was in January in Seville. I felt stronger physically and mentally and was looking forward to being part of the team again. But Seville was one of the worst camps I have ever endured as I was in a more vulnerable state. I wasn't quite back to normal training yet, and although Thommo initially said that we'd just see what I could manage, once on camp the attitude is everyone gets on with the full training programme.

The intensity of the training was displayed when Elise was in tears one day. Thommo's task was to bring success to the squad and so he felt it was his job to push athletes to the edge, especially in an Olympic year. Tensions were high all round and one day as the exhaustion levels rose and the nerves were fraying Thommo and I unleashed our frustrations on each other. Ironically, I had just had a good training session in my single, and he used it to question whether my rehab had been right – my back was so good now, he implied, I could have come back earlier and done more. His tone suggested that I hadn't handled things right, and that my rehab team might have let me down, was the right – or wrong – button to push. My anger escalated fast.

We shouted at each other for half an hour as I tried heatedly to explain how difficult the time had been and that I felt he was undermining me and the amazing staff I worked with, and that he had to trust the experts and also me. And that of all people, I would do everything I could to be back better than ever. He had hated the fact that when I did my fitness test at the EIS at Bisham there were about ten staff watching, staff who had seen me there every day in pain, in tears, struggling with doubt and frustration, and had seen me come out the other side of that darkness. They had gathered to show their support and cheer me on, as it was effectively my last day in the world of rehab. Thommo felt it showed I was overdependent on them – didn't I know I had to make the journey without them? In return I felt insulted that he would think I would be dependent. For me rowing has always been about people I have met on the journey, and those who cheer, support and encourage are part of what makes it so special. That while he would play the biggest part in our careers there was room for other crucial members of our wider team. The medical staff are often the people the athletes open up to. In my own career, physios like Ash and Pam Gardiner became valuable sounding boards as well as lifelong friends, while Sarah Hodson, the team's skilled massage expert, as well as exuding positive enthusiasm and giving wise advice, was someone always available for a laugh and some escapist conversation. These people provided not only support but also an important release valve from the day to day pressure. They all made the days more fun but never distracted from the job at hand. I told Thommo that I was well aware they couldn't be with me on the startline but I would willingly and gratefully use any help and support along the way to make me as good as I could be. As often happened with Thommo's "heated discussions", the last ten minutes settled down to normal conversation.

I went back up to the room I shared with Cath, mildly shaking as the adrenaline still flooded my body. Cath was stunned by the fact Thommo and I had just been yelling at each other, as I described my relief that we had both got things off our chest. To his credit Thommo chatted things through a few days later and advised me of three things: that I should use people to make progress, I should leave no stone unturned and that I should take more control. Although Thommo's temper could be frightening, he always calmed down afterwards and didn't hold any grudges. He also listened and thought deeply about what had been said and often came back a few days later having considered the various points of view.

From my point of view the best thing that came from our fight wasn't the fact that we had each finally managed to express our frustrations, or that we had broken through our communication block. They were very healthy, useful steps, but also crucial to me was the fact that I had fight in me. There were times during injury when I was insecure and had doubts, and the biggest problem would have been if Thommo had gone on the attack and I had sat back and allowed him to, unable to stand up to him. When he tested me I had to be able to fight. He and I had to know the drive and desire and grit were still there.

When we went back to Seville in February, Cath and I were allowed back in our pair and by the end of the camp we raced in the Seville Team Cup. We won everything we raced, and although there were not many of the big names it was great to be racing and great to be winning. The GB team won the overall title and the team manager David Tanner chose Cath and me to collect the award on behalf of the team which we really appreciated. David is an ex-head teacher and is still referred to as

"The Headmaster" within the squad. No one is left in any doubt that he is in charge and his vision of where the GB rowing team should be and the standards he sets has created the most successful rowing team this country has ever seen.

Before the main international season started we raced in the annual Head of the River Race on the Tideway in London. It's the biggest eights race in the country and a highlight of the year. As squad athletes we were released to our clubs and allowed to row in whatever combinations we wanted. When I first arrived on the team the big showdown was between Marlow and Thames Rowing Clubs. Now it was Leander against a random composite. Miles usually coached the composite, based out of Thames or London Rowing Club, and his ambitious and brilliant idea was that half of our eight were top squad people and the other half were development athletes. It was always a tough challenge getting together a disparate group of people to become a fully formed racing machine in the space of a week, but I loved it and we often won thanks to Miles' inspiration.

Over the years the development athletes went on to become Olympic and World Champions and medallists. We had the likes of Annie Vernon, Vicky Thornley and Helen Glover all before they were known as top athletes in their own right. In 2004 we had a real mix of past, present and future stars. Alison Trickey had retired but was back for another race; Cath, Sarah and I were firmly focused on the Olympics, and Annie Vernon was a promising young athlete from Cambridge University. Apart from the race itself I used to love sitting in our meetings to hear Cath come to life. Her quiet intensity in training was given a voice in those meetings, and in 2004 when Miles asked us all to say who we were and what we wanted from the race, Cath led off in her low and clear voice. "I'm Cath Bishop, I'm a World Champion training to be an Olympic Champion." There was no discussion, no hesitation, no doubt. I smiled to myself and was once again thankful to be in a boat with her. I glanced up to poor Annie who was next, her eyes slightly widened and she stuttered her way through her introduction: "I'm Annie Vernon." Pause. "And I'm clearly not a World Champion." She wasn't then, but a few days later she was a Champion of the Head of the River and a few years later would have her own world titles to talk of.

The racing season approached and Cath and I loved the chance to be back in our pair making our boat fly. The big test would be the first World Cup at which we met the Romanians – seeing whether we could beat them again. Unfortunately we didn't and our mental advantage from the previous summer disappeared.

The summer camps before the Olympics were challenging in their own right. Although at our best we were a fantastic combination of crew and coach, as Athens approached the cracks were showing. The Romanian pair were going to be the toughest opposition and Thommo still talked about them with reverence. In hindsight, although they were a superb crew at their peak, we gave them too much respect. Thommo was also going through a painful divorce and he was feeling the pressure of having to get a result in his new role as a GB coach, after winning Olympic medals for Australia. Cath was feeling a lack of confidence, caused partly by our mixed year, partly by not feeling positivity from Thommo and partly by the shadow of her previous Olympics now falling across us. Meanwhile I knew it wasn't a happy time, I felt I couldn't ease communication and I sometimes detached myself mentally, perhaps doing exactly what I shouldn't have done, but doing what I thought would avoid any more conflict. However, there were still moments of magic on the water, our training was actually going surprisingly well considering the difficulties we were experiencing off the water, and we went to Athens reasonably optimistic.

***

Athens was a different experience from Sydney. We wouldn't be staying in the Olympic Village for a start, because of the distance between the rowing course and the centre of Athens. We also needed armed security because of threats the British team had received. It was 2004 and invading countries hadn't made us universally popular. In theory we weren't even supposed to leave our hotel without telling the close protection team and they would shadow us from a distance when we went for a walk. They became good friends with us all and over the next few years I was delighted to meet one of them, Scott, when he was on duty with the Royal Family. The fact that there were also Israeli athletes in our hotel block with their own security added to the international tension in Athens. We left our hotel to watch the marathon go by, stunned at the speed as the women raced past. We fleetingly cheered for Paula Radcliffe before she had to stop in tears. We celebrated as Kelly Holmes brought home the 800m and 1,500m double gold. Matthew Pinsent won his fourth Olympic gold medal by 8 hundreths of a second and was on his way to a knighthood. The men's 4 x 100m relay won the Olympic title by 1 hundreth of a second and Chris Hoy won his first cycling title. Great Britain were champions on the track, on the water and in the velodrome.

Back at the rowing lake we were getting ready for our own moment. The preparation had been good, so we were devastated to be off the pace in the heat. We seemed to lose a length of speed every quarter of the race. And yet nothing had felt awful – which was the worst thing. If we had been able to explain what had gone wrong then it would have been easier, but we couldn't. Steve Redgrave spoke to us and told us to relax and focus on the positives. He reminded us it was a bit like how we had started the previous year in the Milan World Championships. That was true, and we did improve throughout the regatta.

The night before our final Thommo met Cath and me in a room down in the basement of the hotel. Once we had gone through the logistics Thommo looked us in the eyes said he had never seen athletes push themselves as hard or race as well as we did. He was incredibly complimentary with his praise. The first emotion I felt was surprise. All of the things he could have said, this wasn't what I expected to hear. His words were exactly what we had needed him to say in the days, weeks or months before. Sadly it felt a case now of too much too late.

It was about a year later, when I was waiting at the luggage carousel at Heathrow after a training camp, that I felt the need to mention something to Thommo. He had previously been raving to the new athletes on the team about Cath Bishop and about her intensity and level of training and how impressive she was. I said to him when we were alone waiting for our bags that I felt it was a shame she never knew the respect he had for her. He looked at me a little confused. "I told her all the time how good she was. She knew." I shook my head. "Honestly, Thommo, to this day she thinks you thought little of her. She felt she could never be great in your eyes." He looked crestfallen. His admiration of her was clear to me now, but never had been at the time. As I found out over the next few years Thommo is often toughest on the people he respects the most, because he knows he can push them harder and expect more of them. It struck me as crazy how much we can say to each other while still not saying enough.

In the final we had our best race of the regatta. Once again we had a flying finish, but we had left ourselves too much to do and finished in silver behind the Romanians, who added to their medal haul with another two Olympic golds in Athens, bringing their combined Olympic titles to seven. The result was a mix of emotions. We had won a silver medal, a fantastic achievement in itself and especially in the face of all that had gone before. But there was a feeling that if we had got things absolutely right then we could have won the gold. Unfortunately we couldn't quite release the overwhelming desire to get the right result and focus just on the process as we had in Milan. It is still one of the medals I am proudest of, because of the challenges we had to overcome to achieve it, and I am so pleased that an athlete of Cath's calibre won a much deserved Olympic medal and a world title. She retired after Athens, and this time for good. Within a month of racing, Cath was on her way to her first diplomatic posting, in Sarajevo. Never one to do thjngs in half measures, she spent her final rowing year between training sessions learning Serbo-Croat fluently. Although she retired from the team she left me with a powerful message of how much work and effort can be put in every day to achieve a longed-for dream.

The most positive thing for the women's team in Athens was that whereas in Sydney we had left with one Olympic medal, this time every single woman went home with one. Thommo as chief coach had delivered on the vision he held when he arrived three years earlier. Sarah and Elise had won bronze in the double, Fran, Debbie, Becs and Al had won silver in the quad and we had won our silver. The belief that began in Sydney came to fruition in Athens when British women proved they were capable of delivering results. However, with two silvers and a bronze, there was one obvious result missing.

CHAPTER
7

QUADRUPLE
QUANDARIES

The lead-up to 2004 had included some of the toughest tests in my career, and the various stresses meant I hadn't enjoyed the time as much as I'd have liked to. I considered seriously whether or not I wanted to continue in the sport, especially knowing Cath had now retired and I wasn't sure what I would do next within rowing.

I met Thommo for a drink in Marlow and we talked through options. He thought sculling was to be the way forward for the team. As there was no obvious replacement for Cath in the team, I accepted the suggestion of a return to sculling. I said I would want a new challenge if I was going to continue, and we decided I should put myself forward for the stroke seat of a boat. Every seat is different, and vital, in every boat. Ideally you know the individuals well in your team, their strengths and weaknesses, and then exploit them to the maximum by choosing who would sit where. There is a reason why each athlete sits in a particular seat in the boat and the best boats will have every athlete playing to their strengths. I had been in the bow seat in the pair and one of the key things in that seat is to set the boat up so your stroke can feel free to race exactly as he or she wants to. The bow seat generally makes the tactical calls, but when there are two people the jobs are evenly shared. In a bigger boat, like the quad, I would feel a different responsibility. The stroke seat sets the rhythm and in my mind will never say die in a race. You have to lead by example, be consistent, be willing to push yourself as far as is necessary and inspire confidence in the people behind you. I felt I was immensely lucky to have sat behind Cath and her hungry intensity in racing, and I felt it was now my turn to see if I could take on the new role.

The women's team, led once again by Thommo, met in the winter of 2005 and we discussed the results from Athens. Cath and Al had retired but the majority of the Olympic team were still there. We had been more successful than ever before, and yet there was still no Olympic gold medal. It was agreed that gold would now be the aim and that although realistically not everyone in the meeting would be the one to stand on the top step of the podium, everyone would play their part to contribute to that goal. It was a powerful and passionate pledge.

A quad was formed of Sarah, Becs, Fran and me – all now Olympic medallists. We were the first boat to be selected and would lead the new golden charge. We met with Chris, the psychologist, to discuss our new crew and we were introduced properly to the concept of detailed roles and responsibilities. Although in previous years we had always known what each person had done in the crew this was the first time we took it apart in intricate detail. We started with the classic listing of strengths, weaknesses, opportunities and threats for the crew. Then we were honest about our own individual strengths and weaknesses. We were a very varied group as far as personalities went and it was crucial that we worked out how best to operate as a team.

Chris astutely asked us how we wanted to be defined, and after agonizing over various words we settled on "passion and excellence". We wanted to have the heart and soul side of things which was defined by passion, but it was crucial to balance that with a disciplined attention to detail and an exceptionally high standard of work. Those words passion and excellence stayed with us all season and underpinned everything we did.

We also talked specifically about the roles in the boat, so that when it came to racing, to performing under pressure, we would know exactly what was expected of us individually and how we would deliver it. Crucially we knew that our own job was 25 per cent of the boat. Each one of us had to do that job 100 per cent, but never more than our defined quarter. It meant that when we were under the fiercest pressure of racing we would focus on our roles and not try to do anyone else's job. I wouldn't start thinking I needed to do a bit for Fran, or help Sarah. I had to stay focused on my role and trust the others to be doing the same. Shifting focus to what someone else was doing inevitably meant less attention on your own job and so vulnerability within the crew. If we could each stay focused on our own role we would also create a powerful trust between us. The greatest test for this would be the upcoming World Championships which were to be held in Japan.

We flew to Tokyo and took the bullet train past Mount Fuji to where we were staying. Japan was a reassuringly welcoming place. The people could not have been friendlier, more polite, or more helpful as we lumbered into the local shops and buses. That little corner of Japan was suddenly filled with overlarge athletes speaking not a word of Japanese other than the basic "thank you" and a deep bow. Before we arrived David, our team manager, warned us that it would feel like an alien place and we wouldn't recognize anything in the local supermarket. He had been exploring the previous year and brought back stories of confusion and bewilderment as a result of the language being so different. In the intervening year, however, a massive mall had been built, and although we went in fearing the chaos of buying cereal thinking it was washing powder and cleaning product thinking it was juice, we were instead met with every recognized brand in the world displayed in familiar English-language packaging.

Japan was full of memorable moments. None of us spoke Japanese but one evening Sarah and I sat next to our translator as she tried to explain the idea behind certain characters in the Japanese alphabet, using the hotel address as a reference. We had no idea how useful that casual chat would turn out to be a few days later when we had ventured out to the cinema and then missed the last planned bus home. We stood in the darkness trying to light up a bus shelter and, running fingers underneath the writing, concluded, "We need the one that looks a bit like a house with a kite on top and the other one that could be a bird on one squiggly foot next to a picnic table …" We then jumped on a bus that had matching pictures and somehow made it back.

Japan truly was a fascinating place. And the rowing course was no different. After the racing finished I was pulled in for a drugs test. It's always the last thing you want to do; you get taken away from your crew and have to sit in a room drinking water or juice until you can give a urine sample in front of a stranger. It's usually a quiet and sombre affair, with everyone trying to get away from it as soon as possible. Although it is a necessary part of keeping our sport clean, it generally wasn't considered the highlight of a racing day. Until Japan.

As I trudged up the stairs thinking "why me?" and muttering about the unfairness of being selected yet again to Ali Saunders, our team doctor, I stopped as I heard boisterous noise coming from the room ahead. I must be in the wrong place, I thought, but no, my Japanese new best friend insisted. I walked into what could only be described as a party. There were athletes from all different countries joking and laughing and gathering in groups to take photos with each other. The table in the middle explained it all. Rising shakily up above the heads of the athletes and their team doctors was a leaning tower of empty beer cans. Whenever one of the athletes finished another can, there was a general drum roll on the table and a low cheer rising in a crescendo as the athlete had to place the empty can on the top of the moving tower. Huge cheers erupted as he managed to place the can without knocking down the tower, and someone else would lean over to the vast cooler box filled with ice and beer cans. More beer was passed around and the chat and photos started again. Unlike anywhere else in Japan they had allowed beer to be available alongside the usual water and juice, and for the first time ever I witnessed athletes being more than happy to stay in drug testing as long as possible to consume as much as possible. It was a friendly free bar. Quite a long time later I finally left, having made new friends, and started weaving my way back to find my teammates.

Before the racing even began there were new rowing experiences for us all. We were taken to the rowing course for the first time and as the bus drew into the car park I looked out of the window and frowned at the rushing water falling over itself as it flooded past us. We stepped out of the bus and asked the driver if we had come to the wrong place as this was quite clearly not a rowing course. The driver insisted it was the correct place and left us there. Looking out across the white horses we could see no buoy lines or lanes or anything familiar. Then word came through that this was indeed the World Championship course, and the course had been laid the day before, but the floodwater coming down from the mountains had carried it away. But it wasn't necessarily the end of the world because this particular piece of water was also tidal. And so maybe the tide would bring it back.

As the days went by the water calmed down a little, but it was still flowing fast. The lanes were put back out and this time they seemed to be more firmly anchored. Before racing started there was the scientific "orange race", where officials placed an orange at the start of each lane to see if the course was fair or if any of the lanes were particularly fast. At one point we had to lock up all the boats into massive transporter containers because of a predicted typhoon and the course was shut. Luckily the typhoon never arrived and we were safe to venture back out on to the water.

We had a much bigger team in 2005, created by adding an eight and a single to the mix. We had a new flood of enthusiastic young athletes, many of whom had risen through the junior ranks together and had now arrived in a welcome wave of excitable noise and fresh exuberance. In the women's quad our main opposition that year was undoubtedly the Germans. They had a fearsome reputation in the event, having won every Olympic title, every World title except two and holding the world record. In addition to the boat class itself being "owned" by the Germans, they had also recently added their most successful athlete. Kathrin Boron was a legend in the world of rowing. She had four Olympic gold medals to her name from four consecutive Olympics and she was aiming for one more World Championship title that would equal Steve Redgrave's collection. She was an impressive mix of Redgrave and Pinsent success. I had never raced her directly, but when we heard she was being moved into the quad I knew that the stakes had been raised a little bit higher and the odds were now stacked against us. There is, however, something very exciting about taking on the best in the world, those rare individuals who have broken through barriers and blazed trails. This is where we would truly be able to measure our worth.

We were on opposite sides of the draw and we weren't expected to meet until the final. Thommo had videoed the racing and we watched in silence as first our boat was shown on the screen and then the depressingly superior-looking Germans raced across it. The final was going to be special. And very hard. Thommo, however, appeared unfazed and did a great job of keeping the mood upbeat, focusing on the positives. Although he knew with his expert eye that we were up against the best in the world, he appeared to be thrilled by the challenge and believed in what we had worked on. On the morning of the final we woke in our single rooms and found a message that Becs had put under each of our doors. Usually the quiet one in the boat, Becs had written us all an individual note saying great things about what she respected in each of us and why we were so good. It was a lovely, unexpected, heartfelt and genuine gesture.

We arrived at the startline, and the photos taken then show faces lost in serious contemplation and focus. The video of the race has a moment when the commentator says, "Frances Houghton said she would sit at the startline and look across at her opposition in the three seat, Kathrin Boron." At that exact moment Fran did exactly that. It was pure theatre and the stage was now set. In our discussions of the race Thommo had done a shrewd clinical job in analysing the crews we would be racing and deciding on our race plan. The German style was to come out fast but not too fast; their devastating move was in the second quarter of the race when they pushed past everyone and left every crew in their wake. So the decision was made to beat them at their own game. We would come out fast and then, when the other crews were settling, we would attack in the second quarter, surprise the Germans and unsettle them, stealing their thunder and their lead. It was a daring plan, but we were up against the best and so needed to be brave or risk letting the Germans have it all their own way.

We sat silently on the startline going through the plan in our heads. I knew it was going to be tough, but I had no idea it would be the closest race of my career – that for 2,000m there would never be more than 0.7 seconds splitting the lead crews. When the gun went we came out fast, alongside the Germans and slightly behind the Russians. We were leading the Germans at 500m and this was our move. I didn't let myself think about the pain we were about to experience or how early it felt to increase the workload because we had all committed to this move, and it would take total commitment from all four of us for it to be successful. We'd agreed that even if it meant we might not be able to continue for the second half of the race, it was worth the risk to seize the moment and go for the gold. We effectively entered a tunnel and shut down any awareness of the crews around us. For 500m this was our race and we would bury ourselves to make the necessary impact. The other crews didn't matter; this was our moment to throw in something nobody would expect and possibly not be able to react to. I'll never forget getting to 1,000m, looking up and realizing the Germans had not only drawn level but had actually moved through and ahead of us. They had gone from fourth to first. Becs gave a shout of dismay. The plan had failed.

There was no time to regroup, the race was at full speed now and every stroke was critical. We were in unknown territory, not having planned for this part to go wrong. We reverted to those roles we had painstakingly gone through in the months before. I set the solid predictable rhythm and responded instantly to any instruction that came from behind. Fran sat behind me, locking directly into that rhythm and keeping the positive momentum flowing, adding the power along with Sarah, who was also making the race calls and wouldn't let our heads drop despite the change in fortunes. Becs stayed acutely attuned to the race unfolding around us, ready to pounce on anything that might happen and we needed to know about. None of us worried about each other, we homed in even more sharply on raising our own individual standards. By 1500m we had marginally closed the gap. In the last quarter of the race the water became rougher and every bit of precision was needed. Fran called to relax, keep calm and stay in control.

As the crews edged closer together something happened to our right-hand side, although it wasn't clear what. There was noise from the German crew and Becs called immediately for an attack. Without questioning, I lifted the rate and the power and our boat responded with speed. All four of us knew the momentum had changed and we continued the assault on the finish line. We blazed across, 0.3 seconds ahead of the Germans. We were elated, laughing, shouting, slapping each other on the back. We came in to the landing stage with the Germans behind us, their heads bowed and shoulders heaving. Kathrin Boron stepped out of the boat in tears and was embraced by Steve Redgrave, two legends of rowing in a hug of mutual understanding and respect. We found out later that one of Kathrin Boron's blades had clipped the water, she actually let go of the blade and did a sensational job of catching it again before it caused any problems. But it was enough to unsettle the crew for a few strokes and caused enough confusion that when we attacked they couldn't respond.

It was a lesson in just how important it was in a team to know what to do, how to do it and who would do it. In their boat, not being able to react quickly and clearly to a surprise had created a tiny upset, but enough of an upset to interrupt their performance. In our boat, there was a calm clarity even when things hadn't gone to plan. Everyone knew their role and how to apply it, so that when things went wrong, we could adapt and adjust and keep our heads. Once battle is underway, the actions of our competitors and the changing shape of the race can be unpredictable, and so the ability to read the situation and adjust things when necessary is a key skill. It doesn't change the planned outcome, but there just needs to be flexibility in case the route to it needs to be altered. The passion and excellence combination was working and we had taken our first successful step along the gold medal path.

Most years seem to involve some sort of crew change and 2006 was no different. Despite being World Champion, Becs decided to leave rowing and to give cycling a try. She had had back problems and cycling seemed to be a better fit for her. She was also keen to try a sport which was able to be more individual, in the sense not only of competing individually but also of tailoring training. One thing Becs struggled with in the squad set-up was that training often has a "one programme fits all" design. There are so many athletes in the rowing squad that it couldn't be specific to each one of us. Becs chose cycling because the ratio of support staff to athletes was very different there and she felt she could make sure she had done absolutely everything she could to sit on the startline and feel prepared in her own individual way. And it worked for her; rowing's loss was cycling's gain. In 2004 Becs had won an Olympic silver medal in rowing, in 2005 she was a rowing World Champion, and in 2008 she would become a cycling Olympic Champion.

Meanwhile back on the water the mission was still the same. We were aware that individuals within the team might change over the years, but the drive to Beijing was all about gold-digging and that goal was immovable. Becs was replaced by Debbie and we started to plan the defence of our title as World Champions. It was particularly exciting as no British women's crew had ever successfully defended their world title, and also the World Championships were coming to Britain's newest rowing course, Dorney Lake.

We had more meetings in the same vein as the previous year, talking about roles and responsibilities. And as a high-performing team we wanted to improve on the previous year by taking discussions to a higher level. This time we would take it in turns to choose one person from the crew and the other three would name all the positive things that stood out about them, all the attributes that we respected, admired and made us laugh. Then we would discuss what role they would suit best. It was a fun and confidence-building exercise, although inevitably it would never go completely smoothly.

We had been listing all the good stuff that Fran brings to a crew, which were many, and then we moved on to describing the one very crucial and vitally different role that she played. Debbie went for it: "You see you're just absolutely brilliant at ... meetings." "Meetings?" Fran asked in a less than impressed tone. "Well ... yes." "I don't want to be good at meetings." Sarah jumped in, "But you are really good at them." "You're also good at loads of things," I added, "it's just that that's one area that we're all a bit useless at and you're really good at keeping us on track." I suppose that to Fran it must have been like waiting eagerly as superpowers were dished out and, while others got "leaping buildings in a single bound", "flying" or "deflecting bullets with gold bracelets", she was given "organizing the costumes".

Years later I would remember this when I spent an afternoon with Saracens Rugby Club and we discussed how in all great teams not everyone could get the glory role of the kicker, the penalty taker or the forward striker. A team won't operate with everyone in the same role, particularly the same starring role. It's important that everyone plays to their own individual strengths and is honest about what those strengths are. The combination of different skills adds to the ability of the team and does that classic thing of making the team greater than the sum of the parts. A team full of strikers would be an absolute disaster. The best teams have a full variety of key abilities.

Without Fran our crew had the potential to be full of exciting, inspiring, enthusiastic ideas without any crucial structure, clarity or detail. Fran was not just able to keep our meetings on track, but would make Thommo choose only one or two things at a time from his hectic train of thought for us to work on. She made sure we were all clear on the reason behind every outing and what we wanted to achieve. And she wouldn't be distracted by the lure of something new. She added discipline to our natural unbounded exuberance. It may not have been the glamorous or exciting role she would have chosen, but that didn't make it any less important. Fran has a surprisingly loud booming laugh that can dispel tension and she can use her humour to help instil discipline in a relaxed manner. Fran also happens to be a skilled cook and the crew room is sometimes supplied with her latest delicious creations.

With Debbie coming in we had a new element. She replaced Bec's reticence with a slightly crazy sense of humour and enthusiasm. Debbie's greatest attribute and weakness is her inability to say no to anything anyone asks. We lost count of the amount of times she arrived out of breath having just loaned her car to a friend who was stuck, or having dropped off food for someone who was in need, or having slept on the floor while allowing others to use her bed. She is the most generous of fools and would drive Fran to distraction with her often madcap lifestyle, as she used any spare "rest" time to run errands for others or take Charlie, her adorable, boisterous labrador, for a walk. Debbie and Fran had known each other for over ten years, and although they could be complete opposites in their approach to things, they were like sisters and so had a healthy ability to tease or scold each other when necessary while always remaining supportive.

As the Dorney World Championships arrived there was great excitement, not just for the athletes but also for friends, families and fans of British rowing who this time would get to watch. We moved into a nearby hotel and prepared for our first experience of racing in front of a home crowd. There was a huge expectation for us to defend our world title at Dorney, and on the basis of our performances so far in the season, it was looking distinctly possible. Our greatest threat would come from the Russians, who had an impressive turn of speed, but a speed we had managed to contain all year.

We raced the Russians early in the regatta and beat them. The final was looking good, although we took nothing for granted. In the final we led the field and had Australia next to us, with the Russians on the other side of them. As we raced in front of the screaming grandstands we were ahead of the Australians and I thought ahead of everyone. What I didn't know and couldn't see was the late Russian surge; but then out of the corner of my eye as the Australians dropped back I realized there was a crew on the other side and it was moving ahead. They beat us in the sprint for the line and there was an audible collective gasp from the stands. The British favourites had been beaten in front of their eyes. I couldn't believe it. I was furious at not having known what was happening in the race and desperately disappointed to have let down all the people who had travelled and bought tickets and gone out of their way to come and support us.

We struggled to talk to the waiting press and then were called on to the podium. We arrived without Sarah, who had somehow got lost on the way to the stand. She was in tears and had stumbled the wrong way and was seen being shepherded back towards the medal ceremony area. We stood in front of a hushed home crowd who had come to see British success and instead were witnessing their own athletes struggling with personal loss. When you have only one major international race a year, the result feels very final. It doesn't take long to sink in that not only was that the chance to win the world title, but in all reality that was the one and only chance in your whole career to win the World Championships in front of your own friends and family. That would have been the thank you to everyone who had helped, supported and loved us along this journey. We would have been the first British women's crew to successfully defend their World Championships title. And we had got it wrong.

We shook hands with the beaming Russians and as I congratulated their stroke, Irina Fedotova, she leaned towards me with a look that combined supreme pleasure with an edge of steel and said something in Russian which I'll never know. But I didn't need to understand the majority of what she said because the last few words, "Sydney 2000", said it all. She was in the Russian crew that we had beaten in the photo finish to claim the silver medal back at the Sydney Olympics. This was her revenge. Six long years of waiting had finally given her the opportunity to deliver the perfect, devastating blow. I had so many emotions as I watched the Russian flag being raised and stood with my hands behind my back staring ahead. Ironically I like the Russian national anthem. I find it a strong piece of music with a stirring emotion to it. As painful as it was, the music possibly helped my stoic mindset as I stood with jaw clenched and my expression fixed watching the flags rise up over the Dorney crowd.

That night there was the usual end of Championships party, in Uxbridge this year. I couldn't face the party and instead met my mum and dad for dinner. Cath joined us too, someone who knew exactly what I was going through and knew that nothing needed to be said or done. We just enjoyed a quiet meal, understated and in easy company. The conversation flowed but it wasn't around the race or the Championships. Cath told us about her new life out in Sarajevo, and for a while I remembered there was a bigger world out there, where the result of a race really didn't matter.

I went back to the hotel where we were staying and found Sarah there. She had also been out with her family, unable to face the Uxbridge party. We entered the world of the past 24 hours, reliving the race, talking through what went right and what on earth went wrong, how we could have done things differently. Although it would not change the result we wanted to somehow explain the loss, to find an answer to a question we couldn't quite define. I felt it was a race we should have won and was incensed that we had let such a fantastic opportunity slip through our fingers.

The late-night TV droned in the background as we talked, sitting on our single beds, and finally we both fell into a restless sleep. I woke early while it was still dark and lay torturing myself with unavoidable thoughts and regrets. It is always the same for me: the bad races are the ones that keep me awake as my mind goes over the details again and again. I don't often relive the great races; they just leave me with a sense of contentment but not necessarily highlights playing in my mind. As the grey light of the summer morning shone around the edges of the curtains I heard Sarah moving around in her bed on the other side of the room. "Are you awake?" I ventured. "Have been for hours," she muttered. We decided to get up.

As we were packing up our bags and emptying the room, I leaned outside to look at the papers. Every morning on the way to the course we had stepped over the newspaper left outside the room next door. This morning I thought I'd have a quick look to see if there was any coverage of the rowing. I was flicking gently through the borrowed paper when I saw a write-up of the Regatta. What I didn't initially notice was the enormous photo that accompanied the article. It was a half-page close-up of Sarah's face. I'm not sure when it was taken but quite possibly as she was distressed and lost behind the stands before the medal ceremony. Taking out my own emotion about that moment, I can see it is a striking picture. It is the confused and disbelieving face of someone who has just witnessed horror. Her mouth is open and she is staring shocked at something out of shot, her eyes are rimmed with red, her face streaked with sweat and tears. It is a picture that makes you stop and consider, and it had me frozen to the spot. Unfortunately that meant I didn't have time to react when Sarah came up behind me to see what I was looking at.

She swore in surprise as she saw it. I closed the paper, replaced it outside the room, and we gathered our things and headed for the car. It was very early on a Bank Holiday Monday. Sarah wanted to find a coffee shop, but the first one we arrived at was closed, unsurprisingly. We drove through the deserted streets and ended up at our familiar Marlow Starbucks. We had spent countless hours here over the years lounging on the sofas, drinking coffee and trying to get mentally prepared for the next training session. As we parked we saw a man going up to the door but being turned away because it was closed. I already felt despondent and it seemed right that even our friendly coffee place was going to turn us away. Sarah walked up to the door undeterred as I shuffled along behind like a reluctant child. As the girl who worked there leaned out to bring in the newspapers she glanced up at the two of us, smiling, and then stepped back into the shop. We stood at the glass door. She mouthed through the glass, "We're not open yet." Sarah pleaded for her to open up as we needed coffee and the girl opened the door slightly to apologize and said the shop was still closed. There was a moment of silence before Sarah eyed her and said, "We need coffee." Before the girl could react Sarah added, "And we've just lost the World Championships." This was followed by a longer silence as the girl looked at us, unsure of what to say. "Really?" she finally managed, looking at us a little bit disbelievingly.

Sarah glanced down and saw that one of the papers she had just brought in was the same as the one we had looked at in the hotel. "Let me show you," Sarah said. As the girl continued to stare at us, unconvinced, Sarah opened up the paper to her picture. "See, that's me." The girl looked down and had the same reaction we had had. She looked from the picture up to Sarah and back down again. She then looked up at me and I just nodded. She then ushered us in, whispering, "Oh dear. Come in, come and sit at the back. What do you want to drink?" We were settled in the comfy armchairs at the back of the shop and were soon brought hot coffees along with a sad sympathetic smile. "You can settle the bill when the shop is open and the till is up and running."

We stayed there for hours, with nothing else to do and nowhere to go that day. As a constant flow of customers came and went around us we had a healthy lesson on how little impact our own stories can make on others' lives. On how sometimes the biggest things in your life, whether euphoric or devastating, will register nothing more than a passing interest in others. People arrived and sat opposite us with the paper and either flicked past or stopped at the rowing page before moving on to the other news. It was of mild interest at best and they had no idea of the heartbreak sitting in front of them. Thommo always says, "Today's news is tomorrow's fish and chip paper." This time it felt like we were already fish and chip paper even before the day was through. As we sat in silence the easy listening music flowed over us from the nearby speaker. Despite being in a miserable place, even I could appreciate the irony as the words of Nat King Cole's classic "Smile" started. "Smile though your heart is aching, smile even though it's breaking, when there are clouds in the sky ..."

CHAPTER
8

CHINESE BURN

That winter we entered a dark period of reflection. There was a complete review of all that we had done and where we could have made it better. There was an acceptance that the Russians had beaten us but no acceptance that they were better than us on every level. There was more a sense that we had underperformed. We still felt we had got things almost right and we went into a full debrief to look at all aspects of what worked and what didn't to put things right for the next time. If it was to be a painful experience, then at least it should also be a useful lesson so the summer wasn't completely wasted. With any loss, there is usually fertile ground for learning things. Everyone looked deeply into where they could have done things better individually and collectively. There were no bad feelings towards the Russians, just a very internal review of what we as a team, a crew and as athlete or coach could have done things differently. The reviewing process of our racing is a crucial part of how we progress, and to learn the most it must be as honest as possible, even if that meant potentially facing some painful truths. There can be objective criticism without personal blame.

We were back in the midst of winter training on a cold January day when Thommo came into the weights gym in Bisham. Sarah and I were lifting together and he came over and said, "Can I have a word?" We looked at each other and immediately wondered what we'd done wrong. He said, "Let's talk outside you two. Or should I say World Champions." We were really confused and I tried to understand what Thommo was meaning. We stepped through the doors and Fran and Debbie were standing there looking equally confused.

Thommo told us he'd just heard from a friend that FISA (the international governing body for rowing) were about to announce that one of the Russians had been found guilty of drug abuse by taking testosterone and the quad would be stripped of their world title. The title would be awarded to us. The news came as a complete shock. It is (thankfully) a rare situation in international rowing and there is no expectation that something like this might happen. We stared at each other in disbelief and didn't know what to say. Thommo had had more time to get used to the news and he was buoyant with the change in fortune. He told us that soon the media would have it, so we should be ready to speak to the press about how we felt. The problem was we didn't know how we felt. It was a lot to take in and didn't seem real in any way. There was no explosion of joy or relief or sense of justice done. There was disbelief, surprise, disappointment and frustration. And more disbelief.

As the news became known and people talked about it, the situation became more real but somehow no more acceptable. The disappointment remained but a new, more powerful emotion was added to the confusion: anger. Pure rage. The realization that someone in the Russian boat had deliberately cheated to rob us of our winning moment in front of our home crowd. That those friends and family and supporters would never enjoy the experience of watching us crossing the line as Champions of the World and that we would not stand in front of that crowd with the National Anthem playing and the Union Jack flying high. I have a picture that Jo, my good friend from University, sent me of her two boys who had come along to watch "Auntie Katherine" racing. They had their faces painted in full Union Jacks and were having a fantastic day out until we crossed the line. Although they were too young to understand the significance of the result, they knew from the reaction around them that something bad had happened. And they started crying. Their mother Jo told me the result had ruined their day, and the photo shows the two boys with tears streaked through the red, white and blue face paint, the Union Jack slipping off their faces.

All four of us reacted differently to the news. Debbie felt utterly let down by the cheating. She has always done a lot for anti-doping projects, fighting to keep sport clean, and this was the ultimate betrayal by fellow athletes. When we later met the Russian team at various competitions she would coldly ignore the athletes. Fran felt robbed of the moment of winning in front of the home crowd but was also left with the sense that they may have cheated to beat us, but that was a race we should have won regardless. That the result was more because of something we had done or not done than because of what the Russians had done. I was desperately disappointed that people had brought drugs into our sport, tainting it. I was also angry that they had stolen that moment from us. Competing at home has a special pride to it, a real ownership of the event, and losing fair and square is one thing but to lose because of cheating leaves such a bad taste. However, I agreed with Fran that I felt we hadn't raced as well as we could have and it was actually our own performance that let us down, not the cheating. If we had raced to our full potential then we would have won regardless of how many of the Russians were taking testosterone, so in some ways the silver medal was what we did deserve. Sarah was hit with a deep sense of depression. She went into a very dark place and ultimately spoke to Dr Steve Peters to try to get help in sorting out her thoughts. The difficult thing is although the result is reversed and we were given the world title and history is changed on paper at least, these are all things that happen *to* you. It is a very passive process and we didn't actually do anything different. We didn't cross the line first. Someone telling you that you are now a World Champion doesn't mean much, as you don't cross the line first or feel you've earned that result. It's an underwhelming experience at best.

British Rowing did everything they could to improve the situation. About a week after we were told the news we had the GB Rowing Dinner. This is an annual event for the international squad and also partners, parents and supporters. David Tanner, our team manager, hands out certificates and framed pictures to medal-winning crews, and it is a general celebration of the team's success from Junior up to Senior. It is also very hierarchical and the gold medallists are kept until the end. The programmes were printed long in advance and on the programme we were still silver medallists. Our moment was left until the end of the awards and when summoned on stage David had a surprise for us. Aware we could never get our moment on the podium, he had done all he could to make this special for us. There was a drum roll and the National Anthem started. Then the room stood as new gold medals were brought in. GB Rowing and FISA had acted fast to secure the medals in time to award them at the dinner so as to make it something of an occasion for us. It was a highly emotional experience as a roomful of our peers sang the National Anthem and the medals were put around our necks. People knew what we'd been through, from the disappointment after the result to the months of soul-searching and debriefing, and on to the anger and emotion of the change in result. This was the team trying to help us through it all.

On a positive note the Russians gave us a gift they couldn't have foreseen. They gave us the urgency and the focus of a crew who believe they are second best in the world. Training as if you're second best is a common mantra for top athletes. It stops any complacency and keeps the hunger and desire there. Even if you are the best in the world it can help to feel more needs to be done in the relentless drive to improve. The Russians let us believe for the early part of the long winter that we were second best and needed to be better. To be fair, I felt the same regardless of the changed result, because on the day we did come second. But then we blazed through the second half of the winter as rightful World Champions, with renewed confidence and a sense of injustice that fuelled every session. We had been robbed of the moment and we would do everything to make sure that wouldn't happen again.

Unfortunately that spring Sarah once again suffered an incredibly ill-timed injury, tearing her cruciate ligament in the gym. It would mean time out of the boat and she wouldn't be able to race in the quad that summer. Debbie, Fran and I continued and were joined by Annie Vernon, the young athlete from Cambridge who had made her debut with us in the Eights Head of the River back in 2004. Since then she had competed in the single scull at the Japan World Championships and the double with

Anna Watkins in Dorney, narrowly missing out on a medal. She stepped into the quad and straight away felt part of the team. She was joining a highly charged boat with athletes who were out to prove a point.

In the lead-up to the 2007 World Championships I had a small scare with my back. There was a slight recurrence of the problem I had suffered in Milan, and this time the medical team leapt on the first signs. I was held back at the beginning of the summer camps when the others flew out to Germany. For a while Annie had to sit in the stroke seat and they temporarily used other rowers in my place. Thanks to the skill and experience of Dr Ann Redgrave and consultant Keith Bush, I made it back in time for the end of the training camp. But it was mentally tough joining the crew again just before the World Championships, as there was a sense of having missed a lot of their preparation and not feeling a part of the process any more. When I returned in the boat I suddenly doubted my role – I wasn't sure if I could be as vocal or give an opinion when I hadn't been a part of the crew in the most recent part of the journey. I was in a different seat and taking on a different role. I was also keeping an eye on my back and making sure it was coping with the increase in intensity as racing approached. The boat was performing well at speed, however, and we unofficially broke the world record in a training piece.

I spoke to Annie when we moved to Italy as she seemed to be struggling too. Although awkward at my request to chat at the bar, she was open about not being particularly comfortable in the stroke seat, and also she had her own personal battles going on as her grandfather was very ill at home and her thoughts were there. She didn't want to leave the camp to go home, but she also didn't want to cut herself off from her family and what they were going through. I hadn't been aware of her personal problems, although I had been aware she wasn't happy. Talking to Annie was a good reminder that everyone you deal with will be fighting their own internal battles, so there should always be as much understanding shown as possible in every situation.

A few days later I felt it was time to talk to Thommo about moving the seating back to normal. I said I felt ready physically and mentally to return to the stroke seat, which I thought had always been the plan. He surprised me with his reaction. He asked why I felt I would go back in that seat at all. He said that the boat had been going well as it was. Why should I feel I would be the best person in that seat? Having won the past two World Championships in that seat I felt I was in a good place to argue, but I didn't. I felt a horribly familiar feeling that once again he didn't rate me, and he didn't value my input. Chris Shambrook joined us at the table to be met by me standing up and snapping to Thommo, "Well, one day maybe I'll be able to impress you in some tiny way and you'll actually believe in me." I turned on my heel (or would have if I'd been wearing them) and marched inside. A few steps later I realized I had left my flip-flops under the table. It had been a satisfyingly dramatic exit and now I had to go back. It wasn't the coolest entrance as I walked back in. Thommo half stood up to say something, but I shook my head and gestured to my flip-flops and strode back out.

Thommo later found me to explain that he did value me and he had thought he was facing the first World Championships without me and he was actually sad about that. It was the first admission of the incredible journey we had been on together and I was touched by his words. We had been bonded since his arrival by the joint goal of winning but over time we had also developed a deep, personal respect for each other, albeit one we rarely voiced. I stated again I was ready for the stroke seat but accepted it would be his decision. We continued with the crew as it was, with Annie as stroke, and then moved to Munich for the World Championships. We won the heat, although it wasn't a comfortable win and the Germans pushed us hard to the line. The next day we met at the boat and the seating order was changed. I would go back into the stroke seat and Annie would be in the bow seat. We spent the next few days settling the crew back and then gearing it up for the final. I know Annie struggled through that time with me and with the change in seat. Although she was happier with the more familiar bow seat, she was disappointed not to have the opportunity to race in the stroke seat for the final. It was an impressive trait that Annie wanted to put more pressure on herself while dealing with so much else at the same time. In training Fran sat behind me and reminded me I didn't need to be trying as hard as I was every stroke. I hadn't realized it, but I was feeling as if I had to do everything perfectly and not make any mistakes or let anyone down. It was as if I was back at the beginning of my career again. But I was adding unnecessary tension.

The focus then fell on the final, and it wasn't about who was sitting where any more, it was about defending our world title and proving to everyone that we were rightful winners of the title and no one, especially not drug cheats, would stop us.

Debbie had missed out on her first gold medal podium moment the previous year; Fran and I had experienced it in Japan but missed out on the rare home crowd podium; and Annie had never won a world title before but was now a key player in this one. The race was ours for so many important reasons. Our warm-up was determined and dominant. Fran was a little concerned about the intensity, but one of the umpires in the launches later spoke to me and said he saw from our warm-up that we were going to do something special. I remember sitting on the startline daring the traffic light to flip to green. I wanted to be out and racing. I wanted to show how good we were. I wanted to put the Dorney World Championships behind us, the drugs scandal behind us, my back injury behind us, the frustration of the past 12 months behind us.

We flew from the start and destroyed the field early on. Pure and simple ruthless devastation was our aim – we were interested in nothing else. There could only be one result in this race and we were going to be sure of it. We had the mistakes of the previous year to put right. If I had to choose one word to describe the attitude it would be defiance. We won convincingly, and when we climbed out of the boat at the end the release of feeling was liberating. Debbie, Fran and I had reclaimed our title and showed we had what it took to own the title of World Champion. Annie had matched our skill and experience and succeeded in the face of a weighty personal burden and threatening grief to win her first world title. Thommo and David met us by the podium and were both quite emotional. I spared a thought for Sarah, the fifth person in the boat, who sadly didn't get a chance to avenge the previous year and was still recovering from her knee operation at home.

Our quad were named as the FISA international crew of the year, an award that Cath and I had been nominated for in 2003 but no British women's crew had ever won. And so there was a sense that for at least some of us the world order had been restored as we entered the Olympic year. The year in which perhaps at long last there would be a much sought-after and long-awaited British women's rowing gold medal.

The four-year journey along the golden pathway was on track. It had been a rollercoaster ride but between us we had managed to win three World Championships back to back and there was the confidence and expectation that an Olympic gold was the next step. The general feeling in the squad was upbeat. Most of the team had had a great Championships in Munich and there were British medals in many boat classes as well as Olympic qualification.

The signs had been there early. The pre-Worlds camp in Italy, although having stressful moments for our quad, had been in general one of the most enjoyable and entertaining camps leading up to a major Championships. As it was the 30th anniversary of Elvis Presley's death, Thommo suggested we had an Elvis night. The team responded with the unashamed enthusiasm of prisoners in solitary confinement suddenly getting an offer of a day trip to the carnival. Quiffs were created with hairspray and back-combing, tracksuit bottoms were worn inside out with the lower bits unzipped to create white flairs, songs were cannibalized and dances invented. Thanks to Darren Whiter, the outstanding lightweight men's coach and unofficial team photographer, we even had a huge wall-filling picture of Elvis in his *Viva Las Vegas* days wearing a garland of flowers, but his face had been replaced by David Tanner's face. Anyone who has met David would agree it was an incongruous image, but it looked hilarious and even David saw the funny side. The team was proof that having a serious job to do didn't mean having to take ourselves seriously all the time. I don't think it was a coincidence that from such a positive fun camp we went on to have one of the most successful World Championship regattas.

The bigger team would mean that selection for the Olympic squad would be tougher than ever and Thommo had hard decisions to make with regard to our quad. Fran, Debbie, Annie and I were current World Champions, Sarah was now back from her injury and fighting to reclaim her place, while Anna and Elise had shown their potential in the double with their close bronze medal in Munich. It was decided early on that Annie, Fran and I would be back in the quad and the final seat would be between Debbie and Sarah. Thommo agonized over it and when seat racing proved inconclusive he had to make a decision. Results to date appeared to show Debbie would be stronger in the first half of the race, while Sarah's strengths were over the longer distance. After a long run around the lake in Italy, Thommo made his decision. With arguments on both sides and no clear answer he chose to go with Debbie, who was the current World Champion. Thommo wanted us to race in the style we had in Munich, coming out fast and dictating the race from the front. The decision was great news for Debbie but devastating for Sarah.

The Beijing Olympics were to hold every emotion possible for all members of the rowing team. There would be tears of joy and tears of heart-wrenching disappointment, with grief, illness and injury all playing a part. The biggest sporting spectacle on the planet would once again show more than mere winners and losers. The Olympics would highlight human endeavour and drama at its extreme. It promised intrigue, breathtaking moments of unparalleled achievement, sacrifice and loyalty, envy and frustration, passion and hope. Whatever might unfold, it would never be dull.

China also wanted to showcase their country on this very visible and global stage. There had been some controversy over whether the Olympic Games should even go to China, with their questionable human rights policies. As competing athletes we were trained in how to answer potentially tricky questions, the kind that are usually reserved for politicians, over sensitive areas of discussion. But whatever the rest of the world thought, China was ready to put on a show.

The Opening Ceremony showed what we might be in for. Every Olympic Games has its own feel, its own DNA somehow stamped through it. Sydney had been the fun Games, and after that people wondered how on earth Athens could possibly follow such a display of entertainment. With Greg Norman, Elle McPherson, Kylie Minogue and Olivia Newton John all being showcased in Australia, where would the big name celebrities and camp entertainment come from for Athens? But Greece followed with the most sensational yet simple display. They needed nothing more than to remind people that Greece, and Athens specifically, was the birthplace of the modern Olympics. They used the original Ancient Greek stadium to host the archery, they used the route from the ancient town of Marathon for the marathon. As an athlete, to go to the home of the Olympics, where it all began, was magical. And although Athens was so far behind schedule that roads were still being built around us, trees hurriedly planted and venues finished off when competitions had already started, it felt as if the Olympics had come home.

In contrast China left nothing to chance. Everything would be perfect, no expense spared. It would be a spectacular showcase. The Opening Ceremony, held in the beautiful Bird's Nest Stadium, would begin at precisely 8pm on the 8th day of the 8th month in 2008 to celebrate China's lucky number. One of the most memorable moments of the Opening Ceremony was when 2,008 perfectly synchronized drummers beat in time. Visually it was stunning. The Chinese drive for perfection was highlighted with a minor scandal when it was disclosed that the beautiful young girl who sang in the Opening Ceremony was in fact lip-synching to a recorded track sung by another young girl, who was considered to have a better voice but was thought less photogenic.

Rather than staying in the Olympic Village we once again stayed in a hotel near to the rowing lake. There were rumours that the hotel was bugged, and rooms and shared areas were being monitored and listened to. This led to team meetings often being held outside or even during walks around the complex. I'm not sure how much truth there was in the stories, but we were certainly aware of people sitting at the end of each corridor and watching the comings and goings. Whether this was merely security or something more sinister we'll never know.

The greatest threat to us at the regatta would come from China itself. Germany had an impressive crew but hadn't made a strong impact that summer. China had put out an impressive new quad and they brought in a new stroke for the Olympics, so we would be racing against an unknown boat. As a result of the seeding we wouldn't meet the Chinese crew until the final. I felt confident, as our own boat had been going well in training. I knew the final would be a blazing battle, but that's what we had trained for. The Olympics should demand everything you have, offering a chance to bring out all the benefits of the exhausting days, hours, weeks and years behind us. Now was the time. In our heat we broke the Olympic record. In their heat the Chinese crew broke the record by a bit more. Everything was set up for the final showdown. The unknown Chinese crew would be racing in front of their home crowd and the pride of their nation. The British challengers were carrying the hopes of history with them and were here to finish off the four-year journey.

We met with Steve Redgrave during the racing week and by the end of his talk with us I was very emotional. The Olympics is a time when sensitivities are heightened and emotions overflow. I remember being in the hotel in Athens and seeing James Cracknell brush past us with tears in his eyes after his crew had been chatting outside. It is not unusual to see the biggest, toughest, hardest of athletes welling up. As well as the usual crew meetings we had before the race, Thommo arranged individual meetings. One at a time we were asked to come to his room, and he sat us down and told us personal inspiring messages. It was powerful, and whereas in Athens I had been unprepared to hear it, this time I soaked it up, and felt myself growing a little taller for his welcome words.

The night before the race we had a final outing under the heavy Beijing skies. As we came in to the landing stage I sat for a few seconds looking down the course towards the startline and under my breath whispered, "We're ready." Fran leaned forward and put a reassuring hand on my shoulder. "Are you all right?" I turned around smiling. "Yes, yes I am." I meant it. We were ready, the boat felt good and we were well prepared. All the lessons we had learned over the past four years, all the minute detail we had worked on, the changes and improvements we had made. Everything had built to this moment. We had accepted nothing less than our best in the relentless pursuit of the gold.

The day of the Olympic final arrived and I wondered how on earth I could use all our knowledge, all my experience, all the help everyone had provided, all the support friends and family had given us; how I could fit all of that into a six-minute race. The race happened fast. We had the start we wanted, we leapt out and dominated the field. We were still leading as we came into the grandstand area, with the loud banging drums of the schoolchildren. In the last few hundred metres, the area where we said if we were leading no one would be able to beat us because we wanted it so much, the Chinese mounted a sprint for the finish we couldn't match. I could see the crew approaching and yet we weren't able to respond. We tried everything and still they came, then drew level, then started to move ahead. The tension grew in our boat as we realized we were running out of time. We tried desperately to raise our speed again but they had the momentum and were moving away. It was close but, as we approached the finish line, I heard the beep of the finish tower and knew it wasn't for us. Our boat crossed the line next and through all the physical pain, the lung-searing gasps for air, the burning legs and aching bodies, through all of that the one thing that pierced like a knife was the awareness that we had come second. That we had lost.

My next thought was an instinctive "What can we do better next time?" – because up until that point every race we did, every bit of timed work, whether we won or we lost, was with a view to making it better for the Olympic final. So my reaction was automatically about how we could improve for next time. That thought had become second nature to me, but then I was suddenly hit by the realization that there would be no next time. My head went down as my mind tried to take in the fact that it was over. With the noise of the Chinese celebrations all around us it began to sink in that our own dreams were finished. We would leave them unfulfilled on the Chinese rowing lake. We slowly limped our way over to the side where the BBC and various other media would be waiting. As we got out of the boat to give each other heartfelt and tearful hugs Debbie collapsed on to the floor. She lay on her back sobbing and gasping for air, inconsolable in her disappointment. Fran went to her but Debbie was unable to move to begin with.

We walked falteringly towards the media area with Steve Redgrave and John Inverdale. They were looking at us with a mixture of concern and sympathy. Debbie was being supported by Annie and Fran, heads were down, and they were unable to speak. John put the microphone towards me. There was nothing to say, nothing that could sum up the emotion, the disappointment, the loss. I felt in that moment that I had let people down – my crewmates, my coach, my team, my friends, family and supporters. I felt it was a race we could have won and therefore there must have been something I could have done differently. John asked about having won silver again and I shrugged, saying something about "always the bridesmaid never the bride".

The medals were given out in front of a jubilant Chinese media who took up the majority of the stand facing the podium. There was no sign of my family in front of us, they were in a grandstand to the side, but I did see Rachel Woolf, who has an uncanny ability to talk her way into areas where she shouldn't be. I found her face in the crowd and she gave me a sad smile while holding her hand to her heart and then clenching her fist. I knew what she meant, she was still proud and she was willing me on with strength. I nodded and kept my head up as the tears rolled. Fran put her arm around me in a protective manner.

At the press conference later few questions were asked of us, the main focus being on the new Olympic champions. I was finally allowed to leave and I walked outside to see my mum and dad. They had experienced their own hell, having a TV camera record them watching the race live. For most of the race the camera captured nervous, excited, happy parents. For the last few hundred metres they captured my mum's reaction turning to utter sadness as she watched her daughter losing out on her dream. I am very aware that my family will always love me just as much if I come first or last in any race, but as all parents do, my mum and dad just want me to be happy, and here they were witnessing my world falling down around me. There were media all around after our press conference but I pushed past them to reach my mum. We embraced for a long time and to their absolute credit the British media melted away, respectful of this personal moment. Not one of the journalists there used that scene in any of the reports of the race, and the only mention was when one wrote an editorial explaining exactly why they didn't want to intrude.

As we hugged and cried my mum whispered something in my ear. It wasn't a general platitude or reassurance. She simply said, "Promise me you'll be in London. You'll do it, I know you will. " Although I was nowhere near making a decision at that point, it stayed with me. That unfailing confidence and support is priceless. My mum has always been a steadying hand through the roughest seas.

I was selected yet again for drug testing but this time welcomed having a quiet moment alone and away from the crazy Olympic world. While still partially numb about our own result I thought about the others. Jurgen had once again produced a brilliant gold medal winning four that had crushed the Australian boat in the final stages of the race. Darren Whiter had masterfully brought together the abilities of Zac Puchase and Mark Hunter to create history with the first British lightweight Olympic Champions in the double scull. Of the women, Miles had coached Anna and Elise in the double scull coming the closest in time to the elusive gold medal. They had had a challenging year of their own and began the Olympics unaware of their potential and with little confidence in their abilities. In an almost opposite reflection of our race, they didn't make an impact in the first half of the race but towards the end they found their belief and almost caused the upset of the regatta in the tightest of finishes. The New Zealand double crossed the line ahead, leading for only one stroke of the race, but it was the only stroke that mattered, the very last one. They narrowly beat the brave German double who had attacked the race from the beginning and led the entire way, only to be beaten in the last stroke. The poor women's eight had been decimated with illness and their early promise faded with their diminishing numbers. Sarah had ended up racing the eight and although she loved her time with the boat, the fifth-place finish was disappointing for all of them. As a team, the eight had shown fight in frustrating circumstances, the double had displayed a clinical focus, and our quad had shown a passionate belief. Between the boats the ingredients were right but individually we still hadn't achieved what we wanted and no one had got it completely right.

It's a strange moment walking back into the hotel room that you last saw before the Olympic final. Only a few hours may have passed, but somehow everything had changed. In Beijing, the room Fran and I shared had been full of nerves but also full of hope. Over the previous days there was a lot of filling in time while the weight of expectation increased. Now the room felt sad and empty. The cards and decorations seemed pointless and were now painful reminders of a time when hope was still there. I pulled open the drawer by my bed. In it I had a few cards still to open. Two were from Jeff Willmore. Jeff has been a supporter of rowing since 2000 when, as a good friend of Tim Foster, he helped to organise the victorious homecoming of the men's four after their Sydney victory. He had also driven Sarah and me to the airport for training camps more often than I could possibly remember. I looked at the cards. They were the same sized square white envelopes but there was a world of difference between them. One was to be opened if we won; the other if we didn't. I lifted the appropriate one out and opened it. Jeff had simply written, 'You are a fantastic person and I am proud of you'. I looked down at the unopened envelope. I couldn't help myself; I had to open it. I wanted to see what message of exuberant congratulations would have awaited me if we had won. The picture on the card was exactly the same as the 'losing' card: a beautiful snow capped mountain. The writing on the inside surprised me. The message was simple: 'You are a fantastic person and I am proud of you.' It was a comfort to know that for true friends, whatever the result, I would still be the same person.

The next week I managed to put the grief mainly to one side and immerse myself in other aspects of the Olympic Games, grateful to be distracted by other events. Now transformed from competitors to enthusiastic Team GB spectators and supporters, Sarah, Beth and I started the second week of the Olympics sitting in the baking sun watching the British women's hockey team. I managed to get into the incredible "water cube" building that was the swimming venue and watch the synchronized swimming. While I was there I overheard a coach discussing an athlete who on the previous day had passed out while training underwater. The coach then said, without a hint of irony, "Y'see, that's commitment for you" – suddenly I thought Thommo's training wasn't so bad. I spent many a day at the spectacular athletics stadium. There I met Denise Lewis, the heptathlon Olympic Champion from 2000 and someone who had become a friend when we did *Superstars* together in 2004. She always has a twinkle in her eye and is great with a hug. She knew I would be devastated with my silver and as we embraced she said, "Well, girl, you still have London 2012 to aim for." I looked at her and admitted I didn't know if I wanted to do it. Denise smiled at me. "I would give anything to be there. A home Olympics? Home crowd? Now that is a once in a lifetime thing. My poor body wouldn't make it again for the heptathlon. But maybe I could try another event …" Her enthusiasm was wonderfully infectious, but it was still too close to think seriously about things.

Once we left the rowing lake there wasn't too much media to do, although I do remember being called into GB headquarters to do a phone interview with one of the written press. I was still raw and not very keen to talk through the disappointment again. Miriam Wilkens, the head of BOA communications, welcomed me at the door with an apologetic look. "I'm sorry about this, Katherine." Her sensitivity and kindness nearly set me off again and she ushered me to a desk in the corner of the busy and buzzing BOA offices. A hush fell as I took my seat and awaited the call, and I was painfully aware of the silence and murmuring voices as I talked through the loss once again. There were a couple of moments when I was aware of my unsteady voice and I had to clear my throat and breathe deeply, but I finished the call without losing the plot completely. But it was painful to relive our final once again and I turned my chair to face out of the window and away from the rest of the staff. Tears were flowing down my face as I saw Shanaze Reade, the British BMX athlete, coming into the Village. She had just lost her final, and although favourite for a medal, and possibly the gold, she had literally crashed out in her attempt to win, finishing with nothing except for a very bruised and battered body. I watched her being helped along the path, looking as if she had been severely beaten up and every step was torture. In the following days Karina Bryant, the judo player who herself missed out on a podium finish at the Games, would be seen pushing Shanaze around in a wheelchair. I thought yet again what a crazy life we lead.

I bumped into Chris Hoy in the Olympic Village dining hall. It was shortly after his magnificent three gold medals in the velodrome but before his knighthood. Chris is one of the good guys, a genuinely lovely big-hearted man who happens also to be a sensational cyclist and one of the most driven and committed athletes you'll meet. I congratulated him on his incredible achievements and he modestly shrugged, smiled almost shyly and said, "I did OK." He said how sorry he was that I hadn't achieved what I'd wanted. A few weeks later we'd meet again on top of a bus going through the streets of Edinburgh as Scotland celebrated its Olympic medallists. Considering Chris had returned with three historic gold medals and Edinburgh was his home city, it was no surprise when the vast majority of the cheers, waves and banners were for him. The rest of us melted into the background slightly, still waving from the bus but a respectful step behind Chris. As we were coming down the Royal Mile to amazing crowds I heard a voice shout "Katherine? Katherine!" I leaned forward over the top deck to see my fan. A man stood there with a big smile and a shrug. "Maybe next time, Katherine." I laughed and waved; it seemed the only thing to do.

By the end of the Beijing Olmpics, the British team had broken records with the medal success. There was a jubilant mood as we filled the buses to go to the Closing Ceremony. The Chinese were about to end their time as hosts and pass the honour over to Great Britain. David Beckham, Leona Lewis and a big red bus showed the world that the next stop for the Olympic cavalcade would be London. The Mayor of London, Boris Johnson, took the Olympic flag and waved it dangerously to roars of approval from the British team. We all gathered back at the Village outside Team GB headquarters. Once the Olympic flag has been handed over and the flame extinguished, the Olympics is officially over and so the blanket ban on alcohol in the Village is lifted. The British team brought in beer and wine and the celebrations continued. It was a balmy night and we carried furniture from the flats out on to the grassy areas in front of the apartment blocks. It was a wonderful night with a very bohemian feel. Athletes, coaches, support staff and members of the British Olympic Association all sat outside, drink in hand, laughing, joking, reminiscing and sharing stories. Once again irrespective of results people relaxed in each other's company. And for me it felt like the last night before having to fly home and go back into the real world.

At various points through the night someone was playing bongo drums that had appeared from somewhere, human pyramids were formed (usually with the rowers forming the base layer and the gymnasts at the top), trips were made to the dining hall to bring back vast bags of chips, and kit was swapped. Sarah had an unnerving talent for kit swapping, having few inhibitions and a friendly demeanour which was hard to say no to. Within about an hour of coming back from the stadium at the end of the ceremony, Sarah was wearing bright red-and-white patterned Canadian trousers (impressively exchanged with a Canadian guy for her navy GB skirt), one Canadian and one USA shoe (she convinced them it was helping world peace by sharing half of a pair of shoes), a striking cream-and-brown straw hat from Colombia, and a brightly coloured Chinese volunteer's shirt (the poor Chinese man she approached stood no chance as she towered over him pointing to his chest), and she was carrying bright green South African crocs. Jess from the eight was keen to "find something Jamaican" and approached Sarah for advice. With a gleam in her eye and a wicked smile on her face Sarah flung an arm around Jess and marched her off into the night. Shortly afterwards Jess returned sporting a big bright yellow-and-green top rumoured to have belonged to one Usain Bolt.

About an hour before we were due to meet for the long flight home I decided to try to get a nap. I went up to our room, but within minutes

Annie, whom I was sharing with, arrived. She decided now was the time we could have a "proper chat", and although I protested and said I wanted just a few minutes' sleep, Annie insisted we didn't need sleep. We chatted for about 40 minutes, both a little the worse for wear from the beer and wine, and then having given up on the idea of sleep I ran up to the dining hall to grab some breakfast. When I returned about 15 minutes later I found Annie fast asleep – and she didn't have to get up for hours as she was staying on in China with her brother and friends. Annie was in her fourth international year. In that time she had raced the single, finished fourth in the double, become a World Champion and an Olympic silver medallist in the quad – far better results than I had achieved in my first four years. But here she was, just as upset by the result as any of us, feeling like a failure. Whereas I had had the unbelievable joy of my first Olympic medal in Sydney, she stood on the podium in tears with her first Olympic medal around her neck. It is to Annie's massive credit that winning a silver medal at her first Olympics was a disappointment, our joint high expectations robbing her of any deserved celebration. It was sad and wrong and something I couldn't change. Leaving her sleeping, I quietly gathered my various bags of Olympic paraphernalia and headed for the door.

CHAPTER 9

TAPPING INTO PHOEBE

The pain of Beijing didn't fade or ebb. It wasn't like anything I'd experienced before. The pain continued at an unpleasant level for months. When I first flew back with the team there was a heroes' welcome and crowds were at the airport to cheer and applaud the British team on their triumphant return. We were all transferred to a nearby hotel, where there was a wonderful spread of food laid out for us and a beautiful lounge area spilling out on to a garden where various families and friends had come to meet their loved ones. My family had stayed on in China to try to enjoy a holiday, and I was quite happy to have a low-key return. At the hotel there was a delay getting the bags from Heathrow. The prolonged waiting time proved awkward as a number of athletes continued their celebrations with their families while others repeatedly looked at their watches wondering when they could leave this place. For some it was time to move on with their lives or go somewhere private to lick their wounds.

I was there with my desperately disappointing silver medal and I overheard a bronze medallist talking to her mum. Their combined sense of pride and utter elation was a stark reminder to me of just how much individual expectations affect the emotion you feel about your result. Being a member of the Olympic team is an incredible achievement; making it to an Olympic final is a rare and wonderful moment – and then winning an Olympic medal is a case of dreams coming true. If, however, any of these things are on a different level from what you were aiming for, then what should have been sheer joy and immense satisfaction is not only diminished but can be cruelly and unstoppably replaced by a crushing sense of failure.

For the months following my return to Britain I felt as though I was experiencing grief. On the days when things didn't seem so bad I could see people, do other things, but then invariably, out of the blue, a wave of realization would strike and immediately I'd be almost breathless with an overwhelming sense of despair. The chance was gone, the moment, the opportunity, the goal we had been aiming for and living with and training towards was over. We had it in the palm of our hands and it had slipped through our fingers. And I had the horrific sense of letting people down. Many of my family, my friends, and lots of people who had helped and supported me over the years in my quest for gold had flown out to Beijing in the belief of a golden ending. I could only think what a waste of money it must have been for them.

Of course no one said as much, and no one even gave the vaguest impression they felt that way, but that didn't stop me torturing myself with such thoughts. In the months leading up to the summer, the Olympics was all anyone talked about and now while the massive shadow of the Games remained it was much harder for anyone to know what to say. Everyone was incredibly supportive, kind, generous, positive, encouraging, proud, but no one could put it right or make it better for me. I couldn't do that for myself.

I met friends, Sally and Phil Tinsley, in Marlow for a drink. Phil had been involved in rowing long before I joined the team. He was one of the boatmen when I started, the invaluable and endlessly patient team who look after our equipment, move our boats around and generally make our lives a bit easier. Phil was quick with a disappointed sigh or a gentle scolding during boat-loading days when invariably, despite all our best intentions, we would manage to put the wrong boats on the wrong trailer racks and destroy Phil's carefully thought out trailer plan. It wasn't only Phil who experienced this. When he left, Maurice and John also found that it was a requirement of the job to be long-suffering and very patient. As quick as Phil was with a dry remark, however, he was even quicker with a hug or reassuring shoulder to cry on. Phil was the one to escort Kate back home when she had to leave Varese early and he comforted Cath when she was ill and couldn't race in Aiguebelette. He was there in Beijing for me when there were no words to say. When I met them in Marlow over a glass of wine I said something about losing and Sally instantly corrected me with a pained look, saying, "But you didn't lose, you won a silver medal. At the Olympics. It is a wonderful thing" and I winced and said, "But it's not. It's not what I wanted. What we wanted. So it is a failure." We failed in what we wanted to do, what we thought we were capable of achieving and for an athlete to leave a race thinking there was something more they must have been able to do is a horrible place. If you leave knowing there wasn't anything more to do, then you can live with yourself. But to feel that somehow we should have found an answer was the unbearable part. And it was the hardest thing to express to people. Sally, like many people, was desperate to fix it, to help me see it objectively as the great result it was, but I simply couldn't. She became tearful as she struggled with the frustration of seeing me in pain and not being able to get through to me the positives of the situation.

Of course there's a complex mix of emotions. On one hand I was painfully aware that it wasn't the end of the world. That at the end of the day we still won an Olympic medal. That no one died. That every day everywhere people are living through worse experiences and actually what we had done was a fantastic accomplishment in many people's eyes. But there is no perspective in the aftermath, and something did die that day in Beijing. It was not flesh and blood but it was a dream and one we had been living for years. And yet in the wake of a successful Olympics the disappointment and despair was not what people wanted to hear about. It was self-indulgent to be upset about winning a medal at the Olympics. And if indeed it had been a choice I would have chosen to feel fine about it; I would have been able to brush it off, look at my silver medal with pride and thrust my shoulders back, facing up to the next challenge. That's what we're supposed to do. Learn from mistakes, know that life goes on and look forward not backward. Focus on when we can put it right. The painful truth of the Olympics is that it'll be four years until you get another chance to fix it, if at all.

I went to the usual post-Olympic events. There were parades, trips to Buckingham Palace, to Downing Street, awards, dinners, lunches, talks to clubs, to schools, universities, charities etc. And some were wonderful, some difficult, some painful, all a reminder of the result.

One lunch we went to was with our sponsor, and I was at a table of about eight of us. There were two Olympic champions sitting near to me, along with a few directors. As the lunch went on I was still a bit fragile when talking about the racing, but aware that I couldn't continue to bring people into my own misery. So I smiled and chatted and enthused about the wonderful summer of sport which it had indeed been. In Beijing I had managed to watch a lot of the other events in the second week and I could appreciate how wonderful the biggest multi-sport event on earth was. But inevitably, and understandably, the people wanted to hear about our own personal experiences. One of the directors turned to the athlete sitting next to him and asked what it was like to win the Olympics. I smiled as he recounted at length the sense of pride and relief. And satisfaction. And happiness. And contentment. The smile stayed on my face as I listened to the words I longed to be speaking for myself. Finally the answer was completed and I breathed again.

At that point the same director turned to the other guy and said, "So was it the same for you?" I knew the guys well and was so proud of them and happy for their fantastic success, but it was still hard to hear the details of that wonderful moment. I took an avid interest in my meal and pushed food around my plate as he said, "Well no, actually, for me it was the sense that we'd achieved what we should have, that we met our potential, that we didn't let anyone down ..." I dug a nail into my palm and waited for the physical pain to overtake the emotion. It wasn't my place to be upset and I certainly didn't want to draw any attention, but the words were tapping into every insecurity I had after our loss. After a while I realized the conversation had ebbed and I looked up to see the director smiling sympathetically at me. He tilted his head to one side and said in a soft voice, "It probably wasn't the same for you." "No," I managed. He followed up with "But we're so proud of you too" in a sorrowful way. I smiled and nodded, unable to say anything, and turned back to my lunch, for which I had no appetite.

One of the last events I went to that summer was also one of the worst. The other girls from the quad were there too, and as we arrived in London and walked towards the restaurant we bumped into a woman, whom none of us knew well, called Rebecca, who although not a journalist did some work on a rowing website. She stopped us and said she had asked readers of the website to email in questions for the Olympic rowers as she knew she'd be seeing us that day. She then handed us an A4 sheet of paper with the typed-out questions on and said we could email her directly if we wanted with the answers. With that she smiled and breezed off towards the lunch. Innocently we looked at the sheet to see what the public had wanted to know. The first question I remember vividly. "Can you ask the women's quad how it feels to have wasted four years of their lives?" I blinked and reread it. Was I being sensitive again? The next few were in a similar vein – suggesting we had let people down by showing emotion on the Olympic podium rather than keeping a stiff upper lip, and questioning how we thought we could win when we technically had the faults of schoolgirls. We walked into the lunch and I went into the toilets still clutching the piece of paper.

One of the BBC producers, Sally Richardson, who had worked with the rowing team was in there. "Are you all right?" she asked as I walked unsteadily towards her. "I don't know," I replied and lifted the paper. "I've just been given this and I don't know how to take it. Maybe I'm being too sensitive." She didn't say a word but gently took the paper from me and started to read. She glanced up at me, looked down to finish reading and then gradually raised her head. Her voice was low and calm but there was a firmness to her tone. "Who gave you this?" I gestured to the door: "A woman who runs a website." She shook her head slowly and said I shouldn't reply to the questions, certainly not in their current form. If names and details had been supplied then we could consider talking to the people directly, but we should not feel obliged in any way. Sally also apologized on behalf of everyone in journalism for the fact we'd been given the unedited piece of paper in the first place. In her mind it was unprofessional and thoughtless. Thankfully this was a very rare occurrence as all our regular rowing and sports correspondents were incredibly supportive and understanding in the aftermath of our loss.

I never did reply to those questions, and the talk from Sally reassured me that I wasn't going crazy. As time went on I wondered what the person who had asked that question had achieved in their four years over that same period – three World Champion titles and a silver medal at the Olympic Games isn't what I'd call a wasted four years, but then, I suppose, everyone's different. As for showing sentiment on the podium, I know that four years on at the London Olympics the whole nation was brought to its knees with emotion. For weeks over the summer there were tears as the Olympians and Paralympians won and lost and strived and inspired and battled in the arena. Never once did I hear anyone saying that there should be more stiff upper lips. As a nation I think we brilliantly embraced the human spirit in all its forms and we celebrated strength and vulnerability and passion in a way we hadn't before. Yes, there were tears on the podium back at Beijing, but it was the honest emotion of four heartbroken girls who had lost their dreams just a few short minutes beforehand. It was certainly nothing I will ever be ashamed of.

I left for a much-needed holiday and went to the wilds of South Africa and Namibia. It was the perfect trip for me at the perfect time. In the previous few months I had experienced exhaustion, pressure, tension, failure, loss and heartbreak. I also knew I had lost perspective and the ability to see and think clearly and rationally. In Africa I slowly began to relax, to unwind and to regain a sense of serenity. I waited by watering holes as herds of elephants lumbered towards the water to bathe together and spray each other with their dextrous trunks. Their close bond and playfulness was stunning to see, especially from such massive animals. I watched lions patiently teaching their young how to stalk prey and cubs chasing each other in mock fights when their parents weren't watching. I laughed at the ridiculousness of a giraffe splaying its impossibly long legs in order to drink from the side of a lake. I was spellbound as a group of meerkats emerged from a hole in the ground and sat alert on their back legs cocking their heads and listening to all around them. The leopards played hard to get, but the hyenas, rhinos, buffalos, vultures, warthogs, zebras and eagles made up for them. Here was a place where medals and sports results meant nothing and it was a healthy thing to experience. Walking across the breathtaking endless red sands of Namibia I knew it was all going to be OK.

By the time I came back I was ready to make the decision that I had probably made a long time ago. I wasn't finished with rowing, I wanted to get more and I wanted to give more. I still loved it and I still felt I had more to learn and I could be better. I also, with the faint reminder of that website question, had to be sure that in four years' time, regardless of the result, I wouldn't feel it was four years wasted. There would be a lot of hard work with no guarantee of a happy ending. It had to be about enjoying the daily challenge and the company, rather than clinging on just to see if I could win gold. Without question that goal would be the driving force, but I had to buy into the entire four-year journey and not just one day in August 2012. So with a stronger heart and a happier soul I returned.

Although I had committed to returning to the squad I spent most of the weeks before Christmas training in my own time to allow for a bit more flexibility. There was a big training camp in Australia in January, and that would be my return to the squad. But I hadn't done as much training as I would have liked to by the time the Christmas holidays rolled around. So I decided that I would use the holidays for an intensive training break and make up for the ground lost in the post-Olympics carnival. It seemed like a great plan until at the beginning of the holidays I picked up a nasty cold. I am generally lucky in that I rarely get ill, but I had been warned about what could happen after the crazy intensity of the past few months, that it is often when everything finally slows down that you become vulnerable to illness. It's amazing how many athletes will get ill at the beginning of the holidays – as if somehow the body finds a way to survive through the training, the racing, the lack of sleep, the other demands, but when those demands slacken off it relaxes and lets other things take over. So now I was ill. I phoned Rachel, who had retired in 2000 from the rowing team. "OK, Rachel, this is the problem – do I train to try to get my fitness up but risk not getting well, or do I not train, to make sure I'm over my illness, but risk not being fit?" There was hardly any hesitation from the other end of the phone. "No question, Katherine. You need to rest and recover. You cannot afford to go out on camp if you're not well."

So when I met the team at the airport, I was almost fully well but certainly not fully fit. It was a daunting proposition. The camp was going to be based in Sydney and Canberra. The first part was a mixture of cycling and ergos around Penrith. This was the site of the rowing competition at the 2000 Olympics, and I hadn't been back to the lake since the day we won the silver. Although the thought of the training was a concern, the idea of seeing Penrith again was exciting. We wouldn't be rowing on the lake but we would cycle to the course. On the first day I was cycling with a group of the girls who were asking about the Sydney Games. I looked around and said, "Of course, none of you were there." Annie, cycling next to me, said drily, "Katherine, we weren't even in Athens." I looked across to laugh and then realized she was right. Could they really be that new and young?

The ergos I just about got away with – although my scores weren't great. I was saved by the fact that everyone was struggling with the combination of time difference, jet lag and change in heat, so my lack of fitness wasn't as obvious as it could have been. The cycling, however, was tough, though – many of the team had fast new lightweight speed machines and flew past seemingly powered by an industrial engine. They attacked steep hills as if the incline were a mere rise in the road and settled in for hours without a care in the world. I was in a group with Jess and Beth, who saved me mentally and physically that January. What we lost out in superior bike skills and lightweight aluminium we made up in a shared stubborn determination and shameless pride. And, perhaps most importantly, a healthy sense of humour. We would help, cajole and push each other around the exhausting rides, and when morale was running low one of us would invariably start a song (ideally based on the name of the place where we were, or with some connection to cycling or rowing), or recount a joke. Whenever one of us was struggling the other two would help out – it was teamwork at its finest. Each of us trained to a higher standard because of the others and there was never a day when we didn't move on. The hot summer Australian sunshine beat down on us and we responded with a grimace, a song and harder pedalling.

The days passed in a blur of swearing, laughing, sweating, aching and the odd excited shout of "Kangaroo!!" as one bounded across the road in front of us. Beth would keep the cadence consistent, Jess was the human map who somehow always knew where we needed to be, and every downhill became a head-down furious clicking of gears and wild pumping of legs to try to reach new top speeds on the cycle computers. Any regard for safety went out of the window as the adrenaline and competitive drive flooded our bodies. The sense of speed was euphoric. At the bottom there would be gulping of breath, shouts of success and comparisons of speed as the bikes spun on easily, cruising on the momentum of the downhill. Water bottles were grabbed for refuelling along with a gel or jelly snake (the sweet of choice at that camp to get the instant sugar hit) before we regrouped and were off again.

My most memorable ride on that camp happened one fateful day when I was put in another group after we moved to Canberra. In the middle of the ride there was a long hill that zig-zagged ever upwards and my group set off up it at a great pace. Uphill was never my strongest cycling suit, and so I slowly dropped to the back and then finally off the back of the group. The others were relishing the challenge and climbed without a backward look. I was now alone in the baking heat, but I decided that this was probably not a bad thing; I could climb at my own pace and push myself as hard as I could without being mindful of bikes around me. The temperature was climbing past 40 degrees and the tarmac on the road was getting sticky. I was going so slowly that there was no cooling breeze created by forward movement, and the stifling heat increased around me. I was going ridiculously slowly even by my own standards and felt like I was dragging my bike up the hill. At that point I looked down to see that I had a rear puncture. I was literally dragging the back wheel across the sticky tarmac with every agonizing turn of the pedal. No wonder I was going painfully slowly. I considered my options as I heaved on the pedals. I was in the middle of nowhere on my own, and although I had a puncture repair kit I didn't have a pump – that was with a couple of the others in my group. They were nowhere to be seen, or even heard, and probably by now were whooping and hollering their way down the other side of the mountain. I could start walking, but that might take even longer. It was then that I heard the noise of an engine behind me.

We had a couple of safety vehicles, packed with a variety of coaches, physios, support staff, spare water, sports drinks, snack bars and sweets. Their job was to drive around the routes checking that the various groups were OK and didn't need anything, and also to help with directions. As the van came up behind me I looked up with exhausted relief. It was like a vision of security, reassurance and help, all wrapped up in silver metal. A vision that drew level, then pulled ahead and with a clunking of gears accelerated up the hill. I couldn't believe it. I swore at the receding back doors and gritted my teeth, dragging my bike onwards and upwards at a slower and slower pace. For every revolution of the wheel I drove my entire bodyweight on to the pedals and although with hindsight getting off and pushing would have been more sensible, on pretty much every level I was now in a place of anger, frustration, pride and delusion. The salty sweat was pouring off me and I was gulping in air that was hot and heavy. I stopped looking ahead and entered a world where I only saw the tiny bit of road ahead of me and everything else around me faded. The physical and mental pain was taking me to a different place, where I couldn't actually make rational decisions. It was now my own personal hell and I had to find my way through it. It became a test for me, and the bloody-mindedness was probably fuelled by the various disappointments from the previous months. In a strange, slightly unhealthy way the pain was welcome, as was the challenge. Here was a (completely insane) way to prove something to myself.

I was in a different world, and so was almost surprised when the climb ended and I finally reached the top. The road slowly flattened out and I saw Sandy, our friendly cycling guru, coming towards me on his bike. "Ah, there you are," he shouted in his Scottish accent. "We thought you'd got lost." I couldn't speak properly but managed to blurt out "puncture" between gasps. "What? Well then, get off yer bike for heaven's sake." He looked at me as if I was a madwoman – which at that point I probably was. The safety van then pulled up and Thommo bounded out. "All right?" I flashed him a look of uncontrolled rage and he physically stepped back. Sandy saved the moment without realizing. Still looking down as he fixed my wheel he said, "She had a puncture." Thommo's eyes widened. "Yes," I snapped, "and I had it when you came past me. Didn't you notice?" Thommo shrugged and said, "I just thought you were going really slowly up the hill." He smiled awkwardly and offered me a jelly snake.

I returned from the Australian camp a better athlete and was happy to be back in the swing of things once more. The next focus was the spring trials, when decisions would be made about what the summer might hold for us all.

The age-old tradition is that the winner of the singles trials gets the option of competing in the single or entering into the squad and joining a crew boat. I had won trials before and Thommo and I always had a bit of a joke – he'd ask, "So, single?" and I'd laugh and say, "What do you reckon?" And we'd both laugh at the thought of me wanting to go solo in a boat. For me rowing and racing has always been a team effort, a team sport; I love being in a motivated competitive group who go out together and engage in battle. There's something great about starting on the most challenging common goal and pulling together, pooling all of our resources to take on the opposition. Shortly before racing it's a special moment when you look at each other and acknowledge that whatever emotions are flowing through our body, we are in this together, and have each other's backs.

Over time, however, I wondered if it should always remain a joke that I'd ever choose to do the single. Traditionally the single is the ultimate Corinthian event – lone gladiators entering the arena by themselves, with no one to hide behind, to rely on or to be inspired by. I generally think it's a good thing to always question yourself, to push the boundaries, and certainly to test the status quo. As pleasant as it may feel, the comfort zone can be a dangerous place to stay for long.

So 2009 presented me with an opportunity. I knew my heart and soul lay in the team aspect of rowing, but why not for one summer, one season, step out of what I knew and test myself in a very different way? The temptation was helped by the need to do something different after Beijing. I was aware after the previous four years that I didn't want to get straight back into another quad and continue with a similar project. I needed something to change, even if temporarily.

I won the trials in Hazewinkel, Belgium, and for the first time I thought about my options. I saw Sophie Hosking, the lightweight sculler, as I put my boat back on the rack and she asked what I would do. "I don't know," I replied, "any suggestions?" "The single," she said, without pausing to think. This was the clear, no-nonsense, no-compromise attitude that Sophie took to everything – the same attitude that enabled her to win Great Britain's first lightweight women's gold medal with Kat Copeland at the London Olympics four years later.

I was given a couple of days to think about things during the short break that the whole squad was allowed after the trials. It's the brief breathing space that separates the long winter training and the start of the shorter but more intense summer season. In those couple of days I had a message from Anna Watkins asking what I was thinking of doing. I was undecided. It's just that there would be a fast double there, she suggested. I smiled to myself. I thought she was right, but I also wasn't sure I was mentally ready for that project. Of course now I get teased by Anna, who reminds me that she knew before any of us about the true potential of our combined force.

I saw Thommo on the first day back and we had our meeting. It was the oddest feeling, as I knew the rest of the squad were sat downstairs in the gym waiting. The squad would get together after my meeting, as my decision could impact on everyone and nothing could be discussed until my choice was known. The meeting started with just Thommo and me. He congratulated me on winning and asked my thoughts. I said I'd thought long and hard and felt it was the right time to try the single. I knew instantly he didn't agree with the idea. He had pieces of paper in front of him on the desk and continued to flick impatiently through them without looking up or commenting on what I had just said. The silence grew between us. I didn't want to fill it, as I had nothing more to add to my statement, but the urge to end the awkwardness grew.

He finally gestured to the pieces of paper in front of me and pointed out that although I might have won, it wasn't an international-level performance. It was possible to compare my winning time to Alan Campbell's time, and the comparison wasn't favourable to me. Alan was the men's GB sculler and had competed on the world stage, and so we knew relatively how fast times needed to be. My time wasn't good enough as far as Thommo was concerned. But from my point of view I'd done what I needed to do to win the trial; I hadn't won it to prove myself an international-level sculler. To me that work would start now.

David Tanner joined us at that point and asked how things were going. Thommo leaned back sighing and said, "Well, Katherine wants to try the single." David looked up at me, raising his eyebrows and letting a smile lift the corner of his mouth. "Does she now? Well, tell me why?" As the team manager David had the final say in selection. Although he did take an interest in individuals, his responsibility was to the success of the team. I explained where I was mentally, after Beijing, after the winter training. I wanted a different challenge, a new test of myself, and also something to do alone. I wanted to recapture my love and passion for this sport, and not necessarily drag anyone else down a path that might lead to redemption or might lead to disaster.

David looked satisfied that I had at least thought long and hard about the decision. He liked to feel that people had considered their choices, that nothing was done lightly or on a whim, and he liked you to prove to him what you thought and why you thought it. The easiest times were where he actually agreed with you before you started; although you still had to go through the test, it wasn't too much of a grilling. But often he didn't agree, and those conversations were more of a duel, a battle and sometimes ended with the "agreeing to disagree" line. Usually, however, there was respect as long as you knew your mind and had thought through your position. We left the room with David relatively pleased that I was taking on a challenge, and Thommo thinking he now had to arrange a squad which had more disparate elements than before.

One of the hardest parts of that time was the impact it had on Sarah Winckless. Sarah, who had been on the team with me for twelve years and was a close friend, had also had a very difficult time after the Beijing Games. Whereas I struggled with the failure that my silver medal had represented, Sarah had joined the women's eight who were cruelly hit by a virus during the competition and were forced to race with subs and spares. They finished fifth, and after the disappointment Sarah experienced at the hands of drug cheats in 2006, injury and selection in 2007 and then illness in 2008, she wanted to get some level of control back. In her eyes that would be winning the trials and taking the single slot in 2009. She finished fifth at the trials and I had one of the saddest conversations at the airport in Belgium on the way home when she considered her options. She believed the only choices were the single or retirement, and the single now wouldn't be an option as she hadn't won the trials and therefore wouldn't get the choice to race it. When I made the decision a couple of days later with David and Thommo, and then the rest of the squad was told, Sarah walked out of that meeting and out of rowing for ever. Thankfully, our friendship was not affected and although she, like most athletes, struggled with the initial period after leaving full-time sport, we have continued the close bond we forged over the years rowing together.

After the selection meeting, I walked down into the boathouse part of Caversham and saw Jurgen, the ever-present chief men's coach. "SCULLER!" he boomed in his strong voice and thick German accent. "Actually, Jurgen, I think I might be," I replied. His smile lowered for a second and then spread into a huge grin. "Really?" he said. "Yes, I've just told Thommo. I'm going to try it." "Ah excellent!" I was embraced in one of his wonderful bear hugs and clapped firmly on the back. "Ah, Kazren, you must do it and enjoy it, enjoy it all, let the other girls race themselves and see what they can do. For you must step back and enjoy it again and feel no pressure. You have nothing to prove, if you come third or fourth or sixth or seventh that's all OK. It doesn't matter. Just enjoy it." The next day he came to me looking concerned and said, "I know I said you might come sixth or seventh, but I don't think you will, I do think you can do better, but if you don't that's OK too." He was tying himself up in exactly the same way I would a few months later. I took the decision partly to do something where there were no expectations or set standards – where it was a blank sheet of paper. But I am naturally competitive and always want to prove myself. So although there was no reason to have any expectations, the nature of what we do and who we are means there would unavoidably be some.

I had expected the main challenge to be in the training – the hours and hours of endless repetition, trying to make infinitesimal changes, the exhaustion, the need to try new things in new ways – it would be the same as it had always been but this time I would be alone. No friendly faces there in the morning to share the boat and the boredom. No one to discuss how the boat was feeling, how bad the weather was, how tired our legs felt, how much we didn't want to go to the next session or how good last night's TV was. The easy, banal conversation that peppers a workout. The shared joke, the quiet laughter, the acknowledgement of a raised eyebrow or a half-disguised smile.

Training in a single means that you are alone in both a physical and a mental way. You are your own counsel, and I wasn't sure I was looking forward to that. I always made it through the winter season in the single, but longed for the day of being in a crew boat, because for me that was when the racing season began and a team was formed that would take on the world. There is a moment before every race where the coach has his pre-race talk and then leaves you to your own thoughts, and at that point you look your crewmates in the eyes and whether you see terror, excitement, nerves, tension, thrill, pride, defiance or concern, there is something undeniably there. I honestly don't mind what it is that I see (people are motivated in so many different ways) as long as it's not blank. And it never is. Although it may just be a rowing race we're about to do, what it represents is so much more.

That attitude, the look in the eyes, the emotion, is about passion, and that's when I know we're about to do something special. Passion has always been important to me – it's that wonderful, indescribable thing that may mean something different for each person but it's the thing that drives your mind and gets your heart pounding. It keeps you creative, keeps you hungry and feeds the desire to learn. With passion and purpose great things can be accomplished and, crucially, the spark is ignited in the first place. Achieving great things always begins somewhere and it will often come from a passion. Most top athletes I know began their sport because they loved it, and that love and passion for their sport has continued to fuel them through their career, leading them to the highs, taking them through the inevitable lows and back on to the peaks. When the dark questions come in the night it is often the original passion, the excitement, the drive, the enthusiasm, that will help to shine a light.

And for me that passion had always been shared with others in rowing. It is part of what makes rowing so attractive to me – not just the daily physical and mental challenge – but the creation of something special with someone else. The question for me now was whether I would feel the same when I was tackling things on my own.

The day-to-day training actually was a little easier than I thought. Not easier in the physical sense; I usually had to row the same mileage as everyone else, so as the eights, quads and doubles overtook me I was out for longer and it was exhausting. But the time I spent alone was easier than I expected, because in many ways I wasn't alone. The other girls on the team were hugely supportive in a lovely gentle teasing manner. I'd regularly get "Oi, No Mates!" yelled at me as a faster boat accelerated past, invariably with one of the girls looking over and waving, winking, smiling or making a face. Knowing that I was alone, they made sure I didn't feel lonely. And I began to embrace the challenge of moving a boat as fast as I could without anyone to help me.

Thommo and I worked well together, and in some ways the communication was easier as it was just a direct, one-to-one relationship. Each of us could be sure exactly what the other was thinking and if there was any doubt it was straightforward to work out. With just one athlete and the coach, it's not surprising that the single is regarded as the easiest boat for communication. But it is vital that the line of communication goes both ways – Thommo and I both had to feel we could suggest and contribute, disagree and challenge each other as and when necessary, and through that we would gain an even stronger trust in what we were doing. If it were to go wrong it would also be the most damaging communication link to sever.

So the training began to improve and the racing season approached. And that was going to be the true test. Traditionally the top athletes who race in single sculls are single scull specialists – they will compete in that event for years and become masters of their trade. While other athletes can move between boat types, the single scullers usually stay with the lone gladiator role. I knew I was stepping into new territory, and territory that was fiercely protected by those masters. I would race in all three World Cups and the World Championships. I won the first World Cup although admittedly there wasn't a strong field; Great Britain dominated most events. The next two World Cups I was beaten into fourth as the experts arrived from all around the world and flexed their single sculling muscle.

Two hard training camps awaited me between the last World Cup and the World Championships. The first camp was in Germany, the second in Italy. Traditionally the German camp was long and challenging. Often there would be a heatwave and any free time was spent either lying on beds relaxing or down at the local ice cream shop. For me it was a tough camp, but I shared a room with Caroline, the cox, and that did help to alleviate the tension a little for me. Caroline has the entertaining Cockney chat of a slightly dodgy second-hand car salesman and the heart of a lion. She also has the energy of a Duracell bunny and a capacity for asking questions continuously that any Inquisitor would have been proud of. She is constantly concerned about how things are or aren't going, and every day she made me laugh, whether that was her intention or not. Most days at some point I would hear the words "Katherine, can I just ask you something?" and we'd sit and put the world to rights over coffee or occasionally a beer. It helped to distract me from my own concerns and allowed me to feel part of a team.

When it came to the training, however, I was usually alone. Anna and Annie were in the double for that summer and we shared Thommo as our coach. It worked very well, and we'd often play tag team, one boat taking the very early session and the other boat joining in towards the end of the session and passing Thommo on like a large relay baton. There was usually time for just a few words, and those words became crucial in setting expectations for the session. "He's tired", "He's enthusiastic", "He wants to get the catches in faster", "Make sure your legs are connecting first" – we became experts at conveying useful messages in just a few words and hopefully making the session just a little bit easier or better for each other. Occasionally there was nothing that could be done, though – a hard look and a muttered "Good luck, you're going to need it" meant that the standards that day were unlikely to be reached.

I vividly remember getting off the water after a long intensive 5km timed bit of work where the rate and intensity crept up throughout the entire length and by the end I couldn't sustain the work, such was the pain and exhaustion in my body. I kept glancing down at the stroke coach and the numbers were not where they needed to be. Every time I tried to raise the rating, the numbers stubbornly refused to change. It was utterly disheartening. Squeezing my legs harder, trying to accelerate my back more, sharpening up the bladework … nothing was making a difference, and my burning lungs and aching limbs and drained mind couldn't find the answer between them. I dragged myself to the side of the river after the session, bitterly disappointed with my performance and the gap between what I wanted to achieve and what I had managed. Thommo walked over and looked out at the river with me. I remember having dark sunglasses on and being happy that they would hide the angry tears that were threatening to form. I was frustrated with myself and annoyed and exhausted. "Well," he said after a pause, "no one said it would be easy." At that point the tears did break and, much to my horror, ran hotly and silently down my cheek. Thommo would have seen, but thankfully never commented. We stood quietly side by side watching the water flow past. He understood frustration. And although he might have been disappointed on one level, he would rather have seen me push as hard as I could and struggle than stay for ever safely within my comfort zone.

That's what a good coach, like Thommo, will do. Lead you to the edge of the comfort zone and then firmly, with a strong hand on your back, push you outwards. It's not always pleasant, it doesn't always feel right, but many times it is necessary even if you don't know whether you'll fly or fall. If you're not sure anyone will catch you, then it's a particularly scary proposition. But staying on the edge can be more dangerous than risking the fall because otherwise you'll never make progress. It's only later you realize that when you push yourself to those levels and ultimately "fail" in training that you are pushing yourself to a new standard and actually both body and mind grow from it. As long as emotionally you can deal with the temporary disappointment, you will generally be better for having been there. It also means you are working at the right standard where not every session is easily manageable.

The summer progressed and the World Championships approached. They were being held in Poznan, Poland. The organizers had done a great job and the stands were filled with excited schoolchildren. They had each adopted a different country and the seats were packed with noisy kids, waving brightly coloured flags and banners. The energy was wonderful and infectious. It was impossible to look up at the singing, chanting and waving and not have at least a little bit of a smile. The stage was set for the best rowers in the world to come together and let battle commence. And this would be the first World Championships when I would sit on the startline alone. I wasn't sure of what my expectations were.

A few weeks earlier at the Italian camp I'd met with Chris, our psychologist, for a chat. He meets with most of the racing crews to offer advice, be there as a sounding board, discuss issues, problems, talk about the possible opportunities, help to set goals, identify roles, explain behavioural differences, generally whatever is needed. When we sat down I was struggling a little with the training. It was getting closer to the Championships and we were doing more and more timed racing sessions whereby we could compare against all the other boats. In the previous years in the quad and the pair I would be looking at the higher end of the results table; now I suddenly found myself having to lower my view to the bottom half of the results, often the bottom itself. It was fine to get the kick up the backside every now and again with a disappointing result, but it was tough to be getting almost daily feedback that I wasn't going fast. Chris met with me to see how things were going. We sat in the comfy chairs in a quiet corner of the camp and he asked me again why I had chosen to race the single.

I went back to the beginning and talked about needing a break, a different challenge; facing my demons from Beijing and moving on stronger and better for it. About how it was refreshing to not think solely about the result, that actually this was tapping into why I loved rowing in the first place, and for the first time in ages there wouldn't be the expectation of a win or a medal or anything really. I could be free and open to race just for the simple pleasure of racing itself. The simplicity would create the freedom. "So," Chris asked, "in that case how could you possibly lose?" He was right; if I was racing for the sake of racing, then the result was irrelevant and I couldn't lose. But that's when I faced up to the reality that my competitive instinct was too strong, that my pride and standards wouldn't be compromised, even if I wanted them to be. I couldn't completely let go of the result, because in my own eyes it was possible that I might fail. I would fail if I didn't achieve a "decent" result. I couldn't even define what that result would be. But I realized that while I might be able to race with freedom I would always have to race to the best standard I could, and for me that meant high up the field.

I struggled with the dual concept of dearly wanting the freedom, to be able to let go of the result and stay "in the moment", but also wanting the result. I discovered that freedom by letting the result be dictated by the performance. I could allow myself to not obsess about the result, the outcome, if I focused everything on the process, on the how. And by accepting that those were the standards that needed to be high, then I could allow myself to forget about the rest. It was back to the same mindset that had helped Cath and me to win in Milan.

Chris did a magical thing at this point which was stunning in its simplicity. Later that night he emailed me a clip from the TV comedy *Friends*. It shows Phoebe running in Central Park. Her running is quirky and ridiculous. But she doesn't know that it is, so she runs happily in her crazy style, arms waving around, tapping into the original joy of running before you were told of correct form and of right and wrong. I watched the clip and laughed. And then I watched it again, and I kept watching it on and off through the summer. It was a brilliant way to remember that it was ultimately about freedom and fun and pleasure and natural instinct. And that didn't need to be in place of grit and determination and tough racing; it could be alongside and enhancing it. Suddenly, as daunting as the racing might still be, it held an element of fun and a sense of "why not?".

Caroline and I were now sharing a room in Poznan. Poor Caroline seemed to be on call 24 hours a day, and whenever we had a moment to sit and chat over a coffee or tea her phone would invariably bleep, buzz, vibrate, ding, dong or cheep and she would be hurtling towards the door, grabbing paper and pen as she went. I lost count of the number of half-finished sentences and barely begun conversations we shared. She would come back sighing or swearing and sink wearily to her bed before the phone would break her brief moment of calm and the cycle began again. I started thinking that although I missed the camaraderie of a crew around me, at least there was no one demanding I raced around the hotel like a madwoman. I should have told her to run like Phoebe; at least then we would have laughed about it. Or at least I would have.

The competition got closer and as a squad we were a very different group from Beijing, with every boat having changes from 2008. It being the first World Championships of a new Olympiad there was the excitement that anything was possible and the sense that the next few years would be full of changes for all of us.

The single generally has the most entries of all events – and it means more racing on more days through the week of the World Championships. The eight and the single were on different days, so Caroline and I had an entertaining week of watching each other go through various stages of hell. I was due to race first and so I experienced the first "night before". Out of genuine concern she spent the evening asking if I wanted the window open or shut. The TV off or on. The music louder or quieter. Talking or silent contemplation. Every now and then she would glance up from her book with a frown and a look of uncomfortable sympathy. Then the next morning she waved me off with a "You'll be fine", although the look of concern on her face betrayed her real thoughts. Once I made it through my race I returned to the room with the relief every athlete feels when the waiting is finally over and the games have begun. But by now Caroline was experiencing the hell of the night before. As I let myself into our room she greeted me with a direct look and in her honest manner said, "I'll be honest, Katherine, I hate you right now." I grinned and reminded her that in another 24 hours the roles would be reversed again. And then asked her if she wanted the window open or shut.

The days between races are the strangest ones to fill as an athlete. Gone are the exhausting weeks of training camp, when every moment seems to be filled with training on the water, in the gym, on the ergo or in meetings. When it comes to racing, all of that is replaced with downtime, space, relaxation, and that's when the new extra energy and nervous tension become palpable. Some people pass the time with books or DVDs, some with computer games and some with getting together in a crew room where old stories are recycled, rowing myths are recollected and exaggerated, and conversations drift into the world of fantasy. I heard later of the usual list-making – choose three athletes from any country that you'd like to date and why. You could also choose a "Wild Card" – someone a little different from the usual favourites – and no reason needed to be given for that choice. Caroline was a champion in her own version of "Would you rather?" which could wander into the strangest territory. "Would you rather have to chew off your own finger or someone else's?" "Caroline, that is completely ridiculous! What are you talking about??" "OK, OK, well then, would you rather have no eyes or no nose?" And so time was passed, with surreal conversations, games, TV, films, chatting over coffee, walks around the local area, sleeping, phone calls home, meetings, physio sessions, and anything that would fill the downtime before the overwhelming surge of adrenaline that signalled another race was to come.

Owing to the timing of the races I would be the last woman to secure my place in the final. As the semi-final drew close it dawned on me that I could be the only woman not to make the final, and to me that would represent a spectacular failure. Now at last I could define the "failure" that Chris had asked about in Italy. Not making the final would be it. And there were no guarantees; I had a tough semi and would need to get the race right in order to make it into the top six scullers in the world. Remember, I kept reminding myself, you chose this, this was your idea. Idiot.

I met Thommo for our chat the night before the race. This was another time that was so different being in the single. When I was in the quad I was used to there being at least five people in the room at these meetings, and the intensity being split across the room as everyone contributed in their own way to the plan. Conversations flowed in different directions and everyone covered different thoughts, ideas and logistics. This time there was just Thommo and me. The details of the following day were gone through quickly, and then there was just the race itself to talk about. Between the two of us and with Chris's input we had come up with a great personal race plan, drawing on some of my best performances across the years in various events. In order to compete against people with far more experience and knowledge in this event I drew on my own strengths. Which were exactly the opposite to theirs. I didn't have a wealth of international single racing to draw on, but I did have the experience of many other types of racing, in other boats with other people in faster events, and I had learned from all of them. And I was excited to be taking all that with me into my little boat. Everyone I had ever competed with would be there with me in the race.

I didn't win my semi-final but did enough to make it through to the final. Thommo will always tell us that before we can start planning for the final, we have to make sure we get into it first. Now I was there. At the evening meal at our hotel I was deciding on what to eat when I heard a booming voice behind me – "SCULLER!" – and along with the voice came two heavy hands on my shoulders. I turned to meet Jurgen's beaming face once again. "Ah, well done, Kazren, you have made the final! You have done all you need, proved all that you need to. So now you must relax and enjoy it. Every step higher you get in the final is a bonus, a great bonus. So enjoy it, you can do nothing wrong now, it can only get better." I don't know if Jurgen has ever watched *Friends*, but I think he would have appreciated Phoebe running. I smiled back and felt a weight lift. He was right, it could be play now. Competitive, hard racing, but a feeling of just finding out what I can do. Because I really didn't know. And for the first time in a while, that felt OK.

I was nervous going into the final. In the hours before my event I sat on the concrete bleachers at the finish line, watching the races come down the course. Traditionally the single was first, but this year the order had changed and I waited for the women's double to race before me. There was a great hope that Annie and Anna could win the title, but the Poles put in a sensational performance in front of their home crowd to just sneak the gold. I left my concrete seat and headed for my boat to meet Thommo. He raised his eyebrows and asked if I had watched the double. I nodded. He continued, "Yep, it's tough out there. Conditions are getting tough too. It's windy, tailwind, so it'll be fast. It'll all depend on how you race it." I took the boat to the water and Thommo pushed me off with his customary "Race well!".

CHAPTER 9

The waiting at the start is very quiet in a single. There are the glances at opponents as you play the strange dance around the small bit of water that all the competitors share in the warm-up zone before the race. As we were called to the startline I took a deep breath. Remember Phoebe, I told myself. Enjoy it, race it hard, have fun, give it everything, expect the pain, nothing to fear. My boat was in place. Two minutes. More deep breaths. A glance over my shoulder down the course. I could see the blurred end of the course shimmering in the distance. It looked far away. I could also see the wind whipping across the water not too far ahead. The startline itself was sheltered but then the lake opened to a more exposed area, and that is where the small fragile single sculls would be vulnerable to the conditions. I smiled inwardly. I always liked a bit of rough and tumble on the water. It was one last race, no need to save energy now, or hold anything back. I wanted to find out what I could do. All right, let's play.

The gun went and we were off. As expected, pretty quickly the wind gusted across from the side, pushing the boats over and adding a new challenge. I remember the Russian in the lane next to me struggled for a few strokes as her blades were caught by the wind and she had to correct the balance of her boat. I pounced, unaware of anything else around me but thinking I'd use her struggle to put some distance between us. I pulled away and entered the next phase of the race. I let my personal race plan unfold and enjoyed the challenge. What I didn't realize was that I was not only pulling ahead of the Russian but ahead of everyone. For a while I led the field, and at one point when I glanced across I almost did a double take as I saw all five other boats behind me. It was all going well and the adrenaline was pumping as we entered the closing stages, and I was ready for a blazing finish, the feeling of leaving everything on the lake and exhausting myself to all limits. Unfortunately the wind was also gearing up for its finale, and as it gusted and gathered and created white horses around me and the waves got higher and choppier I knew I had to make sure I didn't make any mistakes. The Belarussian was attacking – Karsten was the ultimate single sculler, she had been competing as far back as the 1992 Barcelona Olympics and medalled at the previous five Olympic Games, four of them in the single scull. Her experience showed as she cut through the waves and through my lead, and I raced in behind. It was another silver

ABOVE: Flying solo at the World Cup in
Lucerne 2009.

BELOW: Racing with the freedom of Phoebe,
I attacked the 2009 World Championships.

ABOVE: Jess and I battling the roads of Majorca.

OPPOSITE TOP: The first World Championships title for Anna and I together in the double, Karapiro 2010. A wonderful win thanks to the vision and guidance of Thommo in our first year of the 2012 crew.

OPPOSITE LEFT: Anna and I acknowledge the support from the crowd in New Zealand after our win.

ABOVE: Rachel, Kate and me on our Croatian holiday. A friendship forged through trials that will last a lifetime.

BELOW: The Rowing Team announcement in front of Windsor Castle as we officially become part of Team GB in 2012.

LEFT: Breaking the Olympic Record in the first race at the Olympic Games 2012. The sensational Dorney crowd can be seen in the background roaring us home.

BELOW: That's the moment! Utter joy, utter elation, a dream come true.

BOTTOM LEFT: The long promised hug from Sir Steve. No words were necessary.

BOTTOM RIGHT: Sir Craig Reedie finally being able to give me the Olympic gold medal and understanding what exactly that moment meant.

ABOVE: Mum, Dad, Sarah and Steph with my neighbours Pam and Derek. The day was a celebration for everyone.

LEFT: Jurgen congratulating me after our win in London.

BELOW: We were happy, what can I say?

OPPOSITE LEFT: Thommo gets his well-deserved team hug.

ABOVE: Arriving for the first round of interviews at the BBC we share a sofa with Ian Thorpe and Gary Lineker. The Olympic Park is bathed in sunshine behind us.

RIGHT: The Riverbank Stadium, London 2012. Anna and I are joined by Duchesses and Dames at the GB women's hockey bronze medal match.

BELOW: And the celebrations just continued. We were overwhelmed by the stunning show of support at the various Olympic parades throughout the country.

TOP LEFT: Sharing a laugh with Clare Balding on stage at the BBC Sports Personality of the Year.

TOP RIGHT: The Princess Royal and the Edinburgh University Rowing Gym in my honour.

MIDDLE LEFT: Meeting the football legend, Pele, at a University of Edinburgh Honorary Degree Ceremony.

MIDDLE RIGHT: The Princess Royal awarding me my CBE at Buckingham Palace.

LEFT: In 2014, the Olympic flame came back to life in preparation for the Sochi Winter Games. Naomi Riches, the Paralympic Rowing Champion, and I had fun carrying the Paralympic torch in Marlow.

BOTTOM: Anna and I had the massive honour of being the official starters for the 2014 London Marathon, then ran it ourselves. This was me overjoyed to have finished and to have raised money for International Inspiration.

medal for me, but this one was the happiest silver since Sydney. I had smashed the British record, I had led the field, I had proved to myself that the horrors of Beijing wouldn't haunt me for ever and I had risked personal failure to achieve individual success. Perhaps, most importatly, I had, like Phoebe, embraced the simple joy and loved it.

I spoke to some of the journalists afterwards. In fact they bought me a beer in the Polish sunshine to celebrate and they recounted the moment of my race. The media centre is filled with the constant buzz of TV screens, the tapping of laptops, and the various murmurings of journalists on phones or sharing their wisdom with each other. Someone watching the women's single race shouted out, "Bloody hell, Grainger has gone into the lead," and they all gathered round in stunned silence. It wasn't expected. I also heard that the crew room back at the hotel was deafening with the shouts during my race and one of the guys stood up and yelled "THAT'S my Wild Card!" The support of your own team is the most wonderful thing – when a roomful of fellow athletes all with their own goals and focuses give you a reaction like that, it means the world. A lot of people came up to say well done as I took my boat back to its rack. Thommo met me from the landing stage and his massive smile said it all. Through one of the toughest winters and summers we had spent together we had created something truly special.

As I walked a little dazed around the boatpark, getting various slaps on the back from members of the international rowing community, I suddenly heard that booming voice again – "SCULLER!!" Jurgen was leaning on his bike talking to someone else but had spotted me meandering around. "Ah, sculler," his voice softened with pride and pleasure. He embraced me in his best bear hug and then, gripping me by the shoulders, his grin lit up his face as he slowly shook his head from side to side. "Oh Kazren, you have surprised even me by that performance."

I later spoke to David Tanner, our team manager. Although he was also pleased he is generally more reserved and measured in his reactions. I said how pleased I was but that there was a part of me that kept wondering what if I could have gone faster through the bad water and won. While most people would have been satisfied with the result, David understood and was pleased that for me there was a constant hunger to always do better. He recognized it is the sense of not complete contentment, not complete satisfaction that keeps us all driving on, driving forward and never settling. The year in my single had taught me so much, and it would all be helpful for the future. I could celebrate the medal, but then I needed to refocus on the next challenge. Which would be just around the corner.

Jess found me later – "Amazing, Katherine, absolutely legendary. You know what got you that medal?" We looked at each other for a moment. I smiled and laughed as we shouted together, "That bloody hill in Australia!"

CHAPTER

10

THE RIGHT FIT

During the break after the World Championships of 2009 and before the next year's training began, I left Bisham Abbey, ten and a half years after I first moved in. I still have my original rental agreement that was for three months. In the decade I was there I competed in three Olympics, finished one and started another degree, won titles, lost family members, made valuable new friends and celebrated birthdays. I had seen the national sports centre transformed in the grounds, I witnessed the arrival of the English Institute of Sport, met various national sports teams who came to train and I had listened out for but never met the oldest resident of the site, Lady Hoby, the ghost who haunts the Abbey. It was difficult to leave the place where I had spent such a huge chunk of my adult life. It made it easier knowing that I wasn't going far away and although I missed the friendliness of the staff on site, I instantly loved the escape of walking into my own house and closing the door on the world.

Rowing is an incredibly vibrant, busy, sociable world and I love being part of such a wonderful team. There is still a wonderful moment, however, when I am finished for the day and turn the key in the lock of my home and can enjoy the luxury and privacy of my own space. The one thing I couldn't have chosen when I moved in was who my neighbours were going to be. There's an element of risk in finding out who it is you've committed to sharing a wall with. I could not have been luckier. Pam and Derek live next door and although in their early sixties have the enthusiasm and energy of a couple in their thirties. From the first day I arrived I was welcomed and added to their children and grandchildren as one of the family. In the first few months I was busy with training and unpacking and buying furniture (in fact my mum and I had a possible world record ten-hour session in IKEA one day) and I hardly saw my new neighbours. As I passed they would ask if I wanted to pop in for a coffee. Next time it was whether or not they could put the kettle on for a cup of tea. This went on for a few weeks until I finally managed to have a moment to accept. As I stepped through their back door Pam asked if I wanted a coffee or, she hesitated, maybe a glass of wine? Her face lit up when I said wine and we have been bonded ever since. Every now and then Derek and I will share a whisky and put the world to rights. Through the winter we sometimes share Sunday night TV in front of the fire and through the summers occasional BBQs, after Derek has mowed both of our lawns. From never having watched rowing in their lives before, by London 2012 they were screaming themselves hoarse at Dorney wearing union flags and "GB Rowing Supporters" T-shirts. Sometimes life just puts good people in your path and your world is then greatly enhanced.

After the house move, training took its usual pattern and our midwinter camp that year was in Aviz, a sleepy little part of Portugal. The place where we lived and trained had been designed by ex-rowers and so catered specifically for training camp needs. The water was extensive and stretched in three different directions, so crews could split up and choose either to negotiate the gently winding tree-lined route to the dam, or venture for miles into the wide open space that opened up after the bridge, or take on the challenging complexities of the rock-filled canyon.

Training camp is a place of mixed emotions. On one hand there is a welcoming simplicity to the experience. There is only one main focus to the time on camp and that is work. The team always stays in a hotel or rowing residence designed for the sole purpose of training and so every moment of the day is built around improvement, progress of skill, technique and physical conditioning. The coaches know athletes are being looked after and without the everyday distractions of shopping, cooking, cleaning, washing, driving, balancing finances and the like, so the intensity and workload of the training can be increased. There is no reason or excuse not to have performance as the foremost priority in our lives and so the training reflects it.

This simple focus can be a welcome change from the usual busyness of life at home and I would often look forward to the weeks abroad. However, the intensity of the camp can be a challenge in itself and that very simplicity which lends itself so well to improvement can be a double-edged sword when there is no escape and no release from the daily grind. Knowing just how hard to push yourself every session can take experience to understand the fine line between hard enough and too hard. Too soft isn't an option. Water session was followed by water session and then long hours in the gym. Deafening music would blare out from a stereo even though most athletes would be plugged into their own music to try to form a distraction from the pain and boredom as the kilometres were ground out on the ergos. The most impressive musical challenge was when Annie and Jess listened to Mariah Carey's "All I Want For Christmas" non-stop for 75 mins on one particular ergo session in the run-up to Christmas. Everyone found their own way to escape from the potentially relentless and claustrophic environment as an essential key to maintaining some level of sanity. Afternoon naps were popular and occasionally essential to cope with the crippling training loads. Endless books are regularly devoured and passed around and increasingly downtime was filled with the more sociable pastime of watching DVD boxsets.

As the years went by we filled our spare hours with everything from the *The X-Files* to *Prison Break*, *Spooks* to *Six Feet Under*, *Boston Legal* to *Borgen*, *Ashes to Ashes* to *Glee*, anything anyone could get their hands on. TV sport was also closely followed and in the summer we would become experts in the intricacies of the Tour de France and in the winter the ice skating coverage meant we could tell our triple salchows from our double axel with the extra half rotation. Films were popular to escape for an hour or two and although the current blockbusters and old classics were always with us there were also a few unusual viewings. I remember Annie gathering us to watch her favourite, *Lagaan*, an unusual genre of "Indian epic musical sports drama" that came in at just under four hours. This cultural classic was in contrast to *Megashark v Giant Octopus* that included the rare scene of a giant shark leaping from the sea to snatch a plane from the sky. Everything had the potential to entertain exhausted minds and bodies on camp.

When we felt we had energy to do something more than lying watching TV then we became a little more creative. Beth always had some sort of creative kit in her bag that invariably involved making puppets or painting or pipe cleaners. Helen Casey was a genius with the knitting needles and for a couple of years knitting became the new social fashion as hats, gloves, scarves and toys magically appeared from random bits of knotted wool stretching across the rooms. Anna and I filled our 2011–12 season with the entertaining addition of nerf guns and one Breisach camp we collapsed exhausted on our floor on day one after a particularly competitive assault with the foam bullets punctuated by screams of laughter. Italian camps were broken up with trips to Melamangio, quite possibly the site of the best ice cream in the world and often the incentive to make it through the final gruesome training session of the week.

One of the most successful of the training camp pastimes was the arrival of Hester's choir. Hester Goodsell was in the lightweight double and also happened to be a music teacher. One day in conversation there was a suggestion that we form a choir on training camp for a change. The greatest obstacle to this idea was that very few of the team were willing to admit to any musical ability. Hester, however, did not see this as an obstacle. Her theory was that everyone can sing, people just don't know how. Here was a choir I was finally allowed into. And so began a wonderful few years where every few days on training camp we would get together and test Hester's patience and skill. Our own special version of "Hallelujah" was a favourite in the choir, but there was no area of music we didn't attempt. From an attempt at a soulful "Stand By Me", we enthusiastically embraced hits from *Sister Act* (much to our surprise Hester had never seen the film and so we managed to educate our own singing teacher in the ways of Sister Mary Clarence), a girl band megamix, Christmas carols for charity, a two-part "Californian Dreaming" and a harmonious "Ave Maria" that brought tears to the eyes of Jo Cook's mum who had tuned in to watch us on skype. It was a bit surreal seeing parents and grandparents back at home swaying along to the music on laptops.

Hester spent the time moving between benevolent encouragement and stern telling off as we reverted to being schoolchildren and pushed the boundaries of behaviour in class. Jess and Sophie would regularly be frowned at for giggling in the corner as Alison Knowles and I got in trouble for yet again getting distracted and losing our place on the page. Alison has one of the driest wits in rowing and can always be relied on for a perfectly pitched ironic comment. It turned out that wasn't the only thing she could pitch well. Alison and I were similar levels of ability (or disability), so I felt safe until we discovered quite by accident that when it came to tuning to a "D" Alison appeared to have perfect pitch. Just for the note D. As limited as this might have been, I still felt almost betrayed by her newfound ability of tuning, leaving me alone as unaccomplished.

As we all chatted and laughed and elbowed our way through rehearsals, Hester would appreciate the camaraderie, letting us go so far and then with one look could silence us, thereby bringing us bring us back into line. The innate skill of a great teacher. She also attained loyalty from all the choir who were grateful for her time and endless patience. As a result of this loyalty, she managed to encourage occasional public performances from us. Hester's confidence in us was infectious, even if some felt misplaced, and she even managed to get us into The Hexagon venue in Reading where we performed Heather Small's "Proud", the theme for the 2012 Olympic Bid, along with hundreds of schoolchildren. The most unreal moment of all could have quite possibly been when a few of us went to record with the Gamesmakers choir. The wonderful song, "I Wish For You The World" was written by the talented Alistair Griffin for the Gamesmakers and then the Gamesmaker choir performed it along with some members of the GB rowing choir. It was all great fun as we put on headphones and leaned towards the microphones feeling like we were living the Band Aid dream. It was only then I remembered a little too late that as much fun as it was I still didn't have the most obvious "recording" voice and as the introduction started and Hester's face lit up all I could do was try to summon my inner Bob Geldof and pray to the gods of music that Alison would hit that perfect D.

The commitment to camp is unequivocal and unquestioning. Some of my toughest times weren't, however, as a result of the relentless discipline, the exhausting training or the mental pressure. Like everyone on the team I've missed weddings and birthdays because of being away on camps. Twice I had to go on camp literally within hours of very special funerals when my precious grandad and gran died in the same year. In July 2005, my wonderful, irreplaceable, strong, proud, devoted, brave, inspirational gran passed away. I didn't manage to spend time with the rest of the family at her side in her last days because I was training. It was summer and the racing season and there was no possibility of leaving the squad for personal time. I was allowed one day to attend the funeral and held my mum's hand as we sobbed through the ceremony. I then flew out to Germany only hours later to join the training camp and the only thing I had for company was my gran's teddy bear. A few years earlier gran had been in hospital and her neighbour, Elaine Rust, had given her a bear. Gran called him Rusty Bear both after Elaine and his colour, and when gran was released from hospital she sat him in the corner of her living room. Everyday she would chat to him as she went in and out of the room. When gran died I asked what would happen to Rusty and mum said she wanted him to go to a good home. From that day on he has lived with me and has come on every single training camp and competition. I held him close that first night in Germany after the funeral as I cried silent tears into his comforting fur. Since then he has had a hat knitted for him by Helen Casey; Beth regularly moved the fur from his eyes so he could "watch" tv with us; Sarah used to sit him with her varying toys on camp; Anna hid behind him during the scarier films and the more violent nerf gun attacks and, over the years, endless housekeeping staff in hotels have placed him on my bed either holding a remote control or wrapped in a bathrobe or wearing sunglasses. He sits now wearing his very own gold medal; his is chocolate, of course. My gran is gone and she is sorely missed, but her spirit lives on in all of us, not least Rusty Bear.

As much as I love and appreciate the professionalism of British Rowing there were times when I struggled with how impersonal it could feel, such as when little concession is made for bereavement and mourning. Sometimes it's other forms of bereavement that are ignored. In May 2012, only two months before the Olympic Games, I spoke to Alison Knowles the night before she told Thommo she felt she had to leave the team. The choice was not entirely hers as she was in an impossible situation as far as selection was concerned. Her fight was not my fight, but as I hung up I felt the old swell of rage against injustice. The anger and frustration that there were some people who weren't fought for, or protected or given the benefit of the doubt, whereas others were. And even more so that, if and when Alison left, I knew the machine wouldn't pause or hesitate or acknowledge the loss of another great athlete who had won medals for our country. Inevitably there would be hardly a backward glance as the system maintained its forward focus. I knew that because I had seen great athletes every year retire, resign, be forced out through injury and barely a word was said. I am realistic enough to know that the constant forward moment is partly why the rowing system is so successful. But after my call to Alison I couldn't help but feel frustrated still. It was right that the sport moved on, moved forward, that it continued despite even the loss of the greats like Steve Redgrave and Matthew Pinsent. However, I couldn't help but feel that although this organization may be bigger than the individuals in it, it was great because of those individuals, and somehow it would be good if that was acknowledged. Sadly both Hester and Alison were gone by the Olympics and so the choir was never the same again.

In 2010 we were doing most of our training in small boats, so either doubles or pairs. As is normal early in the year we swapped around, rowing with different people, and mixed the crews every few days. On 15 January Anna and I took to the water in a double. Although we had been on the team together now for nearly five years, we had never raced in a boat together. We didn't even know each other very well, having not shared a room or even spent much time in each other's company. As Anna and I put the boat on the water we didn't really know what to expect. There were many reasons why in theory it should be a good boat, but things can feel different in reality from how they look on paper and we waited to see what would happen. Thommo was alongside us in the launch as we pushed off.

Within a few strokes we knew there was something special happening. Anna was in the bow seat and after a few short instructions the boat was moving smoothly and effortlessly underneath us. When we stopped I turned around with a smile on my face. "Well, that feels pretty good." Anna's smile matched mine and from that moment on it was the only boat we wanted to be in. Whereas with most new boats there is a formation time as you work out how the boat should feel and what the instructions mean, Anna and I had the same concept of how a boat should move and how we would row to make that happen. Communication was simple and the basics were already in play, so we could quickly move on to a higher level of training.

Thommo was pleased, but as with everything the proof would be in the speed. The boat looked and felt good, but that was irrelevant if it wasn't fast. A few days later we managed to test it against the other doubles on camp and it performed better than we could have hoped. It felt as if this was something different, something exciting with limitless potential. And so, when the final trials rolled around in April and I came first with Anna second, there was no doubt about what to choose when I was given the option of what I wanted to do. I wanted the double. I said as much to Thommo, but he said my choice was to be in the single or a crew boat; it wasn't for me to specify which crew boat I wanted to be in.

During the decision time Anna and I were out in the double and she asked if I had made any decisions about boats. I suddenly thought I didn't want to be too presumptuous with my thinking. I said I thought I did know, but if she had the choice what would she want to do? There was not even a hint of hesitation. "This boat, I only want to do this boat," she said with a massive grin. That was it then, we would do everything to make it happen.

The first season together was incredibly special. We loved every minute of being in our double and had also fallen into a very comfortable company with each other. Although we were different in many ways, we also were very similar and so it was a healthy, balanced and fresh relationship. The key thing for both of us from the beginning was to feel we had equal status in the boat. I brought my long history of experience, my natural racing instinct and a bagful of lessons I had learned through various successes and failures. Anna brought five years' experience of international doubles racing, a physiology that saw her repeatedly break indoor rowing records and an analytical brain that would prove to be priceless. We both shared a healthy sense of humour, useful intelligence and driving ambition. And crucially we absolutely loved what we were doing and spent most days in the boat reminding each other just how lucky we were.

The squad around us wasn't doing as well, and as we entered the racing season it was without Fran or Debbie, who were both injured. That left Anna and me along with Annie and Beth as the sculling squad. With not many options Thommo suggested we tried doubling up – racing both the double and the quad at the first World Cup. It would be a tough physical test and we didn't yet know how either boat would race on the international circuit, but it was a challenge. And we did love a challenge.

The first World Cup was to be in Bled in Slovenia. The rowing course there is visually spectacular. It's as if someone had asked a small child to draw their idea of a perfect place to row and then with the wave of a magic wand created it. The deep blue natural lake is surrounded by mountains and the distant ranges are covered with snow. At one end of the lake there is a medieval castle high on a hill keeping watch over the startline. Near the finish there is an island covered in green trees, and stretching through the treetops towards the sky is the spire of a church. The finish line is against a wall of rock cut into the mountainside. Swans glide around looking suitably proud and defensive of their lake.

Anna and I had the double as our first event, and so we soon found ourselves waiting at the start for the swans to move at their own leisurely, majestic pace out of the racing lanes. Neither of us knew how our boat would race or what the standard of the opposition was around us but we looked forward to finding out. Our first few racing strokes together were fast but not the smoothest we would ever have. As we pelted out at maximum speed the boat rocked in the slightly choppy water and as one side dipped away I gouged my thigh with my thumbnail. Soon we had corrected our overly enthusiastic and admittedly tense start and we moved easily through the field and into the lead. By halfway Anna was calling for us not to do any more and to start easing off, aware we had another final in just over an hour. By the end of the 2,000m I let the rate drop while keeping a watchful eye on the attacking field behind us. It was an occasional habit that used to get Fran very nervous sitting behind me. Here, however, we had room to play with because of the lead we had built up, and Anna allowed the rate to drop from the usual mid-30s into the 20s and we cruised through the line to our first win.

It had been simple and fun and would define our double racing at its best. High on adrenaline and joy we came back in to the landing stage and tried to come down a little before gearing up for the quad. We had massages arranged to try to get the lactic acid out of our legs, although we had managed to clear most of it by being able to take it easier in the second half of the race. We ate our planned jelly snake sweets and drank recovery drinks. Then it was time to meet Annie and Beth. We were raring to go and excitable but toned it down for the meeting as they were going through the usual pre-race nerves without the flood of endorphins we were experiencing from racing and winning. Thommo gathered us and refocused us on the aims we had for the quad, the simple things we needed to get right to put in the best performance. Anna and I soberly put the double behind us and the only race that existed was the final of the quad.

Although I felt great on the land, I was aware as soon as we started warming up that my legs had just raced. I stayed thinking about the technical details we were concentrating on and reminded myself that behind me I had Annie and Beth who were fresh and determined to win a medal of their own, and Anna who I knew would produce the power whenever necessary. As the race began both Anna and I felt the pain in our legs, but when we weren't where we wanted to be in the race we gritted our teeth and piled on more pressure and made extra demands of our bodies. As we were sitting in the stern end of the boat we couldn't expect Annie and Beth to lead from behind us, so Anna and I raised the intensity to where we felt it should be and Beth and Annie easily matched the work. Soon we were moving through and the title was ours. More celebrations as the medals were handed out beside the fairytale lake.

The original plan had been to double up for just one regatta, but as we moved forward Fran and Debbie were still not back in the team and thoughts turned to trying once again in Munich. The standard would be raised as the weeks went by, with more countries entering the battle. There was also a greater risk, as the gap between finals was even shorter, but once again it was a challenge we were ready to embrace. For Anna and me the experience of racing twice in a short space improved us not only physically but also mentally. It showed beyond all expectation just what we were capable of and so gave us more confidence than ever before.

But although doubling up was the physically hard part, we were aware that in many ways it was the easier and more fun role to have. To be the other half of the boat who had to sit on the sidelines was a greater challenge. I had experienced it back in 1997 when I was in the eight, watching the four race separately. But then I was new and inexperienced and just enjoyed any opportunity I was given. In the intervening years the standards and expectations of all athletes had been raised. It was right and appropriate that Beth and Annie had their own egos and ambitions and weren't as happy to be on the sidelines. They asked if they could race the double too, so we would all be doubling up. Annie in particular wanted to try the challenge of seeing how fast their double could go, and as they were spending a lot of time training in it, it made sense to race it too. There was a suggestion for a while that we could just race doubles and leave the quad, but the decision was made to replicate the Bled racing. Once again Anna and I won our double easily and within the hour we were back on the water for the quad final. This time we didn't have everything our own way. The very experienced and successful German scullers had put together a quad to beat us and knew we could be vulnerable out of the start. They flew from the first stroke, attacking the first few hundred metres, and took a massive lead. Frustrated that we had let them slip away, we chased them down and came very close to beating them, but they maintained a slight advantage. The Germans had won the second World Cup.

After more discussions leading up to the third and final World Cup in Lucerne there was some thought that Debbie might be able to make it back into the squad. In the end it was decided she would race in the single to check her fitness and the four of us would complete our World Cup doubling up experiment. Our loss in Munich still stung and I was very happy to be given the chance to put things right in the quad final. Lucerne is known as the "playground of the gods" and is the rowing course where wins are hard fought and richly enjoyed. Anna and I won the double and made sure we did it as efficiently as possible, conserving as much as we could for the quad final, although constantly pushed by a new and determined Australian double. We were aware that the quad standard had been raised even higher with the arrival of a very fast and very impressive Ukraine crew. This was the Ukraine quad that would go on to win the London Olympics in a display of devastating power and skill. I knew it would be the hardest race of the year so far for us and would take everything we had. This was the race during which as a quad we came together better than ever. Beth was calm and clear in her calls. Annie was aggressive and fiery in her tactics, the rhythm was powerful, and together we stopped being four athletes or two doubles and became a world-class crew, united in a common cause and relishing the chance to test every area of our abilities. Whereas back in Bled Anna and I had taken more of a leadership role, by Lucerne Annie and Beth had seized the baton and were sprinting away with it.

I remember having a wicked grin of masochistic glee as three top quads thundered their way down the course, a blaze of noise and power, blades surgically cutting through the water and voices booming over the top. The 12 athletes from Great Britain, Ukraine and Germany were packed with future and current Olympic and World medallists. The standard was thrilling and it brought out the best in everyone. This is what all the exhausting training is for. The three boats were tied and as the pain started to burn I pushed harder and deeper; this was where we wanted to be, if this was our last race together we had to leave it all here on the water and finish it in the best style possible. The impressive opposition undoubtedly raised our own levels and with everyone delivering an almost faultless performance we moved our boat ahead to win the race. The overall World Cup double and quad title was ours. The loss in Munich still grates a little but it prepared us in the best possible way for the battle in Lucerne. We knew where people would see us as vulnerable, we knew we couldn't give anything away at the start, and we knew the only way to match and better the rival crews was to operate as a committed and united team.

That summer we also had the privilege of racing at Henley Royal Regatta. An annual event, Henley is different from the usual international regattas because it is a two-boat race, operating in a knockout system over five days. The regatta is open to all rowers, from school rowers up to Olympic Champions. The Henley medal is a holy grail for everyone from aspiring university rowers to World Champions. It is one of the rare world sporting events where club athletes can compete directly against the best in the world. And in this picturesque town the racing battles take place just metres from the crowded banks of vocal supporters. The racing lasts a little over 2,100m down the River Thames alongside meadows and local rowing clubs.

Thousands of people fill the bank, from families in their shorts and T-shirts gathered on blankets enjoying picnics in the summer sunshine to the blazer-wearing rowing traditionalists who gather to drink champagne while cheering on the racing from the enclosures. When I first visited the regatta I was a student on a visit from Edinburgh and felt as if I'd entered another world. Amongst the tented enclosures and the jugs of Pimms there is the sound of a brass band playing classical tunes and old favourites. Every day at the end of racing the National Anthem is played. Many of the visitors spend the majority of the time in the car park, where tables are brought out and filled with all manner of food and drinks and groups of people meet to enjoy each other's company.

By the time we raced in 2010 I had been made a Steward of the Regatta. It was a huge honour and one not frequently bestowed on a woman. Previously in its long and rich history there had only ever been two female Stewards: Di Ellis, the Chair of British Rowing, and Annamarie Phelps, a former international rower and the woman who would replace Di at the head of British Rowing. To be the third in this illustrious group was something I didn't expect and found deeply flattering. Although what I hadn't realized is that being a Steward actually meant work. There are around 50 Stewards of the Regatta and it is a lifetime appointment. Once the silver badge is pinned to your jacket you will for evermore be in the town of Henley-on-Thames for the first few days of July. John Hedger was appointed a Steward in the same year I was so we consider ourselves Steward Twins. Unfortunately for poor John that means he spends most years patiently keeping me right as he has the impressive ability to know at all times where we are supposed to be when and what the dress code should be. I am usually jogging a few paces behind him still trying to put my shoes on, while John's genteel demeanour is more representative of Stewards' behaviour. Ironically, it was seeing Henley Royal Regatta through the eyes of the Stewards rather than through the eyes of an athlete that truly made me appreciate how special it is as an event. I had unfairly judged the Stewards to be a group of men of a certain age and certain background, who were far removed from the real world. In reality, they are a wonderful mix of characters of varied age and background united by their deep common love of rowing and of the regatta. There is a strong sense of pride in putting on a new and progressive regatta every year while maintaining the history and tradition that define it.

Unfortunately, however, not all the Stewards show the decorum one might expect. My initial experience of the problem came when I worked on the day of the qualifying races. The available Stewards gathered in the main tent, where we were briefed by Mike Sweeney, the Chairman of the Regatta. He handed out clipboards, radios, megaphones and orders and I felt as if we were in the briefing room in an American police drama, about to hit the streets, with the Captain issuing instructions for the day. Except that the assembled officers were wearing blazers, some had stylish panama straw hats, and I had on a long, flowing white skirt which was the required uniform for women. Looking around, I was aware our outfits wouldn't have been practical, or safe, on the mean streets. Luckily there are not many mean streets in Henley.

I walked up to my designated part of the river, where my main job was to make sure none of the athletes went past the safety marker and risked falling over the weir. I had a radio in one hand, a megaphone in the other and juggled a clipboard under my arm. One of the last instructions we had had from Mike Sweeney was to look out for "inappropriately named boats". There had been one boat the year before that had an unusual name on it, which turned out to be the name for a porn website. As I was keeping an eye on the assembling crews, my radio sprung to life. I was in Steve Redgrave and Matthew Pinsent's team above the startline and Steve's serious voice cut across across the airways. "Uh, we have a boat with a very dirty name coming towards us." I snapped to attention. This was what we had been waiting for. I wasn't actually sure what we were supposed to do about it, and I was armed only with a clipboard and pen, but I was at the ready. The boat would come to Matthew next. His deep voice boomed through: "Oh, I see what you mean, it's absolutely filthy." I was almost nervous as I watched the rebellious boat approach. I squinted into the sun trying to make out the name along the side. When it came close enough I read the name "Katherine Grainger" along the side. It was a boat Marlow Rowing Club had named after me. I lifted my radio and said "You bas***ds" into it. I didn't need to have a radio to hear the laughter from along the towpath. They may be Knights of the Realm, but at their worst, and their best, Steve and Matthew are a pair of giant naughty schoolboys.

My greatest concern about the 2010 competition was the rumours I had heard of what happens to competing Stewards. Sir Matthew and Sir Steve were the only other athletes to have been made Stewards while being international competing athletes (because Stewards work at the Regatta, being a competing athlete at the same time means little useful work can be done, so mostly Stewards are appointed after their international racing career ends). The 1992 Olympic champions Jonny and Greg Searle had competed for their clubs after finishing with international competition and always seemed to experience some sort of abuse from their fellow Stewards on the startline. I warned my crew we might be in for a bit of friendly banter but luckily my fellow Stewards restrained themselves. In our semi-final we broke one of the course records and went on to win the final and so completed an incredible summer of racing. The four of us had won three major international titles together, and Anna and I had completed a run of 15 races, winning 14 of them and loving every minute.

There was now going to be a long period of training before the World Championships in New Zealand. The double was now our sole focus and we entered a wonderful couple of months where we learned, developed, improved and became stronger and better in every way. While still loving the whole process. I had never had such a positive time in rowing, where both on the water and off the water was so much fun. We flew out to New Zealand feeling confident.

When we first took to the water in Karapiro, however, things weren't what we'd hoped. The comfortable control over our boat wasn't there. The natural movement and effortless technical skills had left us. Although we knew rationally we couldn't have lost everything overnight, there was a concern over how long it might take to recover our form. Thommo listened patiently and suggested to us that rather than doing long outings on the course we might want to try leaving the racing area of the lake and row up into the long gulley. The suggestion surprised us, mainly because it would mean he couldn't watch or coach us for much of the outing, and in my experience Thommo had always wanted to watch every session, especially as racing approached. In fact it was a brilliant moment for him to choose to loosen his grip a little, allowing us the freedom to stretch the boat out over a long continuous row rather than the shorter laps we had been doing on the course. As we settled into the outing, managing to relax and feel for the boat more, the magic returned. The concern was over, and we once again enjoyed the fun of seeing how fast we could go.

We also made the most of being in a new country. Most athletes had planned to stay on after the Championships for a holiday in New Zealand. Anna's husband Oli would be coming over to join her, and as an avid fisherman their holiday was going to involve days by the many streams and rivers in the beautiful South Island. To prepare, Anna had been chatting to a guy who worked in the local sports store, and one day he volunteered to take Anna fishing so she could try for herself. She invited me too, for company and safety, and on a free afternoon we jumped into Wayne's car to venture into the countryside outside Hamilton. We drove for a very long time, and as we got closer and closer to the middle of nowhere and mobile phone reception was left far behind, both Anna and I had the same thought about just how sensible this idea might have been. Luckily our new friend Wayne was a true gentleman and far more interested in the state of the fish than in us, and so we spent happy hours in an idyllic clearing, with crystal clear water and gentle green foliage everywhere. I went for a bit of a ramble while Anna was taught the basics of fly fishing. It was a welcome peaceful break from the intensity of competition. It was our calm before the storm.

Back at the course we knew our closest rivals were likely to be an

Australian double. They were changed from the Lucerne combination and in their own minds a better crew. The days of the finals had been troubled by strong winds and very rough conditions, which meant that some races were delayed and some were affected by unfair lanes. There were mixed fortunes for the team. Pete Reed and Andy Hodge came the closest they would ever come to beating the record-breaking New Zealand pair but had to settle for silver. The new women's pair of Heather Stanning and Helen Glover won an impressive silver medal at their first World Championships. It was the first sign that they would go on to even greater things. Zac and Mark turned the conditions to their advantage, dominating the young challengers from New Zealand who had appeared to pose a threat earlier in the week, while the lightweight women's double of Hester Goodsell and Sophie Hosking sadly struggled in the rough water. The men's four were on the unfortunate side of the lanes and slipped out of the medals completely. The women's quad seized their moment and, after an unpredictable and inconsistent training camp leading up to the Championships, they arrived in New Zealand ready to ignore their recent negative history and instead start afresh with a clean sheet and a confident outlook. In the final, as the Ukraine quad never looked dangerous and the Germans struggled with the rough water, Annie, Fran, Beth and Debbie led the way and crossed the line as World Champions.

When it came to our final there was no thigh gouging in the way we had managed in Bled, but we were still a little more tense than we would have liked. Despite the tension we were in our strong familiar rhythm and soon were moving through the field. Without doing anything special we seemed able to continue moving away from the other boats and by halfway we had a comfortable margin. This was the first final of the year when we didn't have the quad race next and so we didn't have to save ourselves. In front of thousands of cheering supporters we sprinted home, over five seconds ahead of the Australians. It had felt sensational and lived up to everything we had hoped. I hadn't realized at the time, but the win also meant, unusually, I now had World Championship medals in every Olympic boat class available to me: single, pair, double, quad and eight.

As Anna and Oli left for their fishing trips, Beth and I hired a campervan and set off exploring the South Island for the next couple of weeks. Beth and I had been friends since she had joined the team but had never holidayed together. Now we would be sharing the same small campervan which became our bedroom, kitchen, car and entertainment centre. Luckily the cramped confines had no negative impact on our friendship and we laughed and sang our way around New Zealand. When rowing Beth is a quietly driven person. She doesn't have a showy manner or a visible ego and occasionally she reminded me of Becs with her silent reticence. She may not choose to be a vocal leader but she is an incredibly consistent and strong performer and an amazingly reliable individual. With Beth in a boat or a team there was always someone who would be responsible and thorough in planning and organizing. I've lost count of the number of times I've had a message from Beth on the morning of flights reminding me of the terminal and flight number. She is the first person to call if you're stuck somewhere and need something done quickly and efficiently with the minimum of fuss. In addition, Beth has a hugely appreciated talent for baking wonderful cakes.

In New Zealand the pressure of the day job was off, we were both World Champions and we had a ball. We climbed glaciers, kayaked through waterfalls, went parachuting, took a jet boat through a canyon and relaxed by the ice blue lakes. I always relish holiday time and love to recharge my batteries and this time was no different. Then, once the holiday break was over, I looked forward to going back and moving the double on to the next level.

Whereas in 2010 everything went smoothly, 2011 was to be a very different story. The winter training had been relatively smooth until I nearly killed myself.

One of the toughest camps we did was the bike camps where we had over two solid weeks of huge rides every day. One day in Majorca the coaches informed us we were going to cycle the "Lighthouse route" because apparently the views to Formentor were spectacular. Unfortunately, the price to pay for the views was a much rougher and more uneven road than the usual ones we rode on. Jess and I paired up again and we grumbled our way along with our bikes shaking under us as the tyres hit loose stones, bounced over holes in the road and we had to focus far more on the tarmac and gravel in front of us than any beautiful views that may have appeared. By the time we arrived at the lighthouse tempers were frayed and while the coaches took photos in the sunshine we sat grumpily eating energy bars. We set off for the return leg with Jess listing all the places she had been to where she felt there were better views than here, but as we arrived at the top of the first hill the sun shone through the clouds and backlit an overhanging cliff up above us. It was indeed beautiful and reminded us of a scene from *The Lion King*. That in turn prompted us to start singing songs from *The Lion King* and as we gathered speed on the downhill I had just started "Hakuna Matata" or, ironic as it would turn out to be, "No Worries". We could generate a lot of acceleration on the descents and there was the welcome feeling of easy gathering speed as we hurtled down towards home.

Up ahead I could see the hairpin bend and I touched my brakes to slow my speed a little. As I did that my bike swerved underneath me and I instantly released the brakes again. I had no idea what had happened or why but I was also all too aware that my speed was still far too fast as the corner raced towards me. I tried the brakes again but there was the same unnerving reaction from the bike. By now it was too late, I saw the crash barrier ahead, the low stone wall and a long drop into the trees over the other side. I had no option, I pulled harder on the brakes and my bike skidded underneath me. I had the time to think it was going to be bad. Bike and body hit the road hard and then spun onto the barrier, bounced off it into the wall and we came to rest separately in the middle of the road. I could hear Jess swearing loudly and repeatedly behind me as she threw her own bike to one side and ran across.

I stood up slowly as I vaguely heard Jess telling me not to move. She lifted my bike off the road just in time, for a car that was coming towards us swept around the corner. I had a moment to be thankful the car hadn't been a few seconds earlier. I had cut my hand but apart from that there were no obvious visible signs of injury. I had a throbbing dead leg but it seemed to be working and my helmet was in one piece. I took a few steps down the road to check there were no obvious problems and then went over to look at my bike. Jess was still staring in disbelief at me. I had a front tyre puncture which explained the loss of control on the bend and when we looked closely we saw Jess had a puncture too. It was then that the shock set in and as we tried to mend the punctures we found everything a little too funny. The laughter meant it was impossible to function properly and it was with great relief that Beth was the next person round the corner and she stopped to see what our problem was. Shortly after that the safety van stopped too and I was given a plaster for my badly bleeding hand. Our tyres were changed, the bikes checked over and then we climbed on for the rest of the journey home. Admittedly at first I felt really wobbly but it seemed the right thing to do. Jess was alongside me shaking her head, "Honestly, Katherine, you are the toughest person I know," and Beth stayed with us frowning in a gently concerned way. Thankfully there were no long-term injuries although the whole of my dead leg had swollen impressively by the time we arrived back at the hotel and over many weeks I watched in the mirror as the huge open graze covering my lower back, backside and the top half of my leg changed through all sorts of colours. Jess dubbed it "Suicycle Monday".

The April trials before final selection were moved to Dorney, the recently announced venue for the Olympic Games. The top scullers would be in singles, and because of our exploits the previous summer the main race was being billed as a showdown between Anna and me. If I were to win, it would be my tenth title; if Anna won, then she would be claiming her first and it would be seen as the changing of the order. Anna had already won the long-distance winter trials and she had been going very well in training. I hadn't been able to find the speed I wanted or row in the way I would have liked. I couldn't quite put my finger on it but I was out of sorts and very unusually for me I wasn't particularly looking forward to the racing. At the Italian training camp before trials I had a room to myself and used it to get some much-needed work done for my PhD.

I had been studying for a PhD in criminal law for years and regularly tested the patience of my impressive supervisor, Elaine. It was important for me to continue my studies, as challenging as that often proved to be. I still believed, as I had since my undergraduate degree, that if I managed successfully to balance my rowing and my studying then each would enhance the other. Elaine didn't always agree but, then, to be fair she thought the bit of rowing I did was a "hobby" and after a year or two was still asking how my "canoeing" was going. London 2012 changed that. In the few months after the Olympics I finally had time to devote to the work and Elaine was as relieved and happy as I was to see it completed and awarded. In the years before the Olympics I would grab whatever spare time I could find on training camp to get some work done and Sarah and Beth used to tape sweets to my work chart as daily incentives. That year in Varese I used the advantage of my single room to get my head down and work my way through the piles of articles and books I had brought with me.

Unfortunately it also had the effect of shutting myself off. It was productive in some ways and yet destructive in others. Anna was great and tried to entice me out of my black hole, suggesting I joined her and some of the others on a trip to the Da Vinci museum in Milan. I declined, in order to get more work done, but I still use the postcard she brought back from the museum as a bookmark to remind me not to be such a miserable loner when I'm struggling. I couldn't wait to get to the crew boat part of the year when we would go back into our double and take on the world together. I didn't like the media hijacking the trial and staging it as a personal fight between the two of us. Of course it made a good story and I should have seen it as inevitable, but I believed Anna and I had created something truly special a few months ago and this seemed to go against everything we had done. The sweep group were luckier, they had to compete in their pairs; it was only the scullers that had to become lone warriors.

I remember having little confidence before the trial and just wanting the racing to be over. I didn't feel any of my usual thrilling killer instinct. At the same time Anna was at her peak and delivered a stunning performance in the final. She beat me and was overjoyed to have taken the title she wanted. I congratulated her and then we gave each other a bit of space. Oli, Anna's husband, had been there supporting her and whisked her off, each of them looking as pleased and proud as the other. I sat devastated on the grass, coming to terms with my loss and the barrage of media questions about being beaten by my partner and whether I was on the decline. At some point my friend from university, James, came over with his wife Sarah and their two young daughters. One of them was the "tickle monster". I laughed and played with them, forcing my own self-pity into a box and ignoring it for a while. Children and animals always provide a healthy dose of perspective and I enjoyed the focus on daisy chains and tickling. Later I could torture myself with thoughts of success and failure; for now I would play on the grass in the sunshine. The "tickle monster" was to later make a prominent appearance on a banner at the London 2012 finish line about 15 months later.

Thommo was very supportive. He understands and respects disappointment in defeat, and he knew the pain I was putting myself through. But he was also pragmatic. His two top athletes had come a clear first and second, and the order was almost irrelevant. The crucial thing was that once again we had to come in the top two, which would make putting us back in the double a straightforward selection procedure. If someone had managed to beat one of us, things would have become more complicated; instead we were close to each other but ahead of the rest of the field.

After a couple of days' break we all gathered again for the start of the crew formation part of the year. This time it was Anna who had the choice of single or double, but there was again no doubt. Anna and I both knew what we wanted to do, and with Anna's recent success we were more equal than ever in the boat. She was buoyant and enthusiastic from the start; I was a little more subdued initially, but soon added the trial result to the large sack of experience I was always filling and got stuck back into the double. This was the fun part of the year and the reason behind every bit of training we did. We both felt there was so much more to come.

And it wasn't always hard work, training and stressful testing. A little over a week after we went back to training there was much excitement in the changing rooms caused by nothing to do with rowing. In honour of Kate Middleton and Prince William and, to be honest, as an excuse to enjoy ourselves, the women's team had decided to have an afternoon tea on the day of the Royal Wedding. As has been said on more than one occasion, if you want anything organized, ask the women's rowing squad. Plans were drawn up as timings were discussed. Logistics of training locations were perfected, while negotiations with coaches begun, and each athlete was assigned a job of either cake making, scone baking, fizzy drink purchasing, paper plate locating, even bunting and decoration planning. As the morning approached we had the most detailed day plan imaginable and it created a welcome air of light-hearted fun after all the pressures of the trials. The wedding added a bit of variety to the training day and another great opportunity for bonding. And eating cake. I don't think I've ever seen quite such an impressive afternoon tea display, and as we ventured back on to the water a few hours later there was a distinct queasiness from the vast amount of tea and cake we had consumed.

Apart from that sugar overdose things on the water were going very well, until a few days after the wedding party. We were only two weeks along from trials, and the excitement of being allowed to play in the double was still high. But that wouldn't last. Things began with Anna doing a little more stretching than usual in the morning before the outing. I asked if everything was OK. "Absolutely fine, just a bit stiff," was the first reply. The next day there was a bit more stretching and then a bit of a warm-up on the rowing machine before we went out on the water. "Nothing to worry about," she smiled, reassuringly, as I looked concerned. The next day I couldn't find her, and when Thommo and I finally did she told us the physio just had to check her over before we went out, but it was "all fine". As she headed up the metal stairs Thommo and I looked at each other.

As time went on it was still "fine", but I had a couple of days rowing with Vicky Thornley in the double so that Anna could rest. When we tried the double again we stopped as her back was feeling sore. Anna is very good at being aware of her body and knowing when and how much to push things. Surprisingly, it is a skill not as common in athletes as it should be – too many of us, used to training in some level of discomfort or exhaustion, keep pushing through the point when common sense should say no. Thankfully, Anna flagged up the problem in a training session and it was an easy decision for us both. Her health and fitness were far more important than finishing that particular session. She went to see Ann Redgrave, the team doctor. Later that day things didn't seem to be so fine when she was sent for an MRI scan. We didn't realize it at the time but the session we cut short would be the last session together for the next five weeks.

Three weeks after Anna went into rehab was the first World Cup of the season, in Munich. I wasn't sure what the plan would be for me, as it took us a little while to confirm that Anna definitely wouldn't be able to compete. Initially I thought that perhaps I would miss out on the racing too. For both Anna and me our double was the sole focus for so many reasons that anything else seemed not quite right to compete in, and I was comfortable with the thought of just training until she returned. But racing is racing and we do it so rarely that it's always worth gaining more experience.

The decision was made for me to race in the double with another partner. The choice was between Mel Wilson and Vicky Thornley. Either would be a great option and I trained with both of them. For the first World Cup Thommo decided Mel and I should team up. Mel came to rowing with a healthy experience of time spent in the real world. She had travelled widely with her family while growing up and was now studying for a medical degree, but was taking time off from her degree to train full time. Mel had a very healthy, open perspective on life, in contrast to many athletes who had been immersed in sport for a while. She was good at pointing out the ridiculous elements of what we did that we had all grown used to without questioning. Mel was also very easy company, often saying hilarious things without realizing and with the wonderful gift of being able to laugh at herself. And she was never afraid to ask questions. We were looking forward to the challenge of Munich.

We made it through to the final comfortably but then on the race morning our bus didn't turn up to the hotel. Luckily we had Maggie. As mentioned before, Maggie is David Tanner's right-hand woman and 13 years on from when I first met her, Maggie was still calmly and efficiently fixing everything. She gives the impression she could sort out all of the world's problems while the kettle boils. A couple of calls later a bus appeared and Mel hadn't shown the slightest sign of being flustered. This was a good start.

As far as racing was concerned our chats with Thommo had gone well, the three of us were all clear about what was needed and how we would do it, and I was looking forward to the race. Mel and I had made it to the course in good time despite the delayed bus and were hanging around in a wooden waiting room at the course watching the minutes tick by. When it was about time we gathered our things and headed downstairs for the last chat with Thommo before the race. As we walked there were the usual nerves but we believed that it was going well and that we just had to go out there and do what we'd be doing and we'd be fine. Mel and I walked down to the landing stage to check the water conditions. We saw some of the lightweight crews boating who were racing after us, and Mel commented, "They're a bit keen." I agreed, while aware that a red flag had appeared in my consciousness. In the far distance I could see our opposition warming up on the lake.

The walk back towards Thommo was slightly quicker and a part of me wasn't surprised when he said, "Yeah right, guys, bit of an odd one. Apparently the race time has been changed but no one told us. You should be warming up by now." There was no panic, just a sense of urgency as we gathered the boat and Thommo escorted us to the landing stage. He gave us brief words of advice and support as we pushed off while trying to stay calm. The message, although unspoken, was clear: "It's fine but don't mess around and don't miss the start." I spent the whole – very shortened – warm-up trying to sound exceedingly relaxed, laughing off the brief time we had and reassuring Mel that there was no way we needed an extended warm-up anyway. I have no doubt that Mel didn't need me to say any of those things, as she is brilliant at taking things in her stride and not blowing anything out of proportion. But I wanted to be certain we would sit on the startline confident, relaxed and with our minds on the race, thinking about what we would do, not thinking about what we hadn't done.

I needn't have worried. Our mini issues made no impact on our racing; we led the race from the beginning and controlled the boat and the opposition exactly as we had wanted. I raced with absolute belief that whatever I did Mel would match, and she did an amazing job. The boat felt comfortable and fast and we were rewarded with the gold medal. Not all of the fastest crews in the world were there and it was early on in the season, but for a scratch double with little time together we had done a great job. Mel's cool head, open attitude and relaxed persona had made it a fun and fast boat to be part of. Thommo bought us a beer at the airport, as is his usual Munich tradition, and we toasted a test successfully passed.

When we came back, the first person I went to see was Anna. I knew how hard it might have been for her having to stay at home, injured, in pain and watching. Mel and I had had a great regatta, we had both learned from it as well as having fun, but we knew it was a temporary thing until Anna could return. Anna's progress had been good and there was hope that she would be back for the second World Cup in

Duisburg. But sadly that proved overly optimistic. Before long we had to face up to the reality that she wouldn't be ready to race in Duisburg. I met Anna for coffee in Marlow, and as I watched her sit down I saw the all too familiar discomfort of someone with a sore back and the tell-tale sign of leaning on thighs as she tried to lower herself onto the sofa. She also sat at an odd angle throughout our chat in an effort to find a comfortable position.

We had met for a coffee and a catch-up, but at one point Anna became emotional. She admitted that things might not be ok: I might have to think about a new partner more permanently as she was beginning to fear the injury could mean she wouldn't row again. It was a massive admission and I had nothing but respect for how honest she was being. Without hesitating I gave her the two things she needed from me. A strong hug and unconditional support. I told her that it didn't matter how long it took; it was worth the wait. Even if it meant not getting back in a boat until next season I firmly believed that we would still be the fastest crew on the water.

So Anna went back into the world of rehab and the safe hands of Ann, Ash, Alex and Liz, and I turned my thoughts to Duisberg. There was the option of Mel and me reuniting to race again, but Thommo wanted to try Mel in the single and Vicky Thornley in the double.

I had raced with Vicky in 2009 in the composite eight for the Head of the River Race and she is not someone you forget easily. She has a striking presence, being a 6ft 4 ex-model who carries her height with style and ease. She only started rowing in 2009, having been discovered at a "Sporting Giants" scheme. In her pre-rowing days she was a showjumper as well as a model. She has a figure to die for and always looks incredible, with the appearance of hardly trying. After an exhausting training most people will be dragging themselves and their kitbags out of the changing room looking about 50 years older than they should and wearing an assortment of flip-flops, trainers, borrowed sports kit – because even doing this every day some item is always forgotten – with maybe a pair of jeans to be really smart. Vicky on the other hand will have blown dry her short stylish blonde hair, added a bit of make-up, thrown on a combination of designer gear, grabbed her handbag and swung herself out of the door looking like a million dollars.

She is the kind of girl you think you should hate just for that skill, and yet any bad feeling towards her is impossible. She has absolutely no pretensions about the way she looks; it's a natural, lightly worn thing rather than something used as a weapon. She laughs easily and often bursts of her excited voice would fill the crew room between sessions. She loves glossy magazines and trashy books and carried the full box set of *Sex and the City* with her on training camp. And amongst all the fun girly stuff is the competitive drive of an ambitious athlete. She often had to be held back in training for fear of overdoing things, and when she first joined the team she was at risk of going too fast too early in the race, such was her need to compete. In the double I sat behind her long easy stroke and looked forward to racing. Unfortunately we didn't get to find out how fast we were, because as the Duisberg regatta approached there was an E.coli outbreak in Germany and it was decided by our Team Manager that we wouldn't travel to compete.

I was sorry to miss out on the chance to race with Vicky, as she is an athlete I have a huge amount of respect for and was a lot of fun to be with. I believe we would have done great things in Duisburg but we would never now get the chance to find out. Being at home, however, meant that possibly Anna and I would be able to get back in the boat together.

The first session back was exciting and the sign that we were back on the path we wanted to be on. It was, however, not the same boat we had left. Understandably Anna was hesitant about her back, and we were missing the natural ease with which we moved the boat and that we had taken completely for granted. Anna is also very attuned to the boat and her calls are always precise and exactly what the boat needs. For the first time Anna seemed quiet, almost withdrawn, as she focused on her body and carefully watched for any signs it might be giving her. I knew exactly where she was, having felt the same discomfort and doubts when I rejoined the quad in 2007 after my back flare-up, and I knew that with time her confidence would return. We only had a couple of weeks before the Lucerne World Cup, however, and we discussed whether or not it was worth going. On the positive side it would be useful to be racing; and otherwise Anna would miss out completely on the World Cup racing season. She was keen to get an international race in before the World Championships. On the other hand, we might risk losing the race with a performance that was realistically going to be beneath our best and thereby throwing away our unbeaten record.

In the end we decided the risk was worth taking, and even if we did lose, we would gain in other ways. Once we openly admitted that, however, any thought of losing was banished from our minds. We were going to Lucerne to win. And we did. It was probably to our benefit that at the time we weren't aware just how far from our best we were. We raced with everything we had at the point we were at, but it was only later in the summer that we realized just how far back the injury had set us. We could still win internationally, but it was way below our best standard.

When we set off for our usual summer training camps we left thoughts of Anna's injury behind and looked forward to focusing once more on seeing how fast we could go. But it was only on camp that we faced the reality of our situation. Although Anna was now completely recovered from the injury, the loss of invaluable training time together had an effect. A year previously we were winning the timed pieces of work easily; this year we were struggling to make an impact on the percentages, which were the numbers that told us how we compared to the other crews on camp. We decided we were just a bit rusty, but as the camp went on we were slipping backwards if anything. The boat had been feeling good but we didn't seem to be getting the response from the stopwatch. Thommo was being very supportive but also seemed at a loss as to why we didn't have the speed we should. It came to a head one day when we had improved a lot in training but once again the timed pieces were slower than ever before. Thommo sent the results through by email at some point that afternoon and then later added a note that we should have a meeting in the morning before the next training session to discuss things. It had been an afternoon off, so he'd wanted to let us enjoy the rare bit of downtime before throwing ourselves back into training the next day. But we couldn't now enjoy the downtime.

Anna and I were in our room and she was poring over the facts and figures from the day. Her ability to analyse data is one of her many strengths and undoubtedly made us a better crew. I judged mainly on instinct in the boat, and Anna more on concrete facts, but the wonderful thing was that those two separate bits of information, rather than being contradictory, almost always backed each other up. It constantly added to our confidence and meant we were good at solving problems. But this problem was proving tough to crack. I was sure from how the boat felt and how we were rowing that we should be going faster, and Anna could see from the data that our angles, lengths, depths, etc were all saying the same. We should be going faster than we were. We talked around and around and finally, exasperated, Anna threw the sheets of paper to one side. She looked at me. "I don't think we should wait until the morning to have the meeting. I think we should have it now." Although I was comfortable relaxing on my bed I knew she was right. "OK, then, make the call."

We met in the reception area of the hotel, Thommo armed with video and laptop and Anna with the data printouts. Between us we agreed that the video looked fine, the numbers were good and the feel was positive. It was the speed that somehow did not seem to fit with any of that, and ultimately that was the most important thing. Then Thommo, for the first time in all the years I have known him, admitted he didn't have an answer. For that moment alone it was a very powerful and very useful meeting. To hear from Thommo that he didn't know what to do was initially a surprise and a concern, but it was also very liberating. It showed just how good our trust in each other was and how honest we felt we could be that our coach, the chief women and lightweight's coach, could admit not having all the answers. Together we would figure it out. As a team, our communication and resolve moved yet another step forward that night.

Between us we decided the only thing we could do was to strip everything right back to the basics. Simplicity would once again be the most important thing for us and we would take nothing for granted. Although still competing against the other boats on camp, we detached ourselves from what the results meant in comparison to others and focused simply on what the results meant for us. Slowly we began to turn things around. Along with Chris, the psychologist, we built a list of what we had and what we would need to be at our best. All kinds of thing from the physical or technical to the psychological or emotional. It was like forming a huge jigsaw, and we were strict with ourselves about only adding a piece in if we felt it was a perfect fit.

This continued as we moved to Italy, and a few days into that camp we turned a corner. The paddling was top quality, the control was back, it felt natural, and the bursts of speed were fast and powerful.

Although we were seeing continuous improvements I was still a little edgy, not sure if the very top end work was as good as it needed to be. However the confidence built with the results, and with the feel of our boat coming back to us all the time. One of the last things we did on camp was a full 2,000m race rehearsal at maximum intensity. Finally everything fell into place. We were fast and only 0.01 per cent behind Zac and Mark, who were racing above their usual restricted weight, so we knew we were going well. In the room afterwards Anna said, "Now I believe we can win. From here it's just about how big that margin can be." Her certainty was reassuring and inspiring and we headed to the World Championships finally feeling ready.

The Championships were being held in Bled, so we returned to the fairytale setting once more. We were in a hotel that looked down on to the course and across to the castle. I watched the Opening Ceremony from our balcony opposite the floodlit castle, with searchlights beaming out over the surrounding hills. Then opera music poured out over the lake from the far end where the ceremony was happening and everything stopped in the presence of the beautiful music. Anna came back out on to the balcony wrapped in her duvet and drawn by the music. At that point the fireworks started. I had thought Bled couldn't get any more magical, but it seemed I had been wrong.

We were excited about the thought of racing again now that we were back performing as we wanted. The last training session on the day before the heat we experienced, unusually for us, a miscommunication. But it was a good one. We were practising a sprint finish and Anna gave a call. She meant it for us to go into rhythm and steady the pace; I thought she meant it as an attacking call, and we scorched up past rate 38 and finished at 44, and it felt great. Anna was very excited that the boat was flying again. That evening we had the usual meeting with Thommo, and as he talked through the plans Anna and I kept glancing at each other and grinning; we couldn't wait to be out there doing our stuff. Earlier Jurgen had come up behind us as we stood at the noticeboard looking at the draw. The first we were aware of him was a strong hand on each of our shoulders. "So, how is the draw?" he boomed. I smiled, "It's good, Jurgen." "Ah yes, the draw is always OK if you are well prepared."

Before the heat we were quite relaxed and just looking forward to racing. The startline of Bled is actually the busiest part of the course. Unlike other racing courses, where the startline is usually furthest from the spectators and in the middle of nowhere, the Bled startline is practically in a park. The path along the lake goes right around the start, so we had the unusual experience of facing crowds of people who were making the usual boisterous summer sounds of families and groups of friends gathering outside for picnics and walks and games. There was chatter and bursts of laughter. Stands had been put up at the start too, so as we sat waiting for our race to be announced I tried not to be distracted by looking at who might be in the crowds. The loudspeakers were also very easy to hear, so we knew the Australian double had won the heat before ours.

Finally it was our time and huge boards were held up saying "Quiet please" and the crowds settled to a low murmur. The relative silence was broken by the odd shout of "Go GB!" or "C'mon Canada!". Then back to a well-behaved hush. The gun went and we leapt out. The Austrians and Germans came out fast with us, but by 500m we were clear and we could change down a gear to a more sustainable pace. By 1,000m we took the rate and intensity down again whilst still trying to move away. We lifted the boatspeed slightly at the end to make sure we stayed out of trouble from the high-rating attack from Germany, but it was all controlled. In the warm-down we were very pleased but agreed the speed was unlikely to be great. We had deliberately taken the foot off the gas, so we couldn't be worried if our overall time didn't look fast relative to the other heat. When we met up with Thommo he wanted to know our rates immediately, and I read them out as he wrote them down. I was increasingly concerned as the rates were getting lower and lower and he remained silent. Thankfully Anna came back at that point. She had checked out the times and despite our low rating we had the overall fastest time. All three of us were surprised but happy. After a challenging few months, we were back to our best.

The next morning we had a stretching session with our physio, Liz, and for some reason it was themed nautical fancy dress. Liz embraced the pirate look, Thommo wore a handkerchief knotted at the four corners on his head, and Anna and I stuffed two pairs of leggings and attached them to our tops so we had octopus legs. We thought we were convincing octopuses, although when Andy Hodge joined us in the lift afterwards he asked why we were wearing udders. Unbeknown to us it would be the last bit of fun of the week. On the way to breakfast Wendy, our fantastic nutritionist, stopped Thommo to say that 17 of the German team who were in our hotel had been ill overnight, and a few of our team too. The kitchen was checking the food. This is the biggest scare that happens at regattas; a whole team's preparation can be wiped out if illness spreads. I mentioned it to Anna, who went quiet and said she had been feeling a bit funny and didn't have breakfast. She went to speak to Wendy and Dr Ann. I walked down with Beth to watch the women's eight from the start, and when I came back to the hotel I saw Wendy, who told me Anna had been moved out of our room. A bit later I had a knock on my door and it was Thommo informing me I was in the black boat today – otherwise known as the ergo. My heart sank, for two reasons. First, not being able to train in our boat at the World Championships was a bad sign. Second, the thought of being on an ergo when we all thought we had finished those sessions for the year was less than pleasing. About ten minutes later Thommo phoned my room to ask when I was planning to go on the ergo. I laughed, asking if he was going to join me, and he wiped the smile off my face by saying yes. And he did just that. It must have been even worse for him to be getting back on the ergo than it was for me, but he accompanied me through the whole session. We both sweated buckets in the hot room, but I was impressed and grateful for his company.

The next day it was back on the ergo for training for Thommo and me because Anna had lost a lot of weight overnight. Her main job for the day was to eat as much as she possibly could and try to regain some of the weight. I joined her for breakfast and she had bread rolls stacked up around her and a face that didn't look happy at the thought of enforced eating. I felt sorry for her as I devoured cereal, wishing I could give her some of my appetite. I never seemed to have a problem with eating. I finished my cereal in the time Anna had managed barely a mouthful of bread and it was looking like a long morning for her. We had a few days yet until the semi-final so it wasn't a huge problem as long as she could manage to eat soon, but until she put some weight back on she would be constantly monitored and checked by the doctor, nutritionist and coach and we wouldn't be able to go rowing.

Meanwhile the rest of the squad still had racing to do, and I was chatting to Caroline, the cox from the eight, while we watched the women's quad race on TV. The quad had raced with Vicky earlier in the season, but she had moved into the eight and the quad was Annie, Debbie, Beth and Mel. Annie, Debbie and Beth were the reigning World Champions from the year before, but their recent training camp hadn't gone particularly well. However, considering they had still managed a great win in Karapiro despite a challenging few weeks I had confidence the quad would be able to secure a good result. It was the year before the London Olympics and every race meant that little bit more because Olympic qualification was at stake. The quad hadn't won their heat so were forced to go through the repechage. They had to finish top two to guarantee a place in the final, which would also assure them of an Olympic place. They led the repechage and I watched quite relaxed as I chatted to Caroline. But as they entered the last 500m the water started to get rough and the lower-rating USA seemed to be handling the conditions better, cutting through the British lead. The Chinese were attacking too, and while the camera angles on the TV made it impossible to know for sure, it looked tight. As the camera cut to the finish line we watched the USA go through first, then China, then Great Britain. There was stunned silence in the hotel reception where we had been watching it. My heart was pounding as if I'd been racing and my hands were shaking, as were Caroline's beside me. We looked at each other shocked. It was a massive upset for the British women's quad, who had finished in the top two in the world for six of the past seven years.

The best they could now come was seventh, and it was crucial that they did, as that was the last Olympic qualifying slot. Thankfully they managed to turn around a crushing loss in the space of 48 hours and rally to win the B Final, securing the Olympic berth.

Meanwhile Anna and I finally managed to take to the water that afternoon for a short outing. Anna was very quiet and admitted to feeling bad throughout. The boat, however, felt relatively good and we were all a little bit reassured from getting out on the water.

One problem was where our attention needed to be. Most of our discussions had become about food, weight loss or weight gain, calories and hydration. Usually the World Championships week is a wonderful week of thinking about nothing but fast boats and exciting racing, but for us the focus had to be different. We couldn't be quite sure how

Anna's fatigued and underpowered body would cope with a full race, or about its ability to recover in time for another one 24 hours later, so we decided to take the semi-final a bit easier than originally planned, saving what energy she had for the final.

The final of the women's pairs was the day before our semi-final and we gathered to watch Helen and Heather, everyone agreeing they could win this race. They put themselves in a great position, leading from the start, but then came under pressure from the New Zealand pair and in a very close sprint for the line the British pair missed out by 0.8 seconds. It was only their second World Championships and a fantastic second silver medal for them but they were devastated not to win. I saw them separately down at the course after the race, both in tears. I reassured them that their time would come, but none of us predicted quite the scale and joy of "their time" when it came about 12 months later at the London Olympics.

One boat that was also on fire at that regatta was the women's eight – only five of the final six boats would qualify for the Olympics, so their race was as fast and furious as anything you'll see. The British eight put in a stunning last 500m to move into third place and win the bronze. There were tears of joy and relief on the podium for the crew and a few hours later many celebratory and well-earned drinks. When Anna and I finally made it on to the lake for our training session I felt alive again. I was suddenly aware of how frustrated I'd been, and out of sorts, and annoyed by our fortunes over the week. And now something had changed, in the boat I felt ready to race – alert, excited, raring to go.

Our semi-final the next day was a bit of an unknown, but mentally I was sure. I felt relaxed and ready to turn recent frustrations to good use. The race went better than we expected. It was comfortable and once again we controlled the second half of the race – I knew that was a good sign and Anna was feeling better. Meanwhile I heard Rachel and Kate had arrived in Bled. Between Anna and me finding our form, the women's and the men's eights out celebrating and Kate and Rachel being on the loose somewhere nearby, I hoped Bled was steeling itself for whatever the next 24 hours might hold.

The morning of the final was quite relaxed. Most of the big boats had raced, so the boat park felt quiet. Anna and I were sharing the GB tent with the massive physical presence of Andy and Pete from the pair and Alan our single sculler. There was a sense of quiet solidarity with the few of us who still had to race. Before Anna and I boated we exchanged a big hug on the landing stage and gave each other a silent look that said everything. Those are the moments everyone shares with their racing partner; it is the acknowledgement of all that has gone before and all that might come. We wanted this to be our race, our moment, in spite of all that had happened, in fact because of all that had happened. In the race the Australians were the closest to us and continually threw challenges at us down the course. In comparison to the year before, the gap had narrowed considerably between us and our opposition, but we had had a tough few weeks to overcome. In the final few metres Anna had nothing more to give, having used up every bit of her available energy. There was a sprint for the line from the crews behind us, but we didn't react because we didn't have to; we had the margin we needed. We won, having led from the beginning, and the closest margin came from the New Zealanders launching a surprise attack at the end and almost beating the Australians. I was asked later what I felt at 100m to go and I said honestly, "I was smiling, I knew we had it."

As we celebrated after the race with our families, there was time to acknowledge the achievement Thommo, Anna and I had managed. A combination of the back injury, underperformance in training and illness had threatened to derail our great vision. But through a combination of honesty, trust, patience, clarity, never losing sight of the great things we could achieve – and a good sense of humour – we overcame everything to win. Whereas the 2010 season had been a complete joy because everything had gone right, this past season had been the true test of how we would react when everything had gone wrong. We did some things brilliantly, some things less well but had learned from it all. And now Thommo, Anna and I had added another powerful and priceless weapon to our armoury. Coming into the London Olympics we had the confidence that even when we were less than our best, we were better than anyone else in the world.

CHAPTER

11

GOLDEN DAYS

I was in Edinburgh for the arrival of 2012. Having been a student there I had enjoyed many a Hogmanay; concerts in the Castle, ceilidhs in Princes Street Gardens and arm-in-arm versions of "Auld Lang Syne" as thousands of strangers joined together to welcome in the New Year. My memories are of singing and dancing, of cheap alcohol and raucous laughter and over-the-top exuberance. This year, however, was a much quieter affair. When the bells rang out at midnight I watched the fireworks explode over Edinburgh Castle with mum and dad from their house with a glass of champagne in hand. The dark skies lit up in various stages of reds, oranges, greens and white as stars exploded overhead. It was as beautiful as ever, just a little more sober and sobering. We turned to each other to toast the New Year and as the glasses clinked there was a sense of "Here we go." We were now in 2012.

235

The concept of "London 2012" had been seven years in the making. The bid for the Olympic Games was won in 2005, seemingly against the odds. There was a general assumption that although London had made it into the final two bidding cities, Paris would win in the last round of votes. Arguably Paris had more existing stadiums and appeared ready to host the Games. In the final presentations, however, while Paris concentrated on Paris, Seb Coe and the London bid team talked about the Olympic Movement, about athletes and dreams, about legacy and inspiring a new generation. It was an irresistible assault on the hearts and minds of the people involved with the Olympic Games. London had already explained from a detailed logistics point of view that it could host the Games; the final sell was focused on aspirations and inspirations. When the IOC President, Jacques Rogge, read out the name of London as the winner, Britain was in equal parts surprised and overjoyed.

Twenty-four hours after the London celebrations, the city was brought to a shuddering halt by the bombing of a bus and underground. It was a sober reminder of the frailty of any city, and the emotional extremes of those 24 hours were thrown into sharp contrast. There was a deep sadness at the loss of life, an anger at the assault on the city and a defiant refusal to allow terrorists to change a way of life. It may have stopped the celebrations of the winning of the bid, but it wouldn't crush the spirit of the city or the country. The journey to London 2012 had already begun.

A few months later at the annual rowing dinner I was on the same table as Liz Nichol, the impressive Chief Executive of UK Sport. A discussion started about the success of the bid and what it would mean for sport in the country. She turned to me smiling. "You must be very pleased at the thought of a Home Games?" I agreed that it would be the most fantastic experience for the British athletes competing. "And you'll be one of those athletes." It was a statement rather than a question. I choked over my coffee. "Liz, I don't think I'll be competing when 2012 rolls around." At this point it was still nearly three years before Beijing, with London a distant four beyond that. Liz just looked at me for a while in silence. She finally said lightly, "Well, it'll be an incredible event, so let's just wait and see." Liz was the first person to suggest I should be in London 2012, seven years before the event.

As I stood watching the 2012 fireworks I thought about the journey that had taken me to this place. Anna and I were entering the Olympic year as favourites to take the Olympic title at our own Dorney Lake in front of our home crowd. When I left school struggling with what I wanted to do I didn't for a second imagine it might be this. I knew how lucky I was. I understood that some people may never get this level of opportunity, anticipation, excitement, so when the pressure came on, I had to remember I was lucky. In the words of the great Billie Jean King, "pressure is privilege".

Earlier in the season I had had a conversation with my mum that left me a little sad. She had just been to the local shops and been asked a couple of times what she thought would happen at the Olympics. Would this be the year Katherine might win a gold medal? Mum came home weary saying she just wanted this year over. She saw a long few months stretching ahead, being asked by lovely, well-meaning people how my training was going, how fast Anna and I were going, were we confident, were we able to win, etc. It added pressure that mum didn't need. That's when it hit me properly. That my life is my choice, the highs and the lows, the tests and the trials, the pressure and stress, the public praise and criticism, all of these things may not have been what I wanted but were a direct result of what I had chosen to do. The fact that my family were taken along on this crazy ride was not their choice. And I didn't want my mum wishing this year away. I said as much, explaining it could be the most amazing year imaginable ahead or it might be awful, but we'd only find out in August and until then we should enjoy the trip, as much as we could. As usual, my mum wasn't down for long. At New Year she gave me a card saying, "Let's celebrate that 2012 has finally arrived! It's been a long time coming but it's going to have so, so much in it that we'll celebrate and remember for ever."

The last major individual test was once again the April trials. Shortly after the win in Bled, Anna and I had sat down with Thommo and discussed the year ahead. Anna and I were already agreed that in the previous year there had been too much focus on the final selection trials in April. Anna certainly felt that was when she had peaked in 2011 and the most important thing for us this year was to peak once, on 3 August 2012. We also didn't want to risk damaging our partnership by having weeks trying to beat each other. We would always be competitive and we knew that helped to push us on individually and collectively, but we didn't want it to go too far and risk ruining confidence or communication. Trials should be a goal but not the main focus of the year. For Anna and me those points were unarguable. But we were wrong.

Our meeting was at Oakley Court, deliberately chosen because that was to be our base for the week of the Olympic regatta. As the three of us settled to a lovely afternoon tea toasting the success of Bled, Anna and I looked forward and talked about our plans for the year. Thommo remained quiet. As we finished he put his plate down. "So, you think you should miss trials, then? At the moment there is no guarantee you'll be in the double. There's no point in planning for 3 August until you've been selected in the boat. You need to come first and second at trials to prove that you should be back in the boat. There may be a faster double we can put together, and that's what we'll look at during the trials process. The best way you can prepare for August is to come first and second in everything you do." It wasn't the "discussion" we were expecting, but it was a reminder that there would be no assumptions and no favours. Even as a crew that was unbeaten for two years we were told quite clearly that either one of us could be replaced. We left feeling a little deflated but even more determined to prove ourselves. It was no doubt the outcome Thommo wanted.

Once again we returned to Dorney for the April trials. I was feeling like a different athlete from the previous year and part of that inspiration had come from an unusual source. It was thanks to a horse.

I've ridden a horse only once in my life and the closest thing I came to horse racing was our annual team flutter on the Grand National, and that was generally unsuccessful. One year in Varese after Beijing I was the second person asked to pull a name out of a hat for the race. From about 40 possible names I could have chosen, I unfolded "Silver by Nature". Born in 2000, the horse's key assets were his bravery, speed and stamina. He was tough and resilient and Scottish born and bred, so there was a lot to commend him. But his name was a bit too close to the bone for me. Caroline found me later and in a hushed tone told me her thinking: "It's all right, Katherine, it's Silver by Nature, Gold by Nurture." She nodded wisely.

Then, as 2011 came to an end, I read about Kauto Star, the champion racehorse. James Lawton in the *Independent* had written an article entitled "Vintage Kauto Star gets better with age and makes everyone feel young again". Lawton wrote that "there are all kinds of champions, human and equine, who claim a piece of the nation's affection, but some of them offer a special gift. It is the idea that you are never done. That you can grow strong at those places which have been broken and, in the opinion of some, irreparably." The message was that for the people watching Kauto Star's race was an emotional and inspiring reminder that everything is possible, and by being beaten and coming back to win the horse had offered a ray of hope for everyone who had ever been beaten in life. It struck a nerve. And so I continued through the winter with the knowledge that it wasn't about Anna beating me or me beating Anna, it was about enjoying the racing again, focusing on the performance and never feeling that I was "done".

Thommo was fantastic in his support and help through the winter of singling. He listened to where I felt it had gone wrong the year before in the single and showed no sign of believing it was over for me. In his mind he knew Anna and I could be out front battling each other again and he believed the best boat on the day would win. If Anna was having a great day and I was slightly off my best then she would win, and vice versa. It was an amazing sign of how far we had come and the standard we were competing at. We trained in singles for the majority of the winter, but fairly regularly Thommo would allow Anna and me to train in the double. It felt like a treat and we couldn't wait for that session to roll around. With the quality staying high even when we weren't in the double, it gave us the confidence that everything we were doing – in singles, in the gym, on the ergo – was moving the double onwards.

In the waiting time before the race, as the pairs huddled in their groups of two, the scullers moved together in a shared space of understanding. Vicky was listening so loudly to Rhianna that we could all join in, and she constantly let out little squeals of excitement or frustration as she played Angry Birds on her pink phone; Beth had been doing puzzles, with people helpfully, or occasionally unhelpfully, shouting out random answers; and Anna and I were sharing a newspaper. There was an air of mutual respect and support, and we had the knowledge that we could spend this time in each other's company while being able to switch to competitive beings as soon as our boats touched the water.

I was looking forward to the racing again and that's always a good sign for me. With the inspiration of Kauto Star I won my tenth title and put to bed some demons that had accompanied me after the result the previous year. I wasn't past it after all. As I carried my boat off the water, Jurgen came up to shake my hand. "Ah, Kazren, you can't stop now!" There were a lot of people on the bank who had come along to see what all the fuss was about Dorney Lake and rowing. In among the dog walkers and joggers and supporters were a few very familiar faces. Cath was there with her son Jonny, Elise with her daughter Erin, and Carla with her daughter Nella. Our teammates of the past, who were living evidence that there is a wonderful life beyond all of this. But for now and for the next few months, all of this was just what Anna and I wanted to do.

Once again we loved the moment of getting back into our boat, and this time it was with the most important goal ahead, the Olympic Games. Everything we had learned separately and together would now come into play, and to put ourselves in the best possible shape we would draw on every bit of knowledge, skill and experience that Thommo had. The goal was so obvious and so clear, it wasn't something we needed to keep discussing. Of course it was about winning; it felt as if that was the only thing that would do justice to the potential of this fantastic boat. But by having that common understanding we could move past the outcome of winning to concentrate on the only thing that would matter: how we were going to go as fast as we possibly could. We now knew that if we could go as fast as we were capable of then we would be better than anyone in the world. So we left the outcome to one side and focused all our collective energies on the process. In previous years we had concentrated on what building blocks were needed to make the best crew. With that knowledge already clear, we started with making sure those blocks were in place and there was a clinical mindset of taking away anything that might stop us fulfilling our potential. All barriers would be removed, leaving only the essential elements of a winning crew.

One of those barriers could be the pressure and expectation that the Home Games would bring. In order to make sure one of our greatest strengths, our communication, didn't become an issue, Anna and I met months before the Games for a coffee and ice cream, once again back at Oakley Court. It was feeling like a friendly and familiar place by now and that had been entirely deliberate. Over coffee we discussed openly what we both felt the biggest threats to confidence might be, how our behaviour might change when the nerves came, what negative influence the media could potentially have, how we might be able to help each other, and how to recognize signs that there might be a problem ahead. We had to be sure on this; personal sensitivities were less important than getting this right. I had learned from previous experience that not confronting things, not being open and honest, could make things easier in the short term, but when the big pressure moments came, any minor cracks would be split wide open, exposing dangerous vulnerabilities.

It was another powerful conversation, and by having it away from the intensity of competition we were able to talk openly without the threat of causing serious damage. We knew there would likely be surprises along the way and we would have to be flexible to deal with things as and when they came. But we were also going to make sure that any forseeable problems would be ironed out as early as possible.

We knew our search for excellence was going to need many other people too. The principal and most obvious example was Thommo. However we were also making a lot of demands on those around us. The stronger our team was, the better we would be. Alex and Katie in the gym, were charged with finding ways to make us stronger and more dynamic whilst also as resistant to injury as possible. Our nutritionist Wendy was aware of every new advance in food, drinks and supplements and we had regular discussions over the best ways to be fuelled and ready to race. Liz, our physio, and Sarah, our masseuse, kept a watchful eye on how our bodies were coping with training and flagged up any potential issues. Craig, Sarah and Homer, our physiologists, monitored everything they could from training intensity to hydration and from sleep patterns to recovery strategies. Our performance analyst, Ali, and the biomechanics boys made facts and figures our friend with all their useful data. We wanted the best everybody had to offer. We wanted our team to be the gold standard and everyone individually had a crucial role to play. Whereas in earlier years the roles and responsibilities of the crew had been intricately discussed and planned, now we spread that thinking wider. It was important that our entire team felt valued and valuable.

One extra secret weapon we had in our corner was Steve Redgrave. With his five Olympic gold medals and his long and successful rowing career Steve was an invaluable source of knowledge and wisdom. He was also incredibly generous with his time and had many meetings with us to share his opinions and experience. He cared deeply that we achieved what we wanted to. Those meetings were relaxed and friendly and Steve talks with an entertaining sense of humour. But he also talks with a passionate intensity when it comes to racing and it is clear why he won as much as he did. When someone who has led the world and set the standards in his particular field speaks, you listen.

At one point in the summer Anna and I went to meet a woman called Tig, who was a psychologist. It was to be just a one-off meeting to check we were leaving no stone unturned. Over the years many athletes on the team had talked to Britt, a fantastic independent psychologist who had worked with the British Olympic Medical Service. It was often useful to get an opinion from someone outside the rowing set up, a fresh perspective with a different voice. With that same ethos of trying to get different insights in the lead up to the Home Games, a lot of athletes from different sports had come knocking on Tig's door. She had been doing some great work with the women's eight and we thought we'd have a chat with her and find out what her impressions of us were. It felt like a couples counselling session as we walked in, sat down and smiling she said, "Well then, tell me about yourself." Anna and I looked at each other. Anna asked awkwardly what was it Tig wanted to hear – how Anna got into rowing, what she did in the boat, or what? Tig continued to smile, settled further back into her seat and simply said, "Whatever you want to tell me."

After Anna's initial stumbling start – "Am I saying too much? Have I said too little?" – we talked about ourselves individually and then we talked about what we liked and respected in each other. It was interesting and fun to hear each other speak. Soon the chat was flowing out of us, we interrupted each other, adding bits in, explaining and laughing about some of the comments. By the end Tig was still smiling and simply said, "You're going to be just fine. I work with a lot of people who are preparing for the Olympics and of all of them I am the least worried about you. You clearly respect each other, love being in each other's company and have fun together. You are also different from each other in some ways and that actually complements each other beautifully. Make sure you stick to how you naturally are and there won't be any problems." It was a wonderful moment for a stranger, albeit a stranger who was highly trained and experienced in these areas, to have met us, understood us, summed us up and believed we were exactly where we needed to be for what we wanted to do. Another brick cemented into the wall of self-confidence. That wall was beginning to appear so high, so deep and so strong it would soon be impenetrable.

The first race of the Olympic year was Belgrade. Belgrade was to be memorable for two main reasons. Firstly the display of naked men sunning themselves on the banks but, more importantly, it was the closest anyone came to beating us. We were happy with how the boat was going but came into the racing still very much in training mode, and even during the final it felt more like a training piece rather than the final of the World Cup. The German double shook us out of it by sensing an opportunity with 250m to go. We were leading but not by a huge amount and were at a lower rate than most of the boats around us. From a couple of lanes across and almost under our radar the Germans lifted the attack they had already started and launched a full-power, top-rate sprint for the line. Just in time we reacted to hold off the charge, but it was a reminder that racing is racing, and although we use each race as a learning experience they are still things to be won as well as experienced.

Lucerne was next, and this time we were sharper and not taking anything for granted. We were very proud of our unbeaten record and wouldn't give it away lightly by taking our eye off the ball. But crucially we didn't want to race predictably. As summer went on we tried some different tactics to make sure we had everything we might need when it came to the Olympics. We managed to keep testing, keep learning and keep winning. Lucerne had been another success and there was only one remaining regatta of the 2012 World Cup series. Munich would be the last international race before the Olympics and this one was a much-anticipated showdown. The Australian double, who had finished second to us in the previous two World Championships, continued to believe they could win. They considered their role in this drama as being the ones to come to the British Olympics and spoil the party. They wanted to beat us on our home soil and ruin the fairytale ending of our three-year campaign. Reading their interviews in the Australian press,

CHAPTER 11

there was clearly no doubt in their minds that they had the ability. Kim Crow, an impressive and successful sculler, had been the constant in the double, having been partnered at various points by Sally Kehoe, Kerry Hore and now Brooke Prately. This latest combination was confident of being the one to defy the popular expectation of British dominance.

In Munich we would find out for real. We would be racing the new Australian double for the first time, and also the last time before the Olympics. We were drawn in opposite heats and as the results came out it was clear they were faster than us, taking most of that in the first part of the race, an area where we had consistently been strong. The results had Thommo on edge and had us fired up and ready. There would be no chance of letting things slide a little as we had in Belgrade – later Anna would talk about the feeling of grim determination that weekend. We knew we would be focused for every stroke of the race and whereas in all other races we had taken it easy once we were in control, this time we were prepared to fight with every last stroke. For the first time we were given permission to show our full hand if necessary. The balance of the Olympics could be tipped here, and for us it was very important to make sure it tipped in our favour. We blasted from the start and moved away, they closed a little, but as the race settled we took control again, and although we never took our foot off the gas we also didn't have to respond to any attacks and didn't feel in danger. As a result of the smaller gap we had won by in the Bled World Championships in 2011 and the close finish in Belgrade a few weeks before, people had begun to question our dominance. Munich put those doubts to bed and cemented us as favourites. It was a huge win for us, and another very solid row of bricks had been added to the confidence wall.

We would not be seeing our opposition again until the Olympic regatta, so it was now time for everyone to go to their various corners of the world to get heads down, train, and either reinforce the good stuff or come up with better ideas. We went to our usual parts of Germany and Italy. In Germany we were pushed to our absolute limits physically in every way. On the camp we were usually in groups of similar speed boats, so we were with the women's pair and lightweight women's double. It was a hard, competitive group and you had to be absolutely at the top of your game to win. That made sense a few months later when all three boats became Olympic Champions. At the time, however, we didn't know how fast we were all going, we were just aware of how hard we had to push to win. By the last session Anna and I limped our way along the bank trying to create rhythm and power with whatever energy we had left, but the reserves were practically empty. It was perfect. It meant our last timed piece wouldn't be spectacular in any way, but more importantly it meant we had given everything and got everything we could from the camp.

Our escape from the pressure and the exhaustion on the water in Breisach and Varese was a daily dose of Danish crime. For a long time my mum and dad had been raving about the wondrous TV programme that was *The Killing*, or, as Anna used to announce loudly at the beginning of every episode in her best Danish accent, *Forbrydelson*. My dad was famous in our family for enjoying anything subtitled and obscure, and therefore often his recommendations went acknowledged but unfollowed as far as my sister and I were concerned. Even mum agreed at times that the latest Iranian drama was a little tough going. And so I ignored their praise of *The Killing*, *The Bridge* and *Spiral*. What I didn't realize was that, just as when I said as a child I would read only animal stories, by ignoring the whole of European drama I was shutting myself off from a vast world of entertainment. Finally I was intrigued enough to suggest to Anna in Breisach 2012 that we should try *The Killing*.

A few of the girls on camp had already watched, and loved, the exploits of Sarah Lund. Jess, Sophie and Fran were among those who had raved about the series and now envied us for being able to embark for the first time on our journey to find the killer of Nanna Birk Larsen. We had no idea when we began just how it would soon take over our lives. We started with a gentle opening episode to "give it a go". Beth joined us, and the first thing we noticed was how different it was to read subtitles. We realized how much we had all started to multi-task while watching TV – emails, texts and even books could easily be on the go, but with a foreign language and subtitles there was nothing to be done except concentrate fully on the screen. That very focus made it more engrossing. Even when the odd bag of Maltesers or Minstrels was brought out, they were passed around like Braille. Beth would wave the bag to her left without taking her eyes off the screen, while I leaned forward grasping at the air with my fingers, trying to locate the bag, equally fixated by the conversations taking place. As the days went on, the illusion that we could speak fluent Danish grew to the point that we started to look away and reach for the snacks or drinks being offered. There was instant outrage that we had lost part of the plot because for some reason when we looked away we stopped being fluent.

Reality and fiction began to blur. Every break Anna (now known as Anna Birk Larsen) and I would leave the river and cycle up to the nearby bakery where we would take our regular corner table, order coffees and sandwiches and then discuss our most recent theories on the crime. We would talk through the latest developments, discussing potential suspects, alleged alibis and possible motives. We drew on our strengths: as I explained my hunches, Anna relied on detail and analysis to narrow down the suspect list. We loved every minute of it, and it was a welcome distraction from the stresses of the rowing. We even had a mini incident room set up in our hotel room, putting up huge flipchart sheets of paper along the wall and drawing a timeline, adding information as it came. Anna embraced her inner artist and sketched mini pictures of the suspects. With bobbly eyes from Beth's craft kit, we created the "eyes of suspicion" on a Post-it note that could be moved as our suspicions changed. Whereas many people said Sarah Lund was a flawed character, we related to her drive, her obsessive need to find answers and triumph. She was our heroine.

We left the Breisach camp having completed the case and also got our rowing to the standard it needed to be. Now we moved to Varese for a final sharpening up and the addition of the last ingredients. For Anna and me the first week in Varese was devoted to recovering from Breisach and finding our top speed. The days passed quickly. I began to feel the urgency and we wondered if our standards were good enough and whether we could change all that we needed to without trying to do too much. We were on a constant search for perfection. Derek, my next-door neighbour, sent a text message out of the blue. Quoting Dr Who, he wrote, "It won't be quiet, it won't be safe and it won't be calm. But I'll tell you what it will be: the trip of a lifetime." He was right on every point.

With the big event fast approaching, once again distractions were necessary. Before the summer camps we had spotted that Olympic stickers had been released, along with a sticker album. As kids we had all separately collected different things. I remember my big sister completing the *Back to the Future* album which became a well-worn, prized and much-respected possession. Anna and I decided that being an adult meant you could still act like a child but get away with it.

I loved the day I strode into WH Smith in Marlow and handed over my Panini Olympic Sticker album and asked for 100 packets of stickers. The girl looked confused and checked my request. I repeated: "100 packets." She reached behind her to the shelf where they kept the boxes of stickers and in a reverential way lifted over a full sealed box. "This is 100 packets." I nodded gravely, "Yes, that's what I need." I carried off the precious cargo, and sent a message to Beth and Anna informing them of my purchase. It wasn't long before they followed suit and we spent every half day on camp rewarding ourselves with the opening of another few packets and squealing with delight at finding the rare shiny Olympic Stadium or sighing that yet again we had found the all too common Stratford Station. Soon the walls of our room in Varese were filled with the incident room of *The Killing II*, the poster of the Olympic international stars that accompanied our sticker album, and a list of most sought-after stickers.

During the last few days we added the final bits to our on-the-water preparation. The last main bit of work we did was a 2km race rehearsal. Anna and I wanted to make it as close to racing as possible. We wanted the nerves and the pain. It had to be fast and furious, relentless and uncompromising. We started behind the women's pair, spare pair and lightweight double. And feeling relaxed, comfortable, strong and alert we passed them all, in our fastest 2km time and an unofficial world record. We could not have finished the preparation in a better way. As we stepped out of the boat Thommo met us with a broad smile and the comment, "Well, that must have been fun." It was. Later Anna phoned home to Oli to reassure him that things were good. "It's fine, you can stop stressing," she told him. "We've cracked it."

CHAPTER 11

The return to Britain was now upon us. As we had left Heathrow Airport to fly out to Italy we had met various people in departures who, recognizing our British kit, commented, "Aren't you going the wrong way?" It had been a welcome escape to leave the growing excitement in London and go to a quiet part of Italy where you wouldn't even know the Olympics existed, let alone were a matter of days away. Chris, Thommo, Anna and I met to discuss the implications of arriving back into the "Home Olympics". The British Olympic Association had done a fantastic job over the previous couple of years of creating videos and meetings centred around the mindset of the Home Olympics. We knew that as far as racing was concerned we had all the answers we needed, except one: would we crack? Anna was concerned that in that moment her mind might go blank because of a physiological or neurological reaction to the increased adrenaline and pressure. We were about to experience something we had never experienced before and we couldn't prepare for it in any realistic way. We would only find out on the day, in front of the crowds in their thousands and the millions watching at home.

There was an assumption that success would come because of the home crowd, that records would be smashed because of home advantage. It was true that in recent Olympics the Spanish team in 1992, the Australian team in 2000, the Greek team in 2004 and the Chinese team in 2008 had all produced record-breaking medal success when they hosted the Games, and Britain was undoubtedly planning for the same. But there was also an awareness that success wouldn't just come because we were competing at home. There were also pitfalls attached to being the home team. With added pressure, expectation, public awareness and publicity there was every chance that results might be harder to come by than ever.

At the end of the Varese camp we met with Thommo and Chris to flag up when we might possibly feel an overwhelming sense of pressure or stress – moments of terror we called them. There was no use in saying it would all be OK; we had to talk through the points where our own fears or nerves might be damaging and try to minimize the risk as much as possible. We said that arriving back at Heathrow would be the first potential overwhelming moment, followed by the arrival at Oakley Court, where we would be staying during the racing week, and the first arrival at Dorney Lake. Interestingly all three locations were very familiar to us, but in the context of the Olympic Games they could potentially appear intimidating.

We arrived at Heathrow Terminal 5, which was also our accreditation point for the Olympic Games. As we disembarked we were met by the friendliest group of volunteers we could have hoped for. It was like being welcomed by a Disney movie. Everywhere we looked there were people in brightly coloured outfits – the luminous pink of the Heathrow Airport staff and the soon to be familiar orange and purple (or poppy and aubergine) of the Olympic Gamesmakers. Everyone had a spring in their step, a twinkle in their eye, an enormous smile on their faces and if they had broken out into song I would not have been surprised. Perhaps it helped that we were one of the first teams through and everyone was still fresh and eager, but something told me they were ready to high-kick and grin their way through the next few weeks. We sailed through the usually painful and tedious experience of accreditation, and within no time we were on buses outside the airport with bags loaded ahead of us. If only all airport experiences could be this good.

The bus journey from Heathrow to Oakley Court was brief and the excited buzz was palpable in the air. We passed the enormous poles that had been erected at either end of the rowing lake for the overhead cameras. They were extremely tall and could be seen for miles around. A nervousness crept into the excitement as we drove through the hotel gates. Although we had been to the hotel before, none of us quite knew what to expect from our new Olympic residence. In about ten days' time it would be these doors we would walk out of on the way to the Olympic finals, and these doors we would walk back through once it was all over.

Today, however, there was nothing to fear as we walked in. We were welcomed in by familiar members of the GB Rowing Team support all looking unusually happy to see us. Maggie was a reassuring presence and she had fantastic support from Jan Patterson and Jo Bates, who, along with Maggie would fix any problem and were guaranteed to bring a smile in tense times. We were ushered into the dining hall, where feast upon feast would await us over the coming few days. There was a relaxing crew room area too with sofas, Olympic posters and messages from Team GB, tables full of healthy snacks and, thanks to the sponsors Cadburys and Coke, fridges full of cold drinks and chocolate. Once we'd had the official welcome we ventured off to find our rooms, and slowly the corridors began to fill with excitement and noise as one by one the rooms were opened. Inside was a treasure trove of Olympic memorabilia.

One of the fears about staying in a hotel rather than in the Olympic Village was that people might feel cut off from the Olympics, separate and independent of the main event happening a few miles east in London. Because of that, every effort had been made by the British Olympic Association, GB Rowing and Oakley Court staff to make us feel at home but also make us feel special. There were Olympic duvets on the beds and fleece blankets wrapped up ready to take with us to the course. There was an Olympic lion mascot and an Olympic mug by every bed. Olympic bags and books were propped up alongside cards and letters that had been delivered by forward-thinking family and friends. Each person had a special parcel from the hotel with an Oakley Court lion wearing a hand-stitched GB cape, a mug saying "Keep Calm and Carry On Rowing" and a book about 50 things to do when you're stuck in a hotel room. Every little thoughtful gesture made an impression.

Anna and I had kept our door open and soon there were more screams. I put my head out and saw Vicky Thornley. "Oh my god, Katherine, have you been into the bathroom yet? Get in!" Confused, I stepped into our bathroom and found one of the most popular items: the fluffy white bathrobe emblazoned with the Olympic rings and the Team GB logo on the back. Within seconds Fran arrived in our room modelling it like a boxer on the way to the ring. We had all regressed about twenty years and it was Christmas morning all over again. Suddenly we were aware that two of our potential moments of terror hadn't materialized. That left one more. The arrival at the racing venue.

I knew Dorney Lake back when it was just a small puddle. I watched it grow from a short gravel pit to a fully fledged international rowing course complete with conjoined warm-up lake. We had been allowed to train on it years before, when the gravel was still being dug out of it and the necessity to stop after about 800m was often welcomed. None of us knew back then that one day the little ugly duckling of barren grey exposed gravel would turn into the beautiful swan of an Olympic course, hosting some of the greatest crowds that the sport of rowing would ever see. Just as athletes aimed for the top, I like to think Dorney Lake had set its sights on being the best.

The water could be fickle, though. Some days it was beautiful and calm and reflected the blue sky above. On other, gloomy days the water could be dark and unforgiving as ominous strong winds gusted across it and the white tops of the waves were the only thing bringing any sense of light. Dorney Lake had hosted a few major international regattas in preparation for the Olympics. In 2005 there was a World Cup, memorable for very rough and unfair crosswinds. At the 2006 World Championships a few world records fell as the tailwind rushed boats towards the finish line. The greatest hope for 2012 would be fair conditions. Fast or slow was irrelevant; fair was crucial. Nobody wanted Olympic medals being decided by the lane draw. The Olympic regatta would start on 28 July and finish on 4 August. In Britain that would mean we could be in for any weather.

Oakley Court was across the river from Dorney Lake and so it was decided our easiest means of traffic would be, appropriately, by boat. The first day we climbed aboard the little river ferry and enjoyed the relaxed journey, waving to people on their boats moored up along the banks. People recognized the Team GB kit and gave us the thumbs up as we puttered past. Walking across the final bridge we could see the edges of the course, and the sides of the enormous grandstands. It quickened the pulse. The water itself was behind large covered fences, so we aimed for the gate and the first glimpse of the battlefield. Walking through with Anna, I smiled to myself. This was it. And it looked utterly fantastic.

In part it looked so different; it had been "Olympified" and in contrast with how we last saw it there were now flags, Olympic rings, mascots, the grandstands on both sides, cameras, tents, a dining hall, endless amounts of boat racks and flocks of Gamesmakers as far as the eye could see. But in part it was also so familiar; it was our Dorney, the same one I had rowed on before it was 2,000m, the course we had trialled on, raced on, won and lost on. It was ours. There was an overwhelming sense of ownership and of pride. I stood silently next to Anna and felt my shoulders go back and my head lift high. This was our course, and the rest of the world had come here to race us. And if they wanted to beat us on our home course in front of our home crowd then they had better be good, they'd better be prepared and they'd better be ready for one hell of a fight.

Later I spoke to Anna about it and she had felt the same. She felt they had built the whole course for the two of us, as if we were coming home. While we were on camp in Italy, Rachel had arrived at Dorney as a Gamesmaker and she emailed a photo of our boat rack. As we walked over to where it was, it already felt familiar; it had been waiting for us to arrive. I walked around full of happiness and excitement. I remember seeing Frida Svensson, the Swedish single sculler and one of the friendliest rowers in the world, and I high-fived her as she went by. I felt on top of the world and incredibly comfortable to be here. There wasn't anywhere else I'd rather be.

The first outing brought us back to reality with a bit of a thud. I had been soaking up the atmosphere, enjoying seeing the other crews, the stands, the new markers along the edge of the water, the addition of giant Olympic rings, and breathing in our Olympic course. Anna had her mind more on the job and when we came off the water she was frustrated that the standard hadn't been good enough. It was again a rare miscommunication between us. Anna is usually the more analytical of the two of us and she knows that is her job. Her expectation was already for us to be at Olympic final level, whereas I had expected the first paddle to be more of an exploratory row after the travel from Italy. I was just pleased to be here; Anna was already concerned it wasn't good enough.

Thommo arrived on his bike, happy to have been seeing other coaches and managers and had been checking out the course. He was surprised to be met by a slightly awkward silence. After a healthy conversation about differing expectations, we laughed it off and moved on. I later saw Marnie McBean, a triple Olympic Champion rower from Canada. She talked about the "want it" sweet spot – meaning that if it's a case of wanting then it's a good thing, but when it becomes a "must have" or a "need" then it isn't good. It was important to stay enjoying it and remember how this had all begun. How much fun it had been and should still be now. And also that the idea of perfection is a myth. It was a good reminder to try to let go of the stranglehold and enjoy the occasion. Steve Redgrave echoed that sentiment when we saw him for the last time before the heat. "Enjoy it" were his parting words.

On the morning of the Opening Ceremony I nipped out to the local post office. As I weighed my letter the man behind the counter casually looked up and said, "They let you off then, have they?" On the way out a lady with a pushchair stopped me to say good luck. It was the beginning of a realization that the nation knew who we were and were paying attention. During the years before London 2012, as I won my previous Olympic medals and my world championship titles, I had no expectation of any recognition and had continued to be unnoticed in my day-to-day life. I was very soon to discover the difference a gold medal in the Home Olympics makes.

The London Olympics would officially open on Friday 27 July with an Opening Ceremony of which the details were a closely guarded secret but which involved, we gathered, a field and some sheep. And the promise of some real rain. We were all hoping for a bit more than that, but the rehearsals had given nothing away. I had been lucky enough to march at the Sydney Opening Ceremony, and for me it was an incredibly inspiring and moving experience. To be in the stadium when Cathy Freeman lit the cauldron and to see all the countries unified in the middle of the stadium was to understand just what a special event the Olympics Games is. It was humbling and uplifting at the same time. We weren't allowed to march in Athens or Beijing due to the timetable, and so Anna had never experienced an Opening Ceremony. Both of us knew that the London Ceremony would be memorable and we both wanted to be there.

Initial discussions had been less than positive as David, Thommo and Jurgen all recommended that athletes did not attend. The Ceremonies are notoriously long and tiring for athletes and a late night with hours on our feet was certainly not the usual preparation for a big racing event. But this was no ordinary event. Anna and I thought the inspiration would outweigh a shortened night's sleep. Anyone racing on the Saturday or Sunday wouldn't be allowed, but our heat was on the Monday so there was a slight possibility we could make it work. However, after further discussions with the coaches, the team doctor, the psychologist and finally the BOA, it was clear that it would be 2am or 3am before we got back to our beds. That was too much of a risk, and with our teammates starting on the Saturday morning we also thought it would be unfair to arrive back late and potentially disturb racing crews. It meant we could join the rest of the rowing team for an "alternative" opening ceremony at Oakley Court.

With no input from Danny Boyle, the Director of the official Opening Ceremony, we swiftly threw together our own cheaper version. There would be no Mr Bean playing "Chariots of Fire", no Queen jumping out of a helicopter and no James Bond, but we made do. We met in the walled garden of the hotel and had team photos in our shiny white-and-gold official Opening Ceremony outfits. Then I was asked to carry the flag and lead the team to the doors of the hotel. It was a slightly surreal moment as, a couple of hours before Chris Hoy led Team GB in front of tens of thousands and an estimated worldwide audience of 900 million, I led Rowing Team GB in front of one family who were staying at the hotel and an array of local wildfowl. I like to think the ducks are still thinking back to that special night.

Oakley Court with its Gothic turrets had been the location for the filming of the original *Rocky Horror Picture Show* film, so was our atmospheric equivalent to the Olympic Stadium. The staff had transformed the dining room with red, white and blue balloons, paper plates and cups, Team GB cakes and a dazzling display of food. David Tanner was our Queen for the night, officially "opening" our Olympics, and Matt Wells lit the flame (which was actually a large candle). We then adjourned to the crew lounge to watch the real Opening Ceremony. With the racing beginning the following morning, people began to drift off and soon there was only Jess, Anna, Maurice, Ali Patterson and I left. We stoically sat through all 205 teams who marched in, growing mildly horrified at just how many there were. Anna wisely had a nap through the latter part of the alphabet and rejoined us around Venezuela. At one point I suggested a toast to the three surviving athletes. Jess raised her bottle of water, while Anna raised her head and said, "Estonia." As we looked at her, confused, she insisted she thought I had asked her what outfit she liked the best.

We wanted to see how the cauldron would be lit – I'd been intrigued by Steve Redgrave's brief explanation. He had underplayed it beautifully. We moved between impressed silence and cheers of excitement as David Beckham sped along the river in his speedboat and handed the torch to Steve. He then carried the torch into the stadium to a thunderous reception and, along with six other British sporting legends, handed the flame over to seven youngsters. When they lit the edges of the copper petals that had been carried in by every nation, the whole thing ignited and slowly the long stems lifted to meet in the middle, and the formation of the cauldron signalled the beginning of the Games. We looked at each other. This was it.

When we arrived at the course for training the next morning we walked in with thousands of rowing spectators who were ready for the first day of competition. Some people recognized us as we walked through and shouted, "Good luck, GB!" Suddenly the crowd burst into spontaneous applause. Every day we had the same reaction, cheers and applause and good wishes. It was an extraordinary experience and an example of how truly special the crowds were. That first morning the buzz and thrill of the fans added to our own excitement, but we knew we still had 48 hours until we could start racing. Instead we went quietly back to our hotel to relax and watch some of the other sports. Mark Cavendish and the road race was guaranteed to be a highlight. He had the dream team of road racers – out of the group of five, four had won stages of the Tour de France just a couple of weeks previously. It wasn't to be. We watched the gap widen until there was no chance of the British riders claiming the gold, or indeed any colour of medal.

It felt as if the nation was on an Olympic rollercoaster. In the lead-up to the Opening Ceremony there was still scepticism in the newspapers about the weather, the crowds, the tickets, the security, in fact the success of the whole event. By the next morning the papers had pages and pages of photos accompanied by headlines along the lines of "Greatest Show on Earth". Pride was swelling in the nation and everything was going to be brilliant. Mark Cavendish's result was a reminder that it wouldn't be so easy. For the other countries the big aim was to come to Britain and be the best here; there would be no standing aside to give the British athletes the medals and please the Home Nation. The reverse was more accurate; to claim British scalps on British home soil would be the greatest coup. We were aware of that as our own first race approached and took nothing for granted.

The heat was possibly the best we had ever raced. It was clear what we had to do and we executed it. The conditions were good and we loved every second of competing in front of the enthusiastic and vocal crowd. As we crossed the line comfortably ahead, I looked up to see the time. I had thought during the race of lifting the speed to see what sort of time we could hit, but I behaved myself and did what Anna said. She made sure we simply controlled the second half of the race, no unnecessary heroics. As we stepped out of the boat Thommo met us with a huge smile, saying, "Now THAT must have been fun!" As we were enthusiastically agreeing he informed us we had broken the Olympic record. Anna and I looked at each other. We had set a new Olympic record without trying. There were hugs all round and Anna admitted to being aware we wouldn't get a world record but had forgotten about the Olympic record. It reassured all three of us that things were on track. The crowd had been sensational while we raced, and as we carried our boat off the water I asked Anna if we could go back and do it again. This all felt just wonderful; I couldn't get enough and didn't want to have to wait four more days to do it again.

It wasn't just the waiting. It was also the watching while others went out and raced their finals. Wednesday would be the first day of rowing finals and by Tuesday night there were still no gold medals for Team GB. Helen and Heather were favourites to win the women's pairs event the following morning. It was clear that rowing would become an instant focal point for Britain's eagerly awaited first gold medal. Anna and I watched the race from our beds, with the sound turned down and the remote control at the ready. We wanted to watch the race, but without the excitable commentary. We wanted to see the result, but not the medals. So in our silent room we watched history being made. Hardly challenged, Helen and Heather did what no previous British woman rower had managed. They won Olympic gold.

It was the result all of us wanted. And it would have been an incredible honour to be the crew to have done it first. But to me there was something fitting about this young, first-time Olympian crew being the ones to break through. For their win was more than just the result of their undoubted hard work, technical skill and natural ability. It was more than the hours and hours of patient and dedicated work their coach, Robin Williams, had put in. The win was a win for the whole of British women's rowing. In the nineties, when success was hard to come by and rarely repeated, there was no obvious pathway of success. There was no clear consistency about how best to achieve results. It felt like a period of trial and error, of phenomenally hard work that was sometimes rewarded with success but not always – it was unpredictable. From 2003 onwards there was success and repeated success. By 2012 the road to gold was clearer than it had ever been. The methods were tried and tested and perfected. Every member of the women's team over the years had played their part, bringing us to the position we were in now. A position where expectations were higher than ever before and for good reason. Where a relatively new crew could be put together, be given their own coach, awarded every opportunity to train with experts in every available field, have the guidance of a successful training programme and the backing of a professional set-up. And win the Olympic Games. Helen and Heather's joy was shared by millions around the country who had been waiting for Britain's first gold.

Shortly after their win, Bradley Wiggins, recently crowned the first ever British winner of the Tour de France, added the London Olympic Champion title to his collection by winning the time trial. Team GB was on a roll. And we all wanted our chance to go out and try it for ourselves. But patience was needed. It was imperative that we managed to stay calm and not live on adrenaline for days on end. We tried to enjoy the days in between racing. We relaxed, reading the Olympic news in the papers, watching the BBC coverage and sharing the crew room with other members of the team. Cameron Nichol was often in there entertaining everyone with his wonderful dry wit and comments. Hodgey was usually feet up, dwarfing a sofa and adding to the entertainment. Anna spent time watching while knitting, every now and then referring to Beth for pattern advice. It was easy, comfortable company in which to pass the time.

Two days before the final Anna, Thommo, Chris and I met for possibly the last time. The mood of the meeting was surprisingly upbeat and relaxed. We talked through the race and possible eventualities. Towards the end Anna turned to me and said, "And if we're leading and a crew starts to close in on us, we'll be OK." I agreed wholeheartedly. She said it again. I nodded again, wondering now if there was another point being made. As she held my gaze I asked if there was anything she meant by that. She surprised me by saying, "I just wanted to be sure you didn't have any concerns or doubts left over from Beijing."

I laughed out loud. "Seriously? I hadn't even thought about that. Not at all. That doesn't cross my mind at all. Really? Were you really worried?"

"I just didn't want you to be worried."

I wasn't worried and it made me realize that I didn't have any demons left from Beijing.

We had a good last day of training and over the radio Thommo suggested we tried some starts "as if it were the Olympic final tomorrow". At one point Anna burst out laughing in the boat because the boat felt so good. We really were enjoying this. On the journey back to the hotel the guys running the ferry boats allowed me to drive. Each small part of the day seemed to bring us another great experience and I couldn't believe how much we were still enjoying it even with the mounting pressure. Our final meeting was just the three of us. There was no emotion, just belief and conviction. Thommo finished with a "Remember it's like any other race." Then he added, "Except it's not. Don't forget it's the Olympics." It made me smile. He was right, we had to get the balance just right – feeling the familiarity of racing, feeling the confidence of doing something we knew how to do, but also not forgetting that it was a big event and it had to matter. As if we could forget.

I went outside for a last walk in the fresh air and I phoned home to speak to mum and dad and we had a lovely relaxed chat and said we'd see each other tomorrow. I sat watching the quiet river and had a moment of contemplation. I really was looking forward to this race and I had utter confidence in our team of three. It was a good place to be, I had no doubts. Back in the room we decided not to have the TV on because at some point they were bound to preview the next day of racing and we didn't need to see ourselves. We lay in bed reading and wondering how soon sleep would come.

There was no doubt we were both awake before the alarm, but we lay in bed with our own thoughts. Eventually the alarm clock clicked and the music started. I had bought a new alarm clock for the pre-Olympic camps that had an iPod attachment so we could be woken by music every morning. Anna and I took it in turns to choose the music and we often lay in bed laughing aloud at the choice. As for the song choice for the Olympic morning, there had been no need for a discussion. We had known weeks ago what it would be.

In February 2012 Whitney Houston died, aged 48. Her music seemed to accompany me through life. I remember having to create a dance to her music at school. I stumbled awkwardly through school discos with her hits as a background theme tune. Thankfully Anna was also a fan and was keen to revive the classic 1980s and 1990s hits of the great singer. Throughout training camps Whitney accompanied us with powerful singalong hit after hit and she lifted our weary spirits. Anna had recently downloaded the greatest hits on to her iPod and my sister , Sarah, had given me the CD. She gave me a card with the CD, in which she'd written, "Listen to Track Four. And then listen again. And again. And again." Track Four was the song Whitney Houston had sung at the 1988 Olympics, "One Moment in Time". Without question Anna and I both knew that was the song that would start the day of our Olympic final. Most people roll their eyes when they hear that; it is not the coolest or trendiest song. But it has heart. And it has soul. And more important than anything else were the words.

"Each day I live, I want to be, a day to give, the best of me, I'm only one, but not alone, my finest day, is yet unknown. I broke my heart, fought every gain, to taste the sweet, I face the pain, I rise and fall, yet through it all, this much remains. Give me one moment in time, when I'm more than I thought I could be, when all of my dreams are a heartbeat away, and the answers are all up to me."

That morning when the alarm clicked on and the piano started, we lay in silence listening to the words. Today was our moment in time. As the song faded we sat up and looked at each other. And smiled. "All right then," I said. Anna nodded. As we left the room I asked if we had everything we could possibly need. Anna looked at me and said, "We've got a you, we've got a me, we've got everything we need."

There were four boat drivers on our little ferries, Darren, Ed, Jimmy and Lewes, who all made sure the journeys were as relaxed and friendly as possible. The morning of our final race the drivers knew what the day meant to us and were respectful but quietly supportive. Everyone we saw gave us a nod and a meaningful look. There were deep intakes of breath everywhere we went. Each day on arriving at Dorney there was a Gamesmaker sitting in a high umpire's chair guiding people in and always unbelievably positive and upbeat. As we arrived that day he said, "Hey, everyone, I have a gold medal, can you see my gold medal? Are you jealous?" I looked up to see him wearing a big

Cadbury's chocolate gold medal and smiled to myself. Yes, at that moment I was jealous of his medal.

Sonia, our personal security on loan from the Metropolitan Police, was a superstar. Casually dressed and blending in with the crowds, she walked slightly ahead, wearing sunglasses and looking like she was wandering along with other spectators ready for the event. But she walked on constant alert and aware of everyone around us. As soon as it looked as if we might get delayed or distracted, she calmly and politely stepped in to free us to continue our walk. We were a change from the usual politicians and important individuals she protected, and we felt very secure under her watchful eye.

As we headed for the tent we heard the loudspeaker running through the day's events. "And then the women's double sculls which we've all been waiting for. We'll see if Anna Watkins and Katherine Grainger can take the title." The sound dulled as we closed the door of the temporary structure. This would be our world for the next 90 minutes. We felt strangely disconnected from the excited public outside and focused on our job, on finishing our journey in style. We weren't aware at that point of the number of people who had invested emotionally in the race that was about to unfold. It still felt personal to us. We had spent every day together for three years and now had the final step to take. We felt ready and now just had to wait. In the tent there was just Anna and I and our books and music. We chatted a little. Listened to music. Lay down and read. Then the stretching started, the sign that things were getting close. Occasionally someone opened the door and put their head in, only to withdraw it quickly.

Thommo came to see us when it was almost time to go. "Everything OK?" he enquired, assuming it was. We nodded. He told us that there was a bit of a crosswind and so the lanes were being redrawn. In rowing finals, the fastest two crews from the semi-finals always go in the centre lanes, but if there is a wind coming from the side then the lanes are reordered with the fastest crews given the most protected, and therefore fastest, lanes. Lane six would be the most protected. Australia was given lane six, and I was pleased. I believed we could win from wherever and I didn't want anyone claiming our success was due to being in the most favoured lane.

Thommo checked his watch and said he'd meet us over at the boat in a few minutes. Anna and I gathered our things and had a last few words together, just the two of us. We hugged and headed out. The sky above was blustery and threatened rain. Dropping our bags off at the bag check for the last time we were met by the whole team of Gamesmakers giving us silent thumbs-up signs and wishing us well. We had made friends with them during the week and this was our send-off. I had seen Rachel Woolf and Alison Mowbray, who were both working at Dorney for the week, and both had giving me knowing looks. The support came from everywhere.

Thommo was waiting by the boat for his final talk. We all knew what this race meant and nothing special was needed. There were simply words that calmed us and clarified our focus. Words that underlined our confidence and determination. As Thommo reached out and squeezed both of our shoulders, we were united in our purpose. We lifted the boat from the rack and walked towards the landing stage, I saw Matthew Pinsent and a camera crew walk in front of us. It was only when watching the footage later that we learned he was saying the words, "If you could pick one boat out of the whole GB Regatta that was going to win, we'd all pick this one."

Thommo pushed us away from the landing stage and we were off. Through my sunglasses I allowed myself one final look up at the vast stadium of spectators. The next time I would let myself see them would be after we crossed the finish line. Then the focus shifted into the boat as we slipped under the bridge and into the relative quiet of the warm-up lake. It was as if a curtain had fallen on the drama of the racecourse and we were in another world. The warm-up lake was a bit choppy due to the unsettled weather and our hands were moist from the dampness in the air. It rained at some point. Anna and I were both aware of the danger points of slippery hands and seats. We unconsciously factored that into our warm-up, not overdoing the fast work until we were confident it was safe.

When we came back through from the warm-up lake on to the course it was still eerily calm. There were no members of the public allowed in the first 100m of the course. The other crews paddled through with us to the start, and there we were, the six best double scull crews in the world preparing for one enormous blazing battle. There was nothing left to be done, to be said or to be tried. Anna and I had all the tools we needed, all the weapons we wanted and, most importantly of all, we were part of the best team imaginable. Regardless of the confidence and the enjoyment it was still a heart-pounding and nerve-wracking moment. I breathed deeply to keep myself calm. And I didn't think about the past or the future. I didn't think about the opposition or the crowds. I didn't think about what the race might be or how the story could end. I thought about the only thing I needed to. I thought about the very first stroke of the race. It was simple. It was clear. And I could control that.

I turned around to squeeze Anna's leg and look her in the eye. We did this at the start of every race and every time I smiled. This was no different. This was where I wanted to be and this was who I wanted to be with. And I was lucky enough to know Anna felt the same. Today was about delivery. In any other location, any other day of the year, we would have the confidence to blow this race apart. On 3 August 2012, at our own Olympics in front of our own crowd, could we live up to our potential? Could we do our wonderful boat justice? How we coped with the pressure would determine the result. It was ours to lose. Anna said one line: "This is the one."

I sat forward, turning my attention to the red disc of the traffic light. As soon as the disc faded I would be ready to react. Don't wait for the green, wait for the red to fade. Anna wouldn't be watching the light. That was my responsibility. She was waiting to react with me. The starter read out the crews. I breathed. Here we go. "Attention." Think of the first stroke, just the first stroke. The buzzer sounded as the red light faded and we were gone. We attacked from the first stroke and the rating was high. I checked. It was high but not too high. Anna would be watching too, trusting me to adjust if necessary but ready to say something if she thought we were overcooking it. We both knew it was the Olympic final and allowed ourselves a bit of a margin for enthusiasm. But most importantly we had come out in our rhythm. Our wonderful, solid, consistent, dependable rhythm. It was a rhythm that allowed us to apply huge amounts of force and acceleration but with an accurate timing so that the flow of the boat was uninterrupted. It was because of seeing that rhythm that, watching from the sidelines as he followed on his bike, Thommo decided within 30 strokes that we would win this race.

But the Australians were not going to make it easy for us, and the usual confidence didn't come as early as it would have normally. The margin of comfort that was enough at a World Cup race wasn't going to be enough today. We wanted more. The Australians used everything they had to launch repeated attacks down the course, but we were in charge and ready for everything. We had talked about dealing with surprises as and when they came, but they didn't come. Anna knew by halfway that we would win. Her analytical interpretation of the race showed that we had the margin we needed, had more if necessary, and that the Australians wouldn't be able to be faster than us in the second half of the race. Anna knew we would come first in this race but she didn't equate that to winning the Olympics Games, not at that stage. In the third quarter we relaxed slightly and rowed better for it. We had a bag of tricks to use and all the weapons in our arsenal. They were loaded and ready and I knew Anna would let me know exactly if and when we should fire.

It was a racing experience unlike anything I have ever known before in rowing. By halfway the crowds were huge in numbers and noise. As we approached the stands it was as if we were rowing into the centre of the Olympic Stadium. The noise grew relentlessly on all sides and became a physical sensation, something far more than just sound. We felt it through the boat and soon I wasn't going to hear a word Anna said, even though I knew she was shouting as loud as she could. The height of the stands, the passion of the crowd and the effect of the water magnifying the noise combined to create the famous "Dorney Roar". It was utterly mind-blowing. Anna later said she was able to take mental snapshots in the last 200m, of the noise, the sunlight, the Australians behind us; she had no feeling of danger by then. She smiled briefly, giving herself permission to enjoy it. In those last few metres I felt we were invincible, no one would beat us in this boat, on this lake in front of this crowd. We were carried across the finish line on a wave of complete euphoria.

It was about two strokes past the line when I let myself accept the result and I threw off the lid to all the emotion being suppressed underneath. I hadn't heard the finish line beep or felt the change in the water as we crossed the bubble line, so we were past the line before I let myself believe we had just won the Olympics. But then it was instantaneous. I threw my arms wide, punching the air, and dropped my head back. We had done it. I turned to put my arms around Anna – "You are amazing!" I shouted. Anna just laughed disbelievingly. I lay back on to her legs and she leaned forward hugging me. "Did we do it? Did we really do it?" she repeated. I grinned, "Oh yes, we definitely did it." It was a special moment, the two of us in a little cocoon on the water, hearing the sound of tens of thousands of people cheering and applauding all around while we tried to come to terms with what we'd done.

I sat up and bowed to the crowds, who truly had been sensational. As far as we could see were Union Jacks being waved and banners held high. The sound didn't diminish as we paddled over to the pontoon. I leapt out of the boat so I could hug Anna properly, and the smiles felt wider than our faces. I had heard Seb Coe among others talking about the feeling of winning. It is common, when you are the favourite and the expectation is upon you, for the overriding feeling to be one of relief. Relief to have finally made it, to have lived up to the promise. But I can honestly say that for me the feeling was pure joy, deep and undiluted. And I was happy about that, because somehow relief just wouldn't have done that moment justice.

Steve Redgrave and John Inverdale from the BBC were next. They were waiting at the beginning of the media walkway. At last Steve gave me the hug he had promised. After Beijing when we were both in tears he said the next time it would be tears of joy. There was nothing that needed to be said as we embraced. Steve knew what the result meant to me and he had been there throughout my career. But surprisingly there were no tears, even of joy. Somewhere a few miles away in a studio in London sat Sally Richardson, the BBC producer who had been a rock of support after Beijing. She was directing this part of the Olympics and it was her voice that Steve and John had in their earpieces and these pictures she was watching. It was a special day for so many people and lovely that everyone could share the emotion. But at that moment I was too happy to cry. I was somewhere miles above cloud nine, maybe nine hundred and ninety-nine. Anna said she was still waiting for it to sink in properly. She found it hard to change gear from the clarity of doing the job we had done to the enormity of what had just happened. We had rehearsed the race so often that there was a sudden juxtaposition of the familiar, the ordinary, with the completely extraordinary. At some point it had moved from private to public. We stood with arms around each other trying to talk about what that moment felt like. It was impossible to explain. I said something along the lines of this medal being the people's medal because so many people had been behind it and had helped me to get here. Mum later told me off for such a cheesy line, but I had meant it and still do. I didn't win that medal, or any of my medals, alone. And they were better medals for that very reason.

Further along the line was a very emotional Sarah Winckless, reporting for BBC Radio Berkshire. She had enough tears for all of us. As I laughed and hugged Sarah's weeping form I asked what she was crying for. Between sobs she said she was just so proud. With the same generosity of spirit that Dot, Cath and Lisa had displayed 12 years before in Sydney, Sarah felt nothing but happiness for what we had just achieved.

Then it was time to move to the main medal podium. At that point we could look up and see our families in the grandstand. My mum and dad were there with Sarah and Steph, right beside Oli and Anna's parents. Everyone was beaming, waving hands, scarves, banners and flags and hugging each other. As the sun shone down I felt life couldn't get any better. We congratulated the Australians for a great race and waited for the Poles to join us. One of them arrived in a wheelchair; we later found out she had had a bad back problem and held together just long enough to win an impressive bronze medal. They would go home to a heroes' welcome in Poland.

Soon the medals arrived on their formal cushions and Sir Craig Reedie stepped forward. Craig, a member of the International Olympic Committee, had awarded me my silver medal in Beijing, saying he'd hoped to be giving me the gold then. We made a deal that if I raced in London he would give out the medals and I would get the result right this time. We both held up our own end of the bargain. The London medals are much bigger than previous Olympic medals, and as the huge weight was put around my neck I looked at it properly for the first time. With flowers in hand we turned to watch the flags rise as the National Anthem started. Behind us thousands of people bellowed enthusiastically across the water and I was caught between laughter and emotion. This was the moment. This was when everything stopped briefly and the picture freezes. Every sporting idol and role model had this picture: the medal, the flag, the anthem. And now it was here for us. Anna and I held hands and I let the emotions flood over me.

All too soon it was time to leave the podium and get back into the boat. Just before we did, one of the Gamesmakers gave me a tartan scarf for a photo – that's the one used on our Royal Mail celebratory stamp. As we climbed back into our familiar seats in the boat, I had a Union Jack draped around my shoulders, a great big shiny gold medal around my neck and a very happy partner behind me. A safety launch puttered towards us. "OK, girls, the rules are you can row up to the 250m mark." We nodded. He paused. "However, if you were to go any further than that, there is really nothing I can do." He gave a small smile and I nodded again, understanding completely.

We paddled up past the friends and family stand, seeing loads of the BOA and rowing support staff, ecstatic faces reflecting our own joy. We waved our hands and the medals as we passed by the crowds. Then we were passing the tented area where people working at Dorney were based. They waved and cheered us on too. Anna asked if we should stop there and turn back. I said I thought we should continue on a bit. We made it to just shy of the 750m, and had a quiet moment to ourselves. It was probably the last quiet moment we had. We rowed across to the main stadium side. Before we reached the bank another safety launch approached. We were instructed that the men's singles medal ceremony was about to start further down the course and out of respect we shouldn't be opposite the podium during the anthems. So we were asked if we could go very slowly along the bankside. That wasn't going to be a problem.

The crowds there were absolutely incredible. Although racing was now officially over for the day, there were thousands of people lining the bank, still cheering and waving and taking photos. We rowed a few strokes, stopped, waved, showed the medal and rowed on a few strokes, repeating it all over again. We had never rowed so slowly in our lives. We recognized family members, old teammates, godchildren, university friends, neighbours. We read banners, saw flags and grinned like fools. Before we got to the finish two launches arrived to flank us. The drivers were relaxed but told us that as the course was now open for training we were actually on the wrong side, in an illegal place according to the circulation pattern. The boats would stay with us like giant motorized bodyguards to make sure no harm came to us or the other athletes. Anna and I were slightly uncomfortable to see the crews who would be racing the next day starting to come out to train. Knowing how we had been feeling the day before our Olympic final, I didn't think they'd be overjoyed to see athletes with their medals still soaking up the moment. We crossed the finish line for the second time and a final launch came up towards us. It was a friendly face we had seen every day in training. "Well done, girls. Wanna go round again?" he asked seriously. As tempting as it was to enjoy the crowd one last time, we both knew it would be disrespectful to training athletes. We had more than we could have hoped for and it was now time to leave the lake to others. As we passed the giant screen I noticed it said 1.15pm. It had been over an hour since we raced.

As we arrived at the landing stage we finally saw Thommo, whose unfailing drive had been so crucial. At the Olympics, his long-held vision for the women's team was becoming a reality and his reaction said it all. He embraced us both and the ridiculous smiles and congratulations continued. Our success was his success. I hugged so many people in the next few hours, as everyone seemed to be ecstatic for us. The feelgood factor was enormous and infectious but I needed to see my family. I had only seen them from a distance so far. I found dad and then Sarah and Steph. Finally I got a back view of my mum. As I approached I realized whom she was speaking to. Gathered around my mum, in complete contrast to the experience in Beijing, was a range of journalists holding their dictaphones. My mum was holding her own mini press conference. I had to interrupt to attract her attention. As she turned away I heard her saying back over her shoulder, "Well I wouldn't rule out Rio!"

My fantastic family had been there for me every step of this journey. Although over that time we had lost my grandparents and my aunt and uncle, we had also gained new members. On a brilliantly happy day in 2009, we celebrated Sarah and Steph's civil partnership, which gave me another wonderful sister. Steph is a fun and dynamic addition to the Grainger family and Steph's parents, brother and sisters and extended family and friends became enthusiastic rowing supporters, joining in the celebrations when the Olympics came around.

Anna and I had our own press conference and then another interview with Steve and John for the BBC. As I went over to the raised platform where the interview would be, I saw Matthew Pinsent for the first time since he had walked in front of us at the landing stages with his camera crew. Away from the cameras he gave me a hug and a wry smile. "Welcome to the club, Miss Grainger, we've been holding the door open for a while for you."

Halfway through the live interview Ann Redgrave joined us with a bottle of champagne. This was the Olympic version of rehydrating as recommended by our doctor. Champagne. Shortly after I had to report to drug testing. Anna insisted I took the remains of the champagne with me. There were so many people still to see and celebrate with, but eventually David Tanner came to find me. He was overjoyed at our success and the success of the rowing team so far. In 2012 David had overseen the most successful British rowing team in history and the top rowing nation in the Olympic Games. It didn't, however, merely all come together in that one summer. Over the previous 15 years David had developed a stunningly impressive set-up whereby new athletes can come in, be supported, guided by experienced coaches and assisted by world class support staff. The equipment and facilities in rowing are second to none. From the moment lottery funding was a possibility David made sure rowing was doing everything it needed to do to prove it deserved the financial investment and would repay it with international success. David has guided with a frugal and steadying hand to make sure the sport is bigger than any individual and as a result of himself and the superb Di Ellis (the Chair of British Rowing from 1989–2013) the sport has been in consistently safe hands. Their leadership was rightly rewarded with a Knighthood and Damehood and their true success will be to see the sport continue in its winning ways long after we have all moved on. On 3 August, however, David was very aware of his responsibilities of being a team manager. After congratulating us he personally escorted me over to the drug testing to make sure I wasn't late. As we walked over, David eyed the champagne bottle I was holding. "Katherine, I don't want you drinking that entire thing yourself. I would like you to enjoy yourself and remember it tomorrow. I think you know what I mean."

I arrived at the drug testing and was ushered in by two lovely women who helped me through the form. Drug testing is a very serious procedure and even in a euphoric state it was important to make sure the details were right. I placed the champagne bottle to one side and we went through the form together. One of the women looked at me. "I have to write the position that you finished in, so first, second, third, fifth etc. So I've just written gold."

It was there in capital letters. I couldn't help but smile. "OK, thanks, but can we just go through that again?"

"Yes, of course. Katherine Grainger. British. Gold."

"OK, thanks," I said. "One more time?"

"GOLD!" we all said together.

When I left drug testing most of the crowds had gone and I stepped out to a quieter, calmer version of Dorney. It was lovely, and the first real feeling of contentment flowed over me as I gazed out at the still water of the lake. It had really happened. Ann Redgrave then ushered me towards the last ferry, which was waiting for us. Anna had used the time to catch up with her friends and family, and we were now expected on the boat for more media. As I arrived at the dock I was met by two of our lovely boat drivers, Darren and Jimmy, ready with congratulatory hugs and both wearing David Beckham masks after Steve had promised to give me an introduction to David if we won.

The next 12 hours passed in a blur. Anna, Thommo and I were interviewed over the side of the boat as Sky and ITV bizarrely leaned across the water with microphones while trying to keep up in their own motorboats. Then we were allowed five minutes at Oakley Court to change out of racing kit and into Team GB outfits before we were taken to the local boat club for more press and then on to Stratford for the main media interviews at the BOA and the BBC headquarters. In those five minutes Anna had the presence of mind to grab a bottle of champagne that Oakley Court had considerately put in our room. As we sat in the back of the minibus with Thommo we took turns to swig from the bottle, merrily passing it between the three of us and Caroline Searle who sat in the front fielding media calls. Caroline was the team's media officer, being a constant presence in GB Rowing for years and part of the reason why rowing had attracted increased amounts of media attention. Her tireless work had helped to transform our sport and she certainly deserved to be part of our celebrations.

We were all giddy with excitement and laughed loudly when Thommo suggested we should review our race. The laughter continued until we realized he was being serious. Thommo's attention to detail had become invaluable in the way he previewed and reviewed every race. We would know exactly what we had to think about before the race, narrowing it down to two or three key points. Sometimes in the few hours following the race we would sit down as a crew and coach to review what had happened, to assess how far we had achieved our aims for the race and how we could improve next time. Although I teased Thommo about his obsession with graphs, charts, percentages and tables and occasionally felt we were at risk of becoming mere statistics in his laptop, those reviews became crucial to building up how we wanted to race and how we wanted to think.

Even after the Olympic final Thommo recognized the importance of reviewing the race and so he pulled out his laptop and started to go through the familiar questions we'd used after every race. We had to score ourselves on how we felt things had gone in different areas. Anna and I shrugged, had another mouthful of champagne and decided things had gone very well and we deserved full marks. But as we went through the different areas we reverted to our more natural critically astute roles and agreed that there were areas where we could have done better. Even after winning the Olympics there were things that could be improved, and that search for perfection never ended. Thanks to Thommo's dogged attention to detail we now have a very honest and immediate review of the Olympic final.

We arrived at the BBC studios in the middle of Olympic Park for an interview with Gary Lineker and Steve Redgrave. As we arrived in the tiny make-up room I heard a voice through the open door. "Is she here?" Waiting in the room was Denise Lewis, ready with an enormous hug and eyes brimming with tears. "Congratulations, girl, I'm so proud of you." There were congratulations from Gabby Logan and Mark Cavendish, who were also crammed into the tiny space. As we did the various bits of media we were hugged and congratulated by Sue Barker and Ian Thorpe, then by Clare Balding and Chris Evans and Hazel Irvine. After our chat on the sofa with Gary we went to the next-door open-air studio to see a couple of the girls from the England football team, Faye White and Sue Smith, who were doing commentary. The studio was on the top floor, and as we were taken to the edge of the balcony we were met with a deafening cheer from below. Confused, Anna and I leaned over to see a sea of cheering and waving people.

Faye and Sue laughed, "There are crowds there every day waiting to see which Olympians will appear." As we smiled, the crowd smiled; when we waved, they waved; and when we lifted our medals they roared their approval. I grinned and wondered if Eva Peron felt like this. I stopped short of singing.

Then it was off to the BOA headquarters to do more press interviews. As we arrived there were loads of familiar BOA staff whom I had met over the years. Everyone was congratulating us and someone asked if we'd like a glass of champagne. It would have been rude to say no. Soon two beautiful tall chilled sparkling glasses arrived. Anna and I toasted each other, took a sip and then they were instantly taken away so we could continue with an interview. We never saw those glasses of champagne again. At some point we had a Polaroid photo taken of us with the medals, to sign and put on a display board. Anna and I asked for a copy each and it's that picture I carry in my wallet now. It is a picture of two girls who are still in a slight daze at having just become Olympic Champions, and the smiles demonstrate a lovely pure and innocent happiness.

Eventually we were taken back to Oakley Court and met with more TV cameras to do a live interview back to the BBC studio, where Gabby Logan was now hosting her evening show. Our official duties were then complete, and we finally walked through the doors into the hotel. Tip-toeing along the corridor, we were aware that behind some of the doors were athletes who would be waking up in a few hours to race in their own Olympic finals. Our two physiologists, Homer and Craig, were still awake and welcomed us back with hugs and the offer of a gin and tonic. It was lovely to have a quiet moment with two of our amazing behind-the-scenes team. They knew what the win meant to us and we knew how much they had helped us get there. We flopped into the chairs in their room and shared our experiences from the day. They filled us in on all the news we might have missed, including Alan Campbell's fantastic medal in the single and his emotional ceremony.

The next day we woke up for the first time in months without an alarm or music. It was 4 August, a day we hadn't talked about or planned for. To us, it didn't exist. But it had arrived and we were now in uncharted territory. We both woke early, even though there was nothing for us to get up and do. I lay in bed and simply smiled. The feeling of contentment was deep. I had slept with the medal by my bed so it would be the first thing I saw when I woke up and I would know it was real. Anna slept with hers under her pillow. I heard Anna checking her phone, and although it was still early I knew we wouldn't be going back to sleep. We put the TV on to see what the Olympics held for us that day. We were still Olympians, but now spectators rather than competitors. I asked Anna if she wanted a cup of tea and went to put the kettle on. As the kettle boiled I looked around our room. This was the last day we would be here. It had become our home, our haven over the past ten days. There was kit strewn everywhere, Union Jack flags were on the walls, bunting was up, books were stacked in piles, snacks and sweets lay on the table, stacks of DVDs leaned crookedly against the large TV, and flowers and good luck cards covered every surface. I would miss this. This room hadn't held any fears or stresses. It was where we wanted to be and where we could relax and enjoy each other's company as we prepared to take on the biggest challenge of our lives. The noise of the kettle boiling brought me back from my musings.

I made tea for myself in the "MacLund" mug Anna had made for me in homage to *The Killing* and gave Anna hers in her usual tea-stained owl mug. As I carried the drinks over I looked in vain for a place to put them down. "Where do you want it?" I asked Anna, scanning the surfaces nearby. "Oh, I have a coaster right here, put it on this." I looked down to see her gesturing to her Olympic medal. It made a perfect coaster.

Later that day I had my first indication of just what these Olympics and the medals meant to people. I had heard that Dianne Thompson, the wonderful Chief Executive of Camelot who had sponsored the GB team in previous years, was over in the hospitality tent. I went to say hello. As I walked in I met Steve Williams, the double gold medallist from Athens and Beijing. He said Dianne was upstairs and that she would love to see me. I walked into a vast marquee full of tables where people were sitting having lunch. I saw Dianne to my right at a table in the corner, and as I started to try to make my way past the tightly packed chairs I heard a few people comment and point, and then the whole room erupted in a spontaneous standing ovation. Stunned, I looked behind to see Steve smiling and nodding, and I looked forward to try to see Dianne but she was now hidden by the crowds of supporters.

The following day we moved into the Olympic Village and regularly walked into the Olympic Park, where Anna and I were continually mobbed by enthusiastic well-wishers. Having spent years as an unknown athlete, it was very strange to suddenly be recognized wherever we went. Being in the Village brought some element of normality to things, as much as being in a village which is wall-to-wall with international athletes can be. But within the confines of the Village being an Olympic athlete was expected. And it was great to be around other members of Team GB. On our first day there, Victoria Pendleton came cycling past on her bike and stopped to get a hug and say congratulations. She had just set a record of her own on the track and everything felt great. Anna and I met Kate Walsh, the GB women's hockey captain, soon after and we expressed our awe at her courage coming back to compete while suffering from a broken jaw. She shrugged off the praise, saying it was something anyone would do. But to have pain-killing injections into her face before every match and then face balls flying at 70mph at head height seemed particularly impressive to us.

Over the next week I tried to see as many of the sporting events at some of the most iconic sporting venues as I could. Olympic athletes do not get free access to the sports; we need to have tickets to watch the competition. I begged, borrowed and stole from anyone I could to get tickets. Anna and I were lucky enough to be in the stadium for Mo Farah's second gold, and at the amazing party venue of Earls Court for the volleyball, where the Brazilians showed us all how to have a good time as the partying flowed from the stands out on to the surrounding streets. At the boxing on the last day of the Olympics we sat next to Nicola Adams while watching Anthony Joshua win the heavyweight gold medal, and we also visited the spectacular Greenwich Park venue for the equestrianism. At Greenwich Anna joined her husband Oli in the main stands and I went up to the athletes' area. The view was incredible, as I sat looking out over the Naval College and across the Thames to the towers of Canary Wharf. The great thing about the athletes' stand was that there were always familiar and friendly faces.

When I arrived I saw Ash the physio deep in conversation with an equestrian physio, no doubt excitedly comparing notes on different sporting injuries and training. I met some of the members of the team and was incredibly fortunate to find myself next to Will Connell, the personable Performance Director for the British equestrian team. He was extraordinarily patient with my questions and generously explained all about the sport and the competition.

Anna and I were also guests of Sir Craig Reedie and his wife Rosemary at the last session of the cycling. We sat just a few rows from the front and could practically touch Victoria Pendleton as she leaned on the barrier while lining up next to Anna Meares. It would be Victoria's last ever Olympic race. We cheered along with UK Sport's Liz Nichol and Sue Campbell as Chris Hoy won his historic sixth Olympic gold medal. These Olympics would be the last major sporting event with Sue as the Chair of UK Sport. When she retired in 2013 the glowing tributes reflected her inspirational leadership.

Along with the velodrome, another of the great venues was the Riverbank Stadium, where the hockey teams did battle. For the first match I went to see I was in the second row from the back with friends, directly in front of the band that plays at every British match, the Pukka Pie band. "How lovely," I thought as I admired the drum and the brass instruments behind me. An hour later I was having to tell myself how lovely it was when they were still blaring out singalong tunes and British favourites. Possibly my favourite moment was when they played "Rule Britannia", and at the end a smiling Dutch fan sitting a few rows ahead turned and said, "Ah, you need another song. Britain hasn't ruled the waves for hundreds of years." Before anyone else could reply the woman in front of him turned and casually said, "Clearly you weren't at Dorney watching the rowing, then?" I leaned back smiling, anonymous in the crowd.

I watched the women's semi-final when the British team lost to the Argentinians. As the final whistle blew, the scene was one of poignant contrasts, the girls in blue and white celebrating while every British player sank to her knees on the astroturf. Having lost the semi, they had no guaranteed medal and no shot at the gold. Two days later their bronze medal match was the hottest ticket in town. I had a ticket, Sarah and Steph having bought three tickets months previously, not knowing who would be playing, so to get to see Team GB play for the medal was a fantastic stroke of luck. But Anna was keen to go too and we couldn't find a spare ticket. Eventually Anna and I managed to secure two seats through the British Olympic Association. There was just one small catch, as I heard when I took the call. "Katherine, we have managed to secure two tickets. We have to let you know it's in the hospitality area and we are welcoming Kate Middleton for that event too." I looked over at Anna who was sitting next to me. With one hand over the phone I asked, "Anna, do you mind if we're there with Kate Middleton?" "Hmmm?" she asked distractedly, as she answered an email. "The Duchess of Cambridge? Yep, that's fine." I leaned back into the phone. "Yes, that's fine by us."

We ended up sitting in a small group of people including the Duchess, Dame Kelly Holmes, Hugh Robertson, the Sports Minister, and Sally Munday, the CEO of hockey. Team GB put in an impressive display to win the bronze and we stood to applaud as they walked round on their lap of honour. I know one of their coaches well. As Karen walked underneath us she looked up to wave. One of the players next to her looked surprised at her informality. "Oh, I've known Katherine for years," Karen reassured her. The player looked shocked. "I didn't realize you knew her on first-name terms." Karen looked confused and squinted back up into the sunshine where we were standing. It was only then she saw I was next to Catherine Middleton and her look of mock horror was priceless.

But of all the situations we found ourselves in, the most surreal one was probably the first event we saw once we had left the rowing venue. On the Sunday Thommo told us he'd managed to secure some tickets for the beach volleyball, and hospitality was included. So that evening Anna, Helen, Heather, Fran, Thommo, Robin, Nick, Darren and I made our way to Horseguards Parade for our first experience of the Olympics as spectators. From where we sat we could look out over the stadium and see the London Eye and the city skyline. It was breathtaking, and the strangely contrasting surroundings of Westminster and the beach reminded us all again just how weird and wonderful the Olympic Games could be. As we watched and cheered from the stands we were recognized by people around us who bought us drinks or asked for photos. Eventually a woman wearing a Gamesmaker uniform moved along to sit directly behind me in an empty seat. Leaning forward, she tapped me on the shoulder as she cleared her throat. "I'm the Protocol Officer for this venue." I winced. "I'm sorry," I said, "I know it might be a bit distracting having people moving around." I had been very aware of the crowd support we had had, and I thought it might be having a negative impact on the teams playing down on the sand. "Oh no, there's no problem there," she shouted over a burst of music. "I just wondered if you wanted some sand time." I thought I'd misheard. She explained: "You know, we could get you down on the sand and introduce you properly to the crowds." I had a second of hesitation. Mostly I thought this a crazy idea, but there was a voice in my head thinking that that was something that I'd probably never be asked again. "Well, OK then. Can we all come?" She glanced over our group. "Oh yes, that would be great, the more the better."

A few minutes later we made our way down to the edge of the court, where we were instructed to take our shoes and socks off to protect the integrity of the sand. At the interval we were introduced to the crowd and as Helen and Heather conducted an interview with a courtside presenter, I found something else to conduct. In front of me there was a group of men who were enthusiastically singing Spandau Ballet's classic "Gold". They were emboldened by alcohol and their spirits were high. I encouraged them and soon Anna came over to join in with them. All around us there were Mexican waves and cheering and singing. Then we were asked to play "a few points" across the net and Fran, Anna and I proved why our strengths lay in a boat. After the main matches finished we went to the hospitality tent for a meal, and by the end our table was surrounded by a familiar group of men serenading us again with "Gold" and various other hits. In between songs they were drunkenly telling us, "You've changed a nation. Our grandchildren will be telling their grandchildren about you." Much later I sat on the bus on the way back to the Village, watching our coaches' heads drop one by one as the bus rocked them to sleep. I leaned my head against the cold glass and looked out at the floodlit city. Life was good.

On the last night of the athletics Steve Redgrave made good on his promise for me to meet David Beckham. I was called up by the BBC and asked if I could be back on Gabby Logan's evening show, the last one of the Games, to sit with Michael Johnson and Ben Ainslie and review the week. Caroline Searle, the British press officer, gave nothing away as she said it was a great thing to do and important to get a female athlete on the programme. Without suspecting a thing I wandered into the tiny make-up room once more and after greeting Gabby I half turned to see who the figure was in the make-up chair. I froze. It was David Beckham. Being far from cool, I turned open-mouthed back to Gabby, who simply smiled and nodded. I spun around again and David graciously stood up and took a couple of steps towards me, ignoring my shocked reaction. He hugged and congratulated me, asking if I'd got his voicemail. I said yes but that he hadn't left a number to return his call.

Ironically two of the stunning moments of that week were brought to me not by Olympians but by footballers. David Beckham was a joy to meet, and for someone who is a global megastar he was strikingly down to earth, friendly, modest and charismatic. A few days previous to that I had been invited by Edinburgh University to the Victoria and Albert Museum, where they were giving Pelé an honorary degree. There was a man who was a living legend of sport, had been voted athlete of the century and yet humbly talked about the fact that, as good a footballer as he was, he always wanted to be a better man.

Eventually all the fun had to come to an end. The Closing Ceremony beckoned, and unlike the Opening Ceremony we were all going to be there in the stadium watching the show. The biggest cheer of the night sounded when five black cabs drove on to the stage in the centre and out stepped the Spice Girls. There had been rumours about this rare reunion of the famous five, and here they were singing a medley while speeding along on the taxis. It felt so fitting that back in 1997 my first summer of racing had been defined by the new Girl Power, and here they were, 15 years later, joining in with Olympic fever.

Seb Coe gave a speech, saying that when it came to it we could say, "We did it right," and no one would have disagreed. Anna and I stood next to Thommo as Take That sang "Rule the World" and both of us had tears in our eyes as the Olympic flag was lowered and slowly the petals of the cauldron opened and the fire died out. All those individual petals went back to the countries a little more charred than when they arrived but bearing the signs of the 2012 Olympic Games. It was now over. It almost came as a surprise in the end; we were all enjoying ourselves so much that we forgot it had to stop. All the nerves, the stress, the tears, the laughter, the passion, the exhaustion, the fight, the defiance, the pain, the perfection, the focus: everything that had brought us to this point over days, weeks, months and years, was all gone. The Mayor of Rio received the Olympic flag and the Brazilian celebrations finished the night.

The next few months were a blur of strange and new experiences. I've never been in so many parades: in Marlow and Aberdeen, Glasgow and London. I spent more time on the back of buses and flatbed trucks than a southern belle beauty queen. At every location we were overwhelmed again as huge crowds turned out to show their support. While each parade was an opportunity for athletes to say thank you, the crowds gave us the message that it was one of the most memorable summers they could have imagined. The positive support and enthusiasm were infectious. The upbeat spirit was everywhere.

When the Paralympic Games began I went back to the wonderful Olympic Park to watch the Opening Ceremony, and I was there for the Thursday night of athletics when Jonnie Peacock, David Weir and Hannah Cockcroft lit up the stadium just as Jessica Ennis, Mo Farah and Greg Rutherford had a few weeks before. The stupendous summer of sport showed no sign of fading.

Olympians were welcomed everywhere, and the celebrations didn't seem to have any end in sight. Anna, Heather, Helen and I were taken to the middle of the Thames one day on a rickety boat to have photos taken for *Hello* magazine. There were formal lunches, dinners and awards evenings where we gave awards and where we received awards. There were charity events to attend and speeches to give at schools, local clubs, universities and corporate events. We met utterly inspiring people, many of whom are unknown names, continuing to make a difference to people's lives all the time under the radar and away from the spotlight.

One day I had the privilege of meeting the crime writer P. D. James at the Women of the Year lunch. She had just turned 92 and carried herself with style and wit. When she went on stage to collect her award she talked about how she had always wanted to write but had left school at 16 to work and then married and had two daughters. It wasn't until her mid thirties that she decided she had to write, otherwise one day she feared she would be sitting with her grandchildren telling them about her other life but saying, "Well, of course what I always wanted to be was a writer." She is living proof of the value of following a dream. She looked at the impressive eagle statue that had just been awarded to her, and with a glint in her eye she said as she walked off wielding the weighty object, "And I think I've just had a new idea for a murder weapon …" I thought gran would be happy I'd been there to meet a true queen of crime.

I also had the pleasure of meeting Madeleine Albright. She spoke at a dinner I attended in Glasgow and I was introduced to her. She was eager to hear about the Olympics and talked warmly with me about her daughters and grandchildren. But when she took to the stage she spoke with clear intelligent authority on a range of subjects both historical and current. She was not afraid to state her mind and had a striking presence with her sharpness and humour. It was obvious why she had been the first woman to become the United States Secretary of State. She talked fervently about the obligation we have to stand up for and speak out for those who do not have that opportunity themselves. She also happens to be the author of a quote that was put up on our changing room noticeboard: "There is a special place in hell for women who don't help other women." It was a strong message that we believed in. All too often there is criticism of women trying to put each other down. I have lived and worked in a world where women have supported, encouraged, protected and helped each other every single day and that world has been far better for it.

Talking of strong women, we also had our audience with now the most famous Bond girl of them all, the Queen. All the Olympic medallists were invited to a Reception at the Palace. It was a lovely evening of catching up with the other athletes and finding out what everyone had been up to in the post-Olympic whirlwind. Then, at some point in the evening, a door opens somewhere and, without your noticing at first, the Royal Family are walking amongst you. Anna and I had an enjoyable chat with the Queen and I congratulated her on her impressive part in the Opening Ceremony. She gave a small smile and said, "Oh yes, a few people have been commenting on that." But then her face broke into a huge smile as she exclaimed, "But did you see how well my corgis acted!" The performance of her dogs had clearly been a highlight of the night for her.

Throughout those months people repeatedly asked me how bad the "comedown" was from such a climactic event. And I told them honestly that I hadn't come down yet. I don't believe I had any down moments at all until about Christmas, and by then I was so exhausted I was looking forward to a bit of normality. I was aware, however, that I was one of the lucky ones. Most people struggled with more of the traditional highs and lows after such an immense experience. For many, the weeks after the Olympics were confusing, overwhelming and anti-climactic. There is also a sudden change, going from a predictable and controlled life as an athlete into something largely unknown. Even those athletes who knew what the future held for them found coming to terms with life after the London Olympics a huge challenge and not something that could have been prepared for. Before the Games you know what your purpose is and who you are. Things can get a little hazy after such a momentous event.

Anna and I had achieved something very special on the lake in Dorney. It had been a magical few years aiming for that one special day and, along with Thommo, we had spent all of our time together planning and preparing. Anna and I were equal partners throughout and each played crucial roles in the drama. Once we left the lake, however, we realized that the main story used about us in the media was that of my three silver medals and then the gold, which had made me the first British female athlete to win medals at four Olympics. It is a simple and a strong narrative, a tale of never giving up, of climbing back up after being knocked down, of following dreams in the face of sometimes huge doubts, and it has a wonderful happy ending. And many, many people had been part of the journey along the way.

As far as the media were concerned it was a story that people could relate to with a huge amount of human interest. And it was all very true. Unfortunately, though, it was my story, and so to some extent Anna was being marginalized. Our success at the London Games had been our joint success and we shared our moment in the boat having crossed the line, but sometime after that things became blurred.

Ironically the toughest challenge we ever had to face was after we had won the Olympics. It was something neither of us saw coming. Our partnership came under threat but, even worse, our friendship was at risk. Anna felt her role was now less clearly defined and in part her identity had been altered by the media. She felt our partnership had been split where it had always been solidly joined and that she had no element of control. At any time it would have been painful, but at a time when emotions are unpredictable and there seems no stability underfoot it was an impossible situation. It was a bad time for both of us. I hated seeing Anna upset when we had just achieved the most fantastic result that we had worked so hard for. I thought back to all we had overcome and accomplished together, and resented the new situation we found ourselves in. Also, I was feeling guilty every time I was recognized or congratulated, guilt that often took away enjoyment from what should have been celebratory events.

I was so concerned about it that when I was phoned by an excited Caroline Searle to let me know the good news about being shortlisted for the BBC Sports Personality of the Year award, instead of leaping, my heart sank. However, in the end it proved to be a positive turning point. It was the catalyst for Anna to speak to the media about the coverage she felt she had been edited out of. Having had the conversations she needed to have, happily she felt once again in control. In the lead up to the Sports Personality evening Anna campaigned on my behalf and on the show itself she deservedly had a prominent part. I had the public opportunity to express my gratitude and respect for her. Afterwards, with many friends we partied the rest of the night away, feeling we had managed to make sure that the story of our year was back to being about the boat and the racing and the simplicity of our rowing partnership. On a very small scale it had been a lesson in the power of "celebrity" and how alienating it can be. In the end the Sports Personality night was a huge celebration of the summer Olympics and Paralympics.

The last time Anna and I met in 2012 was in a hotel on the Strand in London. It was shortly before Christmas and there were fairy lights in the trees and decorations hung across buildings. The air was chilled and the summer felt a long time ago. We sat anonymously in a corner of the lounge, feeling relaxed, drinking coffee. We caught up with each other's news and hearing about the festive plans. Anna would be leaving on 1 January for a two-month holiday with Oli. As we chatted there was a mixture of happy contentment but also some sadness that our golden year was coming to an end. One of the managers of the hotel was having a meeting in another corner of the lounge, and as she walked past she looked at us twice. A few minutes later she came back with two glasses of champagne. Without drawing any attention from the other people in the room she said quietly, "These are on me. What you both did was just incredible, you should be drinking champagne every day." It was a lovely gesture and very subtly done. As she disappeared back to her meeting we raised our glasses. What we'd done was indeed incredible. We had been through such a huge amount together that, although 2012 was ending, we knew we had forged a bond that would not be broken and created happy memories that would never be forgotten. It was an emotional hug we gave each other outside on the Strand an hour later. I pulled my collar up against the December day and turned away, not knowing what lay ahead for me but feeling ready to move forward and find out.

... AND THEY LIVED
HAPPILY EVER AFTER

How does it all end? Do they live happily ever after? On my desk I have a card saying 'Everything will be okay in the end. If it's not okay, it's not the end'. I like the simple sentiment and it has helped me through some of the tougher bits of the rollercoaster. At the end of the London Olympics it was certainly more than just okay, but it wasn't the end of everything. The story isn't over and can't be neatly wrapped up in a conclusion. But as in all good fairytales many people in these pages are indeed living happily ever after in various places in various different situations at this very moment. As for me the future is still unclear. Life is an exciting place full of many wonderful opportunities that I could not have imagined when I was at school considering career options.

The months following on from the London Olympics were a whirlwind of exciting highs but as I danced the year away at a Princes Street ceilidh in Edinburgh heralding the ending of 2012, I was ready for life to return to a more familiar type of reality. The nerves and excitement of 2012 were replaced by a welcome contentment but also an unfamiliar uncertainty.

One good thing at the beginning of 2013 was having a very simple focus. After more years than I, or my patient supervisor, would care to count, I finally had time to devote to completing my PhD. I again had a clear goal and an aim for each day. The drive I had channelled into my rowing was turned to my thesis. It was a pleasure to interview fascinating and sharply perceptive people and to sit in front of a computer devoting my time to a goal that had always sat somewhere a little out of view and frequently out of reach. It was another proud moment when I defended my thesis and officially became Dr Grainger.

I am aware that although the great summer of 2012 is behind us, it has not disappeared from people's minds. There is constant talk of what the legacy is from those Games. Many question if anything has really changed. I can only talk from my own experience but I know that not only do we have the physical legacy of the sports facilities, but also, while there are accounts that participation rates in a few sports have dropped, in rowing and in many other Olympic sports the story is of clubs, schools and universities experiencing lengthening waiting lists of people – young and not so young – wanting to join. People who have never tried sports, people who had left sport for years and want to go back to try again, or to recapture the fun they once had when they did take part. The success of women at the Games has created a whole new team of role models of all different shapes, sizes, ages and backgrounds for girls to look up to and learn from. Alongside health and well-being, sport reminds people about teamwork, communication, goal-setting, how to deal with failure and success, responsibility, and a myriad other things, all without feeling that lessons are being taught. On the grander scale it is about endeavour and the human spirit challenging current boundaries. On the smaller scale it is individuals having a personal goal or simply having fun.

For me one of the biggest legacies has been the change of mood. There continues to be a powerful sense of pride in the country and the people about what was achieved last summer. When I talk to people about the summer of 2012, there is a light in their eyes and a smile on their faces as they think about their own memories of that time.

Inspiration is a priceless thing and for a few weeks in 2012 we all had the feeling anything was possible. That spirit should not be underestimated. It is the kind of spirit that makes history and changes the future.

It is now time for contemplation, for gathering energy and then looking forward once more. I don't yet have the answers for what comes next, despite being asked daily. Luckily although I like having a plan and a goal to aim for, I am also relaxed enough to let things happen for a while. As Abraham Lincoln said ' the best thing about the future is that it comes one day at a time'. I know what I'm doing today and that's a good enough start. I believe that life is great, is there to be cherished and lived with passion. I'm aware that it's too short and should not be wasted and that it can hold untold pleasures.

My great aunt, who is now 90 wrote me a letter after I had sent her a postcard from one of the various training camps I'd been on. On the camp I was no doubt exhausted, stressed, had doubts and at some point wondered what I was doing. But Aunt Edna saw none of that. In her letter she wrote 'Thanks for all your cards from your travels. They have made me realise I was born too soon'. It made me appreciate all over again that, for all the down times, how lucky I am to be living in the time I am, knowing the people I do, experiencing the life I have. I am often asked about the things I have sacrificed while being an athlete. For me this is a very important point: I don't feel they have been sacrifices; I believe they have been choices. For everything I may have missed out on, I have gained much more and even if I hadn't, every decision has been my choice and my responsibility.

Oliver Wendell Holmes wrote that 'Many people die with their music still in them. Why is this so? Too often it is because they are always getting ready to live. Before they know it, time runs out.' That's why friendships should be made, challenges faced, places explored, music sung to (whether or not you were told at an early age you can't sing), books read, conversations enjoyed, mountains climbed and laughter shared. Life is about taking part: win, lose or draw. And there's no time to waste.

Whatever the result of the challenge it's worth being out there in the dust and the dirt. It's worth the battle and the scars and the possible heartbreak. There are no guarantees in life but in a way that's what makes everything come alive. And, of course, it's worth having dreams because you never know when and how they might come true.

FOR THE RECORD

1997

NATIONS CUP
(Under 23 World Championships)
Milan, Italy......................................U23W2-...........Gold..............07.25.40

WORLD CHAMPIONSHIPS
Aiguebelette, France.........................W8+.................Bronze............06.10.00

1998

WORLD CUP 1
Vienna, Austria................................W1x.................7th.................07.59.35

WORLD CUP 2
Hazewinkel, Belgium ....W1x.................9th.................07.49.30

1999

WORLD CUP 1
Hazewinkel, Belgium.........................W4x.................4th.................06.49.96

WORLD CUP 2
Vienna, Austria...............................W4x ....Bronze 06.52.69

WORLD CUP 3
Lucerne, Switzerland........................W4x.................5th.................06.29.23

WORLD CHAMPIONSHIPS
St Catherines, Canada ....W4x.................7th.................06.16.93

2000

WORLD CUP 1
Munich, Germany............................W4x.................5th.................06.44.66

WORLD CUP 2
Vienna, Austria...............................W4x.................Gold 07.09.87

OLYMPIC GAMES
Sydney, Australia.............................W4x.................Silver..............06.21.64

2001

WORLD CUP 1
Seville, Spain ....W2- ....Bronze 07.37.05

WORLD CUP 2
Vienna, Austria...............................W2- ....Gold 08.26.44

WORLD CUP 3
Munich, Germany............................W8+.................4th.................06.37.67

WORLD CHAMPIONSHIPS
Lucerne, Switzerland........................W2- ....5th.................07.08.86

WORLD CHAMPIONSHIPS
Lucerne, Switzerland........................W8+.................6th.................06.09.64

2002

WORLD CUP 1
Hazewinkel, Belgium.......................W4x.................Bronze 06.26.04

WORLD CUP 2
Lucerne, Switzerland........................W4x.................5th.................06.24.55

WORLD CUP 3
Munich, Germany ....W4x.................Bronze 06.29.75

WORLD CHAMPIONSHIPS
Seville, Spain ....W4x.................5th.................06.20.15

2003

WORLD CUP 1
Milan, Italy...W2-..................Silver.............. 07.07.55

WORLD CUP 2
Munich, Germany............................W2-..................Gold 07.24.21

WORLD CUP 3
Lucerne, Switzerland......................W2-..................Bronze 07.13.01

WORLD CHAMPIONSHIPS
Milan, Italy.......................................W2-..................Gold 07.04.88

2004

WORLD CUP 1
Poznan, Poland................................W2-..................Silver.............. 07.14.79

WORLD CUP 2
Munich, Germany............................W2-..................Gold 07.39.79

WORLD CUP 3
Lucerne, Switzerland......................W2-..................Bronze 07.15.66

OLYMPIC GAMES
Athens, Greece.................................W2-..................Silver.............. 07.08.66

2005

WORLD CUP 1
Eton, England ....W4x..................Gold 06.36.96

WORLD CUP 2
Munich, Germany............................W4x..................Gold 06.50.85

WORLD CUP 3
Lucerne, Switzerland......................W4x..................Silver.............. 06.22.06

WORLD CHAMPIONSHIPS
Gifu, Japan ....W4x..................Gold 06.09.59

2006

WORLD CUP 1
Munich, Germany............................W4x..................Gold 06.32.00

WORLD CUP 2
Poznan, Poland................................W4x..................Gold 06.15.32

WORLD CUP 3
Lucerne, Switzerland......................W4x..................Gold 06.31.27

WORLD CHAMPIONSHIPS
Eton, England ....W4x..................Gold 06.12.50

2007

WORLD CUP 1
Linz, Austria..W4x..................Gold..............06.26.90

WORLD CUP 2
Amsterdam, Holland.......................W4x..................Silver..............06.28.55

WORLD CUP 3
Lucerne, Switzerland........................W4x..................Gold..............06.20.54

WORLD CHAMPIONSHIPS
Munich, Germany............................W4x..................Gold..............06.30.81

2008

WORLD CUP 1
Munich, Germany............................W4x..................Gold..............06.54.38

WORLD CUP 2
Lucerne, Switzerland........................W4x..................Bronze...........06.24.38

OLYMPIC GAMES
Beijing, China...................................W4x..................Silver..............06.17.37

2009

WORLD CUP 1
Banyoles, Spain..................................W1x..................Gold..............07.56.40

WORLD CUP 2
Munich, Germany............................W1x..................4th..................07.55.19

WORLD CUP 3
Lucerne, Switzerland........................W1x..................4th..................07.39.45

WORLD CHAMPIONSHIPS
Poznan, Poland.................................W1x..................Silver..............07.13.57

2010

WORLD CUP 1
Bled, Slovenia....................................W4x..................Gold..............06.26.65

WORLD CUP 1
Bled, Slovenia....................................W2x..................Gold..............07.06.14

WORLD CUP 2
Munich, Germany............................W4x..................Silver..............06.31.96

WORLD CUP 2
Munich, Germany............................W2x..................Gold..............07.02.39

FOR THE RECORD

2010 CONTINUED

WORLD CUP 3
Lucerne, Switzerland.........................W4x..................Gold 06.23.50
WORLD CUP 3
Lucerne, Switzerland.........................W2x..................Gold 06.50.53
WORLD CHAMPIONSHIPS
Karapiro, New Zealand....................W2x..................Gold 07.04.70

2011

WORLD CUP 1
Munich, Germany ....W2x..................Gold 06.57.52
WORLD CUP 3
Lucerne, Switzerland.........................W2x..................Gold 06.54.34
WORLD CHAMPIONSHIPS
Bled, Slovenia ....W2x..................Gold 06.44.73

2012

WORLD CUP 1
Belgrade, Serbia ....W2x..................Gold 06.50.35
WORLD CUP 2
Lucerne, Switzerland.........................W2x..................Gold 06.52.52
WORLD CUP 3
Munich, Germany ....W2x..................Gold 07.09.90
OLYMPIC GAMES
London, England...............................W2x..................Gold 06.55.82

GLOSSARY
W1x........ Women's Single Scull
W2x........ Women's Double Scull
W4x........ Women's Quadruple Scull
W2-........ Women's Pair
W8+ .... Women's Eight
U23W2-.. Under 23 Women's Pair

PICTURE CREDITS

The publishers would like to thank the following sources for their kind permission to reproduce the pictures in this book.

All photographs are from Katherine Grainger's own collection except the following:
Section One
Page 1:   (bottom left) Milngavie & Bearsden Herald
Pages 2-3: (bottom left) Ted Colman
Page 5:   (top) Adam Pretty/Getty Images
Page 6:   (top) Harry How/Getty Images; (centre) Robert Laberge/Getty Images; (bottom) Jamie Squire/Getty Images
Page 7:   (top left) Piotr Malecki/Getty Images
Page 8:   (top) Alexander Hassenstein/Bongarts/Getty Images; (centre) Shaun Botterill/Getty Images; (bottom) Jeff J Mitchell/Getty Images

Section Two
Page 1:   (top) Alex Domanski/Getty Images; (bottom) John Gichigi/Getty Images
Page 2:   (top) Sandra Mu/Getty Images; (bottom left) Hagen Hopkins/Getty Images
Page 4:   (top left) Damien Meyer/AFP/Getty Images; (centre) Francisco Leong/AFP/Getty Images; (bottom right) Ian MacNicol/Getty Images
Page 5:   (bottom) Francisco Leong/AFP/Getty Images; (top left) Chris Shambrook
Page 7:   (right) Pascal Le Segretain/Getty Images; (bottom) Paul Gilham/Getty Images
Page 8:   (top left) David Davies/Press Association Images; (right) Dominic Lipinski/Press Association Images; (bottom left) Karwai Tang/Getty Images

Every effort has been made to acknowledge correctly and contact the source and/or copyright holder of each picture and Carlton Books Limited apologises for any unintentional errors or omissions that will be corrected in future editions of this book.